Memoirs

Kern Holoman
Paris, early 1945

SECOND EDITION

REVISED AND CORRECTED

MEMOIRS

and Other Writings

Kern Holoman

EDITED BY

D. Kern Holoman

AU VIEUX LOGIS

MÉRICOURT — RALEIGH — DAVIS

2023

Memoirs © copyright 2023 by D. Kern Holoman

AU VIEUX LOGIS
sites.google.com/view/dkholoman

ISBN: 978-1-7356907-4-2 (print)
978-1-7356907-5-9 (ebook)

Cover and book design by Mike Corrao, Mayfly Design

Library of Congress Catalog Number: 2023913433
First Printing: 2023
Printed in the United States of America

CONTENTS

Introduction vii

1. RICHMOND (1920–25) 1
2. RALEIGH (1925–50) 9
3. CHAPEL HILL (1938–42) 25
4. FORT BRAGG AND CAMP WHEELER (1942) 32
5. CAMP GORDON AND FORT DIX (1942–43) 51
6. RUTGERS (1943–44) 61
7. OVERSEAS TO ENGLAND (1944) 67
8. LONDON TO PARIS (1944) 77
9. PARIS (1944–45) 89
10. LETTERS FROM PARIS (1944–45) 100
11. GERMANY (1945) 163
12. KAYE 193
13. LONG BEACH 221
14. DALLAS HOLOMAN, SR. 243
OTHER WRITINGS 259

APPENDIX: Correspondence with Jeff Holoman 271

INTRODUCTION

My father would, he often said, have been an English professor had World War II not intervened. When the war was over, it simply made more sense for him to join his father and brothers at their department store in Raleigh, Boylan-Pearce, Inc., in order to provide for his wife and, soon enough, for me.

The long letters he wrote from Paris in 1944–45, two of them published in a popular magazine, show the style and descriptive panache of a born writer. He's good with detail and pacing, and you keep turning the pages. He had been, after all, editor of his high school paper. And he had learned to type, the value of which he impressed on me and probably my brothers from a very early age. (I got my own office typewriter for my 15th, I think, birthday.)

I had these wartime letters in mind when I first went to Europe in 1967, sending home long, long epistles meant, in part, to show that I could do it too. Maybe I'll get around to finding and presenting these someday.

When my father surprised us all by retiring in 1980, he spoke a good deal of his intention to resume his writing. After my mother died in 1997 and he moved to Whitaker Glen, he went at it diligently indeed. His grandson Jeff Holoman was especially interested in fostering the memoirs project, finding in my father an intriguing voice from the past, especially as he recounted stories of life in the military. Beginning after the beach trip in 2003, my father would ship Jeff an envelope full of typescript every few weeks; he was still going strong in the holiday season 2004–05, after which his interest tapered off a little.

Between the letters of 1944–45 and the memoirs project in the first decade of the new century had come countless Sunday School lessons, a vibrant correspondence with his children and grandchildren, and what he called his "papers" for the Sandwich Club. He did a little fiction (see "Halloween Story," below) and a number of short non-fiction vignettes ("Smiley," "Stearns," "Crabbing," all included here). He typed, in all, some 400 or so pages of manuscript, the majority on the simple electronic typewriter that had come to replace the old uprights. He's never showed any interest in computerized word-processing (though the reappearance of his friend Morris Springer in the 1990s was made possible by the nascent internet). The wartime letters were retyped from single-spaced carbon copies, now fragile and crumbling.

I began to think of getting these materials together in conjunction with a personal project I had undertaken with respect to my own retirement from the UC Davis Symphony Orchestra at the end of 2008–09, where it became necessary to see to the preservation and digital safekeeping of many thousands of pages and images: another two or three hundred pages, I reasoned, would be a piece of cake. Then the 90th birthday celebration began to loom, and the goal became obvious.

It took awhile to snare the manuscripts from my nephew, and longer still to assess what we had (and what we didn't). On a stormy Saturday after the beach trip, 2010, I sat at the Kinko's not far from the Raleigh-Durham Airport and scanned the manuscripts and several dozen historic photographs. The conversion to text and editing I did here in Europe.

My father wrote most of this material just after the fact or from memory, without consulting notes. In one or two instances (i. e., the case of Matthew Fontaine Maury, the Confederate "Pathfinder of the Seas") I've provided the detail that slipped his memory. But I've not tried to correct errors of chronology or facts remembered differently by me—and of these there are precious few. I've standardized the punctuation and spelling and tried to get the various essays into as close a chronological order as they can be made to go.

D. Kern Holoman
Méricourt, 10 August 2010

NOTE ON THE SECOND EDITION

The original version of *Kern Holoman: Memoirs* was presented to my father and brothers at the Angus Barn in Raleigh on August 10, 2010, his 90th birthday.

The speed with which it was assembled—from scanning his manuscripts at the Raleigh Kinko's on July 17 and 18, 2010, to affixing the color title page and e-sending the file off from Méricourt to that same Kinko's on August 8 for publication and pickup the next day—seemed at the time miraculous. PDF had become an open standard only in 2008. I fully expected the one-day turnaround time for the printing and binding to fail, but it worked like a charm, and the copies were there at table for the birthday party.

But I knew Dad's *Memoirs* would someday need fixing. For one thing we went to press knowing that at least two chunks were missing. A hand-list of his writings he dated on December 28, 2004, cited an essay he called "Rutgers: Living with Kaye in New Brunswick, 1943–44" that seemed to have disappeared altogether. And the only copy I had of his "Halloween Story" on the Devil's Tramping Ground near Siler City, N. C., was lacking a page right at the climax. The number of typos I began to find was monstrous, due partly to the primitive OCR and spell-checking software available at the time, but mostly to the unyielding print deadline. I'm fairly certain that in France we never had a full printout to read one last time.

We found the missing materials when collating his archive after his death in 2015. They included also another essay not found on the list from 2004: "Christmas Leave, December 1942, Kaye," now chapter 12, part III.

I have adjusted the chapter order and titles. I wanted to leave the major essay on Dallas Holoman, Sr. (my grandfather, Dad's father) near the end, where it would fall just before the related essay "My Father and My God." There was not a perfect solution to ordering the essays on Kaye, "the defining entity of my life." They now appear chronologically in chapter 12, with the exception of "A Visit from Kaye" [1942], in chapter 4, part III; and the description of the wedding itself, which occurs at the end of chapter 5 in the passage on relocating to New Jersey.

My editorial remarks are given in italic blocks within the chapters. All the footnotes are the editor's (mine), not the author's (his).

All the manuscripts that went into *Kern Holoman: Memoirs* are found in the W. Kern Holoman and Katherine H. ("Kaye") Holoman Archive, now housed at the Olivia Raney Local History Library in Raleigh.

See also sites.google.com/view/dkholoman for amplifications, updates, and many more images.

DKH
Méricourt, 10 August 2023

Richmond, 1921

1

RICHMOND

(1920–25)

I moved from Richmond to Raleigh when my father accepted a job there in the spring of 1925. So everything that I remember about Richmond occurred before I was five years old. I am really astonished at how much I *can* remember from such an early age, although, of course, all of my recollections are disjointed and episodic.

We lived at 1514 Floyd Avenue, a few blocks from the center of town. It was a respectable neighborhood in those days. Later on it deteriorated to be sort of slumish, but lately has been rejuvenated and is now considered quite a desirable place to live. We had electricity, but there were still operational gas jets in the wall in case there should be a power failure—although I can't remember one ever happening. The house was heated by a large (5' x 5') grate in the center of the hall, although, come to think of it, there must have been some heating in the upstairs rooms, perhaps electric standing floor heaters. (The "parlor" on the downstairs floor was so cold that one year we kept the Christmas tree in it until Easter.)

There were two staircases, one at the front of the house and the back stairs that descended into the kitchen.

I ate in the kitchen in a wooden high chair. It had a wooden bib that swung overhead and formed the tray for my meals. I must have been quite young for this, or else was kept eating in a high chair for a good, long time.

I had two dolls. One was a large baby doll with a bisque head. She was named Bertha. The other doll was named Rachel. She was a rag doll with a black "mammy" face. I had a big cloth bag full of alphabet blocks with which I learned to spell out my name at quite an early age.

My playmates on the sidewalk were George (Jr.) Ross and Grace Wilson. There was also Jimmy McCracken, a few doors down the street. But he was one of a large family of Catholics who were "not nice," so we shouldn't play with him.

The Pulleys, who lived across the street, did not have either electricity or gas. When we went to visit them we did our socializing by the light of kerosene lanterns. But they always had some delicious cooking on the stove. Also across the street was Mrs. Wade, who won my heart when I came by giving me a rag to chew on which had been soaked in sugar water. Old Mr. Tyree wasn't much of anything, but we were scared and in awe of him, because they said he was a hundred years old.

When I was very young—I don't know just when—my mother had to go to the hospital for surgery (kidney ailment from which she never really recovered). She was gone a long time, and she told me that when she came back I wouldn't have anything to do with her, as I much preferred the company of my black "nursemaid" named Bessie Smith, whom I simply adored. Bessie used to take me to Monroe Park, a couple of blocks down the street, for playtime (sliding board, see-saw, and swings). I seem to think she pushed me in a stroller, but we may have walked.

Down the street a few blocks was the handsomely kept Monument Avenue. At each street crossing it had an awesome equestrian statue of JEB Stuart, Stonewall Jackson or Robert E. Lee. There was also a monument to the naval commander of the Confederacy, but I have forgotten his name [Matthew Fontaine Maury].[1]

One block up the street at 1414 Floyd was where my grandmother (my mother's mother) lived in a house similar to the one we lived in. I remember her as a very decisive, outspoken person, the epitome of an old woman, though she was only in her sixties. We were somewhat in awe of her, but I'm sure she was kind and caring in her way. We all called her "Granny."

Granny was born Addie L. Bailey. She had a sister, widowed when I knew her, named "Jinny" Jeffries. Aunt Jinny had a retarded daughter named Lath(?). Their house always smelled like cabbage cooking. Granny had a brother named Uncle Dan Bailey, a red-faced jovial kind of fellow who lived a few blocks away with his wife, Aunt Annie. They always made us welcome and were fun to visit.

Granny married Nathan B. Lockwood when she was 25 years old. I know nothing about him. Four years later their daughter, Edna Pleasant Lockwood (my mother) came along. She was Granny's only child. Lockwood died about a year later, and after five years, Granny married William D. Kern.

William Kern was a retired, or disability-pensioned, postal employee. He had had a stroke, walked with a cane and shuffled his feet when he walked. He had a big, drooping mustache, slurred his speech, and didn't smell very good. Later on he

---

1. The monuments were removed in 2020.

had another stroke that rendered him helpless while Granny took care of him in bed for the last two years of his life (in 1927). My mother said that in his younger, healthier days he was extremely kind to his step-daughter, and she named me after him—for which I am very pleased. Mother always called him "Poppy." And we did the same.

Granny owned the house she lived in. (We rented.) She rented the upstairs for income. She also owned a string of six or eight garages which she rented out in the back alley behind her house. She had a back yard, but it was solidly bricked in, and I don't recall that anything ever grew in it.

One of the garages that Granny owned housed her own car. (We didn't have a car until just before we moved to Raleigh, when my father bought a Chevrolet sedan.) Granny's car was a Reo. It was a "touring car," which is to say that it didn't have roll-up, roll-down windows. It came equipped with eisenglass panels which you could snap in place if it should start to rain. I don't remember that we ever did. Granny just kept the Reo in the garage if the weather turned bad.

She would frequently come by in the afternoon and take us for a ride around the city. We would drive through Byrd Park and by the picturesque old waterworks. When she said she was going to drive by the "depot" (the railway station complex), I became frightened, because I thought she was saying "deep hole" and I was afraid we might fall into it.

Occasionally in Richmond we would see electric runabout cars. They were one-passenger vehicles operated by a "joy stick" rather than a steering wheel. They seemed to move very slowly on the avenues and were driven by little old ladies.

Another thing we used to see on the thoroughfares were "jitneys." These were T-Model Fords that plied the bus lines and charged only a nickel whereas the buses charged 8¢. They were a pretty good bargain because you could get three or four passengers in them by paying only one fare. My cousin Paul Holoman tried to make a living driving a jitney. Paul was an older sort of ne'er-do-well who had either run away from home or been cast out by our Uncle John Holoman. Paul's wife was named Lillian. She used to babysit for me, and I was very fond of her. I called her "Neeah." Later on Paul gave up jitney driving, and they moved to Edenton, N. C., where Paul became a Baptist lay preacher, and they both lived there for a long time to extremely old ages.

Granny's hobby was making artificial flowers and trees. I don't know where she got her materials or what they were made of, but I remember that she gave my mother a wisteria tree in full bloom and an apple tree in full, red fruit.

On at least two occasions (after we had moved to Raleigh) Granny drove her car—alone—to see us. This was quite a feat for a lady in her sixties over those mostly dirt and muddy roads.

We had a lovable collie dog named Mack. When he was not quite full grown he contracted distemper which later afflicted him with St. Vitus Dance. This rendered him palsied and half-crippled, but we loved him. Once while we were away Granny called the SPCA, which came to take him away and euthanize him. I am sure that it was the wise, kind and merciful thing to do but at the time we were very angry with Granny for doing this.

Many years earlier a fortune-teller had told Granny that she would live to be 68 years old. Granny took this prediction as an accurate foretelling of her death, and she spoke of it fairly frequently. Sure enough, when that age came along she sickened, gathered her tent and peacefully passed away. She was a very memorable old lady. She is buried—along with both her husbands—in the Kern-Jeffries plot in Riverview Cemetery

[Richmond]. She said she wanted me to have the old family Bible—which I do have. I treasure it and keep it in full view in my apartment here at Whitaker Glen.

A block away from Floyd Avenue there was a grocery store, where Mother used to buy our food. The proprietor, Old Man Ambowls, had a genuine peg-leg wooden leg, the only one I have ever seen for real. He also had a jaw bone that had a way of becoming dislocated, and it would hang open grotesquely until his wife would come over and snap it back into place.

Heaven for us kids was John's store, around the corner on Lombardy Street. That's where we bought our penny candy. Surely he sold other things there, but that's all we ever bought. For a penny you could buy a Tootsie Roll or a tiny Baby Ruth bar or a "Mary Jane" (caramel and peanut butter) or a jelly orange slice or a chocolate drop (with cream inside). There were, no doubt, other goodies too. You could buy twisted shoe strings of licorice (your choice of black or red). We didn't like John very much, but his candy counter was heaven on earth.

Catty-cornered across Floyd Avenue was Mr. Cumming's Drug Store, where an ice cream cost a nickel—if a parent would take you there for a treat. You could get a milk shake or a banana split for a dime, but they were expensive, and I don't remember anybody ever getting one.

My father and my mother were married in 1907. He was 34 and she was 18. Neither of them had had even a high school education. He was a traveling salesman for Richmond Dry Goods.

Their first child arrived a little less than a year later and was named Dallas, Jr., after his father. He was in John Marshall High School as I remembered him. John Marshall had an ROTC corps of cadets with fancy uniforms modeled after the "Richmond Blues." I was disappointed by the fact that he chose not to join them. He would sometimes ride me on the crossbar of his bike to the nearby bakery and buy me a cookie. Dallas got his driver's license before we left Richmond, and it was he who actually drove us on our first trip to Raleigh.

Chreston was two years younger. His first name was "George" after his grandfather. His middle name came from a Shakespearean actor named Creston Clarke. Mother thought the name was pretty and so she chose it for her second son. He dabbled in chemistry and had a smelly room in the upstairs back hall.

My third brother, Boyce, was four years younger. His name was our paternal grandmother's family maiden name. He attended Stonewall Jackson Elementary School around the corner. He used to tease me a lot. But he taught me a lot, too, and I am indebted to him for many of the "street smart" things I learned from him.

We used to attend Grove Avenue Baptist Church a block and a half away, and all of our family were faithful churchgoers. One time my mother's Sunday School class put on an amateur minstrel show. When she put burnt cork on her face to black it up, I screamed in terror and wouldn't have anything to do with her until she came home and took it off.

My Dad taught me a catechism-like set of questions and answers out of the Bible: several dozen, I'm sure; maybe more. Questions like "Who made you?" "What did he make you out of?" "Who was the first man?" "Who built the ark?" and onward for many more. He delighted to show me off to neighbors and visitors of how much I knew about the Bible. Of course, I knew nothing about the Bible; I had just learned all those answers by rote. But I enjoyed being the center of attention.

I'm sure I could dredge up many more recollections out of the sink-hole of my memory. But this is enough, and is about where things stood when we pulled up stakes and moved into a new sort of existence in Raleigh.

Boylan-Pearce, 1942
Fayetteville Street, Raleigh
showing also Briggs Hardware [L.] and W. T. Grant Co. [R.]

Albert Barden Photograph Collection
Courtesy of the State Archives of North Carolina

❰ 2 ❱

RALEIGH

(1925–50)

I moved to Raleigh in 1925. My father had been a merchandise manager for Thalhimer's in Richmond, and had accepted the position of General Manager of Boylan-Pearce department store, at that time one of the leading fashion outlets in North Carolina. And of course he took his family with him.

Richmond and Raleigh are about 160 miles apart, and you had to allow eight hours to make the trip. The turnpike to Petersburg, twenty-two miles away, was paved. It actually had a street car that ran all the way. After you left Petersburg the pavement ran out, and it was a dirt road all the way to the North Carolina line. Virginia built its roads on a pay-as-you-go system, whereas North Carolina had floated a road bond issue in the early 1920s, and had paved roads along most of the major routes. Including this stretch of US 1. We used to say you could tell when you crossed the state line, even with your eyes closed, because the road changed from bumpy to smooth.

There was no bridge across the Roanoke River, and no Kerr Lake or Lake Gaston. You crossed on a flat, wooden ferry that was tethered to a cable that ran from each side. It had an outboard motor on the back, and was run by a black man who charged fifty cents to take you to the other side. I don't remember whether it would hold more than one car. Certainly not more than three or four. And the traffic never built up.

When the "Steel Bridge" was built there a few years later it was a major event in highway travel.

You considered yourself lucky if you didn't have at least one flat tire on the way. Although the cars carried a spare, you always carried a patching kit. If you had to you would pull the inner tube out of the casing, glue a rubber patch on it, stick it back in, and then pump it back up with the hand pump that every car carried.

You had to watch your gasoline level carefully, because filling stations were few and far between. When you did buy gas, the attendant would hand pump it into a clear glass cylinder at the top, and then let it gravity-drop into your tank. You bought gasoline five gallons at the time: paid for it with a one-dollar bill, and expected to get change.

When we were anticipating the move to Raleigh the local Chamber of Commerce said its population was "about forty thousand." When the 1930 census came out we added up to about twenty-eight thousand.

Our first view of Raleigh's "sky line" was of the twin steeples of the Baptist church and the Methodist church, each about 200 feet tall. There were no other [tall] buildings. In the intervening years the steeples have been dwarfed by office and commercial buildings, but you can still see the same steeples as you approach via the old Wake Forest Road.

We spent our first night at one of a number of boarding houses that clustered around Capitol Square. Ours was on Edenton Street, just about where the History Museum stands today. I can remember looking out our window and seeing a beautiful brown granite horse-watering fountain at the head of Halifax Street. It had water running from a pipe on each of its four sides into a basin below. There was nearly always at least one horse—wagon attached—drinking at the basins.

We had dinner that first night at an elegant restaurant down Hillsboro Street called The Elms. I was fascinated by both a monkey and a parrot that they kept in the foyer. The monkey bit me.

Raleigh, like Washington, D. C., was a planned capital city. It was founded in 1792 when the state legislature decreed that a central location be created to house the governmental and administrative offices. The locating commission met at Isaac Hunter's Place (or tavern) on what is now Wake Forest Road and decided that the new city should be built within ten miles of there. While looking for a suitable location they stayed at the home of Colonel Joel Lane, a Revolutionary War figure. There were numerous offers to sell land for the project, but the commissioners decided to buy from—guess who?—Col. Lane. He sold the state a parcel of 1,000 acres, of which 440 acres were developed as the original capital city. It was surveyed and laid out in a square by William Christmas, and was bounded by streets appropriately named as North, East, South and West. In the center was the large Union Square to accommodate the projected State House, whose construction began promptly.

Other squares were located in each of the four quadrants of the city and were named in honor of Revolutionary War figures: Burke, Caswell, Moore and Nash. The streets leading from Union Square in each direction and the streets bounding the square were named for the state's eight judicial districts. The wide ones, Halifax, Hillsboro, Fayetteville and New Bern were towns which had at one time served as seats of government for the state. Mr. Christmas surveyed three times to locate the exact center of the city; and his three markers are still in place near the Southeast corner of the square.

In 1925 Capitol Square looked pretty much as it does today. The squirrels and pigeons were in abundance then as now, with a roasted peanut stand for them at the head of Fayetteville Street. Most of the statues were in place then: the Houdin replica of George Washington, the one of Henry Lawson Wyatt, our first Civil War casualty, done by Gutzon Borglum, who also did Mount Rushmore and Stone Mountain; the one to Ensign Worth Bagley, brother of Mrs. Josephus Daniels, and our Spanish American War casualty, the touching one to the Women of the Confederacy of a mother presenting a sword to her young son. And, of course, the big one To Our Confederate Dead with the cavalryman, the artillery man and the infantry soldier.

The statue of our three presidents, Jackson, Johnson and Polk, was not erected until post- World War II, in 1948 when President Harry Truman, running for re-election, came to its dedication. Once I was leading a tour group of visitors through the city and pointed out the three presidents which North Carolina had given the nation. Unfortunately one of the participants in my tour spoke up and said, "Yeah, but all three of them had the good sense to move to my state of Tennessee before they got elected."

The floodlights were first turned on the Capitol Building in 1929, on the 50th anniversary of Edison's invention of the electric light. Franklin Roosevelt, then governor of New York, came down to make a dedicatory speech.

The Hall of History which grew into the North Carolina History Museum was housed on the second floor of the Justice Building at the head of Fayetteville Street. It was built around the Civil War collection of Colonel Fred A. Olds.

The business section of almost all of the retail stores was lined up in the first three blocks of Fayetteville Street. The City Hall and Police Station were on the corner of Martin Street. The National Guard unit used to meet on the second floor of the Briggs Hardware building. In the next block down was the old County Court House on the right. Out in front was an attractive marble monument honoring our service men of World War I. It had a fountain on each end, one inscribed "White," the other "Colored." The colored one was broken as long as the monument stayed there.

Across the street from the Court House was the old Yarborough House, three stories tall, the mecca for politicians and VIP visitors to the city. After it burned down in 1928, Hudson Belk put up its store there, and the Sir Walter, one block down, took its place as the local hotbed of influence and intrigue.

Beyond that there was nothing until Centennial School where Memorial Auditorium now stands. It was on the site of the old Governor's Palace where Grant and Sherman had come in 1865 to dictate the terms of surrender to Confederate General Johnston. On its left was the old Rex Hospital, and on its right Shaw University, still there today.

All of the roads into and out of the city were routed right down Fayetteville Street. The city had two electric traffic signals, one at Hargett Street, the other at Martin. The lights were red and green only—no yellow caution—and each change was heralded by an electric bell. (Richmond didn't have any lights at the time. They stationed a traffic police-man on a platform at their major intersections.) There was angle parking on both sides of the street. When my father was president of the Merchant's Association he had the temerity to suggest that it was not really necessary for all of the out-of-town traffic to be routed down the main street; and he was afraid his fellow merchants were going to run him out of town.

The street cars, electric trollies, all went right down Fayetteville Street too. They were owned and operated by Carolina Power and Light, which also operated a retail store, selling ovens and other electric appliances. One of the car tracks led to Bloomsbury Amusement Park, just beyond the present-day Carolina Country Club, and was also operated by CP&L. The park closed before I got to Raleigh, but its principal ride, the famous Dentzel Merry-Go-Round, can still be seen and ridden in today's Pullen Park.

Other car tracks ran as far as Peace College and another out Hillsboro to the CP&L sub-station. I don't remember if there were any others. Probably there were.

Going out New Bern Avenue past the old City Cemetery, where Joel Lane is buried, was the Old Soldiers' Home. It had a veranda all the way across the front, where the Civil War veterans would sit and rock as they watched the sparse traffic go by.

Where the Motor Vehicles Building now stands was a large, open field where Barnum and Bailey and the other circuses used to pitch their performance tents when they came to town. Across the street was the baseball park where the Raleigh Capitals used to play in the Carolina League.

Hillsboro Street, like New Bern, was mostly residential. It ran past Saint Mary's Academy for young women and N. C. State College of Agriculture and Engineering. (My father-in-law called it "A & E" for as long as he lived.) No bell tower then. It was begun in the late 1920s and discontinued during the

Depression for lack of funds. It stood, half complete, until after World War II, when they finished it.

Across Hillsboro Street from State was the Fair Grounds. If you turn right on Pogue Street and follow it around you'll be on the old race track, with the Little Theater and Rose Garden now standing in the infield. The new fairgrounds with its Spanish-style facade, was located further out on Hillsboro about 1928.

The Victorian, gingerbread-style Governor's Mansion had been built on Burke Square. (When I was growing up I used to think it was the ugliest building I had ever seen. Now I kind of like it.) On the next block down, built in that same style, was Meredith College for young Baptist women. When Meredith pulled up stakes and moved to its present location the old structure was operated for many years as the Mansion Park Hotel, mostly a low-rent facility for permanent residents. All along the street north of the Mansion were the gingerbread homes of the wealthy and influential families. Some people called it the Blount Street Aristocracy.

Other than state government the city's principal area of concern was education. We had six colleges then, all still in operation, though each of them has experienced some rough sledding. There was one high school: Hugh Morson, about where our main post office now stands. The black students, of course, went elsewhere, to Washington High somewhere out in the hinterlands. In 1928, I think, Needham Broughton became our second high school, serving our expansion into the west. The athletic teams, including students from the Methodist Orphanage, competed as one unit called Raleigh High School. (I think it's worth noting that the year I entered as a sub-freshman Raleigh High won the state championships in football, baseball, basketball and boxing, the only time, I believe that this has ever been achieved.)

There was a junior high school for 7th and 8th grades. It was on Morgan Street across from what had been the city's water tower, since converted into an architect's studio.

When the Depression hit, the state had to cut back its budget for education along with the other economies. Therefore we ran schools for only eight months a year and only for eleven grades. (And this shortfall lasted until 1939, all the time I was attending.)

By the late 1920s Raleigh's manifest destiny was to the northwest. And so the developers gave some of the streets cozy suburban names, like Glen-wood, Fair-view, Ridge-crest and Wood-land. To the suburb they gave the name of Hayes Barton after the estate of Sir Walter. The next one out was named Budleigh after the little town in Devonshire where he grew up.

West of Raleigh, on Crabtree Creek, there were three grist mills: Whitaker Mill, Edwards Mill and Lassiter's Mill. All of them burned down at different times. Lassiter's was the last to go, but its product was so highly regarded that for several years they paid another mill to produce it and still bagged it under the name Lassiter's Water-Ground Corn Meal. Yellow bag, red letters, tied at the neck with a string.

Our house was beyond Five Points, just a few yards outside the city limit. We paid a black man fifty cents to come by twice a week and haul away our garbage with his horse and wagon. We had running water, natural gas and, of course, electricity—although the first house we lived in also had gas jets in the walls. We left the back door unlocked so the meter readers could get into the basement for the readings. The house was heated by a coal-fired furnace which my father would "bank" every night at bedtime and stir up first thing in the morning. It was steam heat, which meant a big metallic radiator in each room. When the heat was coming up the radiators would clank ominously.

Nobody had an electric refrigerator. We had an "ice box" on the back porch, and we would hang the sign on the front of the house each day to let the ice man know how much to bring—25, 50, 75 or 100 pounds. The man would bring in the ice with big tongs and install it into the ice box. But emptying the drip pan was a daily chore. We kids would clamber up onto the back step of the ice truck and help ourselves to the little chips and slivers that had broken off.

We sent our laundry out, and the red Sanitary Laundry truck would pick up on Wednesday and bring it back on Saturday so we would have clean clothes for church the next day. Some homes still did the washing and drying in tubs and tanks and outdoor clothes lines. In the spring and summer months the vegetable truck would come by from the farm and ring its bell. Then the housewives would come out and bargain for the day's veggies and fruits.

We had a telephone. Not everybody did. Ours was not the old-fashioned kind, fastened to the wall, but the up-to-date "candlestick" style with a receiver hanging on a hook at its side. You would pick up the receiver, put it to your ear, and pretty soon the operator—called "Central"—would say "Number, please," and after you gave it through the mouthpiece, she would say "Thank you," and make the connection. If she didn't answer promptly enough you would jiggle the hook to get her attention. We were on a two-party line, which meant we shared the wire with a nearby neighbor. If you picked up the phone and heard a conversation going on, it was polite to hang up and wait a reasonable time before trying again. Sometimes curious people would stay on the line to find out what was going on at the neighbor's house. Some telephones were four-party and even six-party lines because they were cheaper. And that frequently made for congestion on the line. Numbers were shorter in those days. Ours had four digits and a Letter: 3436-W. The drug store was 106, and the police station was 56. Incidentally we still use the phrase "hang up" when we complete our calls, although it's usually a matter of putting the phone down.

One thing we used the telephone for was to order groceries. We dealt with a credit grocer, and we would call him in the morning to order our food and other supplies. He would write down our order, and it would be delivered by truck that same afternoon. At the end of the month we would receive a bill for the things we had bought.

Davis' General Store, which was at Five Points where Hayes Barton Pharmacy now stands, did not deliver and did not give credit. But if you called in your order, he would assemble it and have it waiting for you when you came in to get it. Mr. Davis had a chicken yard out behind the store, and if you ordered one—or two—for Sunday dinner, he would go out and catch them for you. He would tie the legs together and put them head-first into a paper bag with the heads sticking out of the hole he tore in the bottom of the bag. He would write your name on the side of the bag and put them over with the other groceries until you arrived.

There were no grocery super markets. Piggly-Wiggly and A&P—The Great Atlantic and Pacific Tea Company—had a number of stores at strategic locations around the city. You got a basket when you entered the Piggly and paid for your things at a checkout counter not unlike today. At A&P you stood on one side of the counter while the man stood on the other side. You told him what you wanted and he would get it for you. He had a long pole with a hook on the end with which he would pull down the items on the upper shelves. He would figure out in pencil on the side of the bag how much you owed for your order.

Some Saturday mornings we would shop for groceries at the old City Market, across from Moore Square, right where it is today. The farmers would bring in their produce on converted T-Model Fords and vie with each other for the parking spaces all around the outside. We would bargain with them for vegetables and for the chickens that they brought along in open wooden crates. Inside the building they sold meat and fish. We never bought any; we suspected that their hygienic practices did not meet our standards.

About the chickens: usually they were the gray and white variety that we called "Domineckers" [Dominique, or domestic chickens], frying size, also called pullets. That afternoon the colored servant would take them to the backyard and wring their necks. When they were no longer flopping she would dip the carcasses into a pot of boiling water and pull off the feathers by hand. Then she would eviscerate them, cut the edible parts into eating size, and roll them in flour to be fried the next morning. The livers and gizzards were considered particular delicacies.

Nearly every household of any means at all had a household servant called "our colored woman," or "colored girl" if she were younger. The going wage rate was a dollar a day—five dollars for Monday through Friday, seven if she worked on Saturday and Sunday, which many of them did. You had to negotiate the hours she worked, but you always had to furnish "car fare," which was ten cents a day, five cents each way on the trolly.

I haven't said much about the black people because, frankly, we didn't have much to do with them. Segregation was total, most of it dictated by law. Schools, of course, but also waiting rooms, buses, rest rooms—if any for blacks—were clearly designated and rigidly enforced. The colored were not allowed in restaurants—remember the Greensboro lunch counter sit-in at Woolworth five-and-dime? Even the take-out places had separate windows for blacks to apply. The good movie theaters, the Strand, the State and later the Ambassador, all admitted blacks, but they had to use a separate entrance and sit in the upper-level "peanut gallery." They had their own theaters, the Royal and the Lincoln, though I'll never understand why they went to movies, where their race was invariably depicted as either servants or clowns. They were truly second-class citizens in every sense of the word.

They worked as domestic servants, yard men, maids and janitors and other menial offices of all sorts. At the end of the day they would disappear to some nameless spaces in Southeast Raleigh, until time for them to show up for their jobs the next day. Looking back, I don't recall that I ever had any contact with a black child or young person. The two races just didn't mix on any social level at all.

No refined person ever used the word "nigger." The proper word was "negro," pronounced "nigra." Most often we just used the word "colored," and let that cover the designation. Colored people were always—always—called by their first names only. Frequently we didn't even know their last names. If they were elderly and respected we would add "Uncle" or "Aunt" before their names. If we saw children on the streets or in farm yards we referred to them derisively as "pickaninnies." From our perspective today this seems incredible. But that's the way it was within our own lifetimes. And not all of seventy-five years ago.

Dining out wasn't much of an adventure, as there were few choices and even less variety. The S&W Cafeteria on Fayetteville Street a block above the Sir Walter was where everybody went. You could be sure to see several of your friends there each time you went. They had a free step-on scale at the entrance where you could see how much you weighed both before and after. Thursday was Family Night, and downstairs they showed old cartoons and Our Gang comedies to the kids. Generally the others were sit-down cafes, many offering the "Blue-Plate Special" with meat, two vegetables, bread, drink and dessert for thirty-five cents. Young people's delight was the Manhattan Lunch on Hillsboro Street where a hot dog, a hamburger or a coke all cost five cents each. Coffee was a nickel everywhere. In the mid 1930s the Canton, Raleigh's only Chinese restaurant for many years, opened up on Hillsboro Street. The 42nd Street Oyster Bar came into being about the same time. For a good steak you went to Mr. Proescher's place in Cary. We didn't get an Italian restaurant until after World War II—Mario's on Fayetteville Street. And as late as 1955 you couldn't buy a pizza in Raleigh.

The main-line churches were clustered near Capitol Square: First Baptist, First Presbyterian, Christ Episcopal and black First Baptist on the square. Methodist, Catholic and another Episcopal were a block away. The Lutheran church, Layton, was away out Hillsboro Street, just beyond Glenwood. Several churches supported and subsidized on the outskirts what they called "mission churches." Less popular denominations and splinter sects like the Seventh Day Adventists and the Pentecostal Holiness were generally in the Southeast section. And there were the black charismatic churches headed up by Daddy Grace and Sister Garry. White people used to drive by Sister Garry's church on South Street Sunday nights to hear the congregation singing. There's a hoary old joke that used to make the rounds about a visitor to town asked a native crossing Capitol Square where he could find Christ Church. To which the oft-repeated reply was, "Well,

I don't know. There's Mr. Weatherspoon's church and over there is Mr. Hudson's church. Mr. Dillon's church is down the street. I don't think Christ has a church anywhere around here."

The Methodist Orphanage between Glenwood and St. Mary's Streets was an active, working farm, self-sustaining, raising its own crops, meat and dairy products as worked by the orphan wards of the church.

We had one radio station. And it went off the air in the afternoons. It was a subsidiary of Durham Life Insurance Company, and it took its call letters, WPTF, from the company's slogan: "We Protect the Family." It was situated in a basement location on Fayetteville Street. It had three studios with glass panels through which the visitors could look and see the entertainment being aired. Visiting WPTF's studios after a dinner at the S&W was very much the "in" thing to do. You could see the Neapolitan Trio, Kingham Scott at the organ and Warren Barfield, tenor. The Children's Birthday Party where the kids could actually visit and be interviewed on their birthdays was immensely popular. Carl Goerch had a remote-broadcast program outside called "The Man on the Street," one of the first radio quiz shows I can remember.

Fred Fletcher's WRAL came on the scene in the mid 1930s, but it was just a disc-jockey and news station. It was roundly ridiculed by the public, who said that its call letters stood for "We Really are Lousy" and "We Rest After Lunch." Which they did. But they progressively improved, and by the time the first television franchise was awarded they had done their homework so well that the city populace was stunned to see that WRAL was the winner. WPTF was the most stunned of all, from which they have never fully recovered.

PRESENTED TO THE SANDWICH CLUB, APRIL 12, 2001

with Bill Tope and "Dub" Martin
Chapel Hill, 1938

❦ 3 ❧

CHAPEL HILL

(1938–42)

When I entered the University of North Carolina in the fall of 1938 the enrollment was about 3,500. All boys. There were no undergraduate girls at UNC in those days. The only ones were a few graduate students. The situation was so dire that when we saw a member of the opposite sex, it was customary to say, "Look. There goes a girl!"[1]

Freshman classes were pretty much no-choice affairs: English, Math, Social Science (History), Foreign Language, Science (Physics, Chemistry or Geology). I chose Geology because it was easiest—one of my smart choices, because it has given me a lot of pleasure since then. Hygiene (Sex Education, required), Physical Education (Gym, required), and one afternoon lab per week. Our freshman teachers were almost always graduate students pursuing a higher degree. Though they taught their classes conscientiously this was a "chore" to them and a burden to their own educational pursuits.

---

1. See also "Where the Girls Are: Chapel Hill to Greensboro in 1938," appended at the end of this chapter.

I lived on the third floor of Steele Dormitory, one of the most desirable locations on campus, near to the Bell Tower (Administration) and the Old Well. In fact I lived in the same room for all four years, I liked it so well.

Housing was short in 1942, and students were assigned three to a room. There was one set of bunk beds and one single, three desks, three dressers and two closets to share. There was a bathroom (toilet, wash basin and shower) to serve twelve students, although I don't recall any particular hardships in sharing and taking turns.

Of my two roommates one was "Dub" Martin, a classmate of mine at Broughton High School in Raleigh, whom I idolized. He was smart, attractive and outgoing and destined to become a BMOC. (Do we still have that abbreviation? It means Big Man on Campus.) My other roommate was Bill Tope from Pennsylvania. He was large, slow-witted but thoroughly amiable. We became close friends and made an excellent team of bridge partners. We roomed together in harmony until he flunked out of school halfway through his junior year. Bill had an attention deficit, and was unable to concentrate on his studies for more than a few minutes. He had come to Chapel Hill to study pre-med, but was unable to pass even the most basic courses. After a number of failures, his grades finally caught up with him. His departure was a sad personal loss to me. Bill's place was taken for the remainder of the year by an All-American lacrosse player named Coleman Finkle. We got along fine. We were about the same size and even shared some clothing.

Meals on campus were taken at Swain Hall Cafeteria. At noon times the lines would stretch out into the street. You would buy a book of meal tickets for $5.00. Each ticket was worth 25¢. It would buy a meat, two vegetables, bread, drink and dessert and was reasonably good, though, of course, everybody complained. Of course you didn't have to eat on campus. There were a number of restaurants and cafes on Franklin St., but they cost more—35¢, 50¢ or, even a dollar for a steak if you could afford it.

An early event at Chapel Hill was the "Freshman Smoker." This was held in Swain Hall, was sponsored by the various tobacco companies and was free to all freshmen. There were soft drinks and an unlimited supply of cigarettes. Everybody came and socialized and many enjoyed the taste of cigarette smoke for the first time. Each company had student representatives who gave away free sample packs of four of Camels, Luckies, Chesterfields and the other brands.

Fraternity "Rush Week" was early on. I guess it's pretty much the same everywhere. Bill pledged Phi Kappa Sigma, Dub held out for a couple of years, and I never did pledge.

But what to do on the weekends? 3,500 boys, all with hormones that raged even back in those days. We learned, however, that fifty miles away in Greensboro was the Woman's College of the University of North Carolina, affectionately known as "WC," where 3,500 delicious females were equally lonely and panting for male companionship. What a treasure trove, what a garden of fruit and flowers just waiting for the plucking.

But how to get to them? It was a rare Carolina man who had a car in those days. No one could afford bus fare—in fact, I'm not even sure there was a bus run to Greensboro. The thing to do was to stand out on West Franklin Street and thumb a ride from somebody—anybody—who was going in that direction. On Saturday afternoons sometimes there were fifty or more students hoping and thumbing for a free pick-up and a travel to the promised land. And surprisingly, they eventually did get rides, though sometimes it took an hour or more.

A friend of ours who went to school at Oak Ridge College just outside Greensboro lined up blind dates for each of the three of us and invited us to join him for the good times. So we took our turn on Franklin Street and exercised our thumbs until the rides came along. It took four hops to get to Greensboro. To Mebane, to Elon, to Burlington, and finally to paradise.

Our blind dates were, well, blind dates. None of the three of us ever went back to these girls for a second helping. Besides that, there wasn't much to do on a girls' campus. We walked around a little, went to a campus movie, went to the campus "dope shop" and bade them a chaste good night. Face, it, you don't do much hugging and kissing—we called it "necking"— on a first date. And we didn't. Nice girls, I'm sure. But if they were panting for us, they kept it pretty well under control.

Getting back to Chapel Hill was an even bigger problem than getting up there. It had gotten late—after eleven I guess, and rides had gotten mighty scarce. After a long time we got as far as Burlington, which is where the trail turned really cold. We stood out on the highway until after one. By that time nothing was coming by. Zilch. We finally gave up and spent the rest of the night in a third-rate hotel. (They didn't much want us to take a room because—I suspect—they were accustomed to renting the rooms on Saturday night by the hour.)

Anyway we spent a miserably disgruntled night in Burlington, went back to the highway on Sunday morning and finally free-loaded back to Chapel Hill by about noon. It had not been a red-letter weekend for us three roommates.

But hope springs eternal. This was our first try. It was by no means our last. I can recall trying our luck several more times in the months that followed. But I really don't recall any of these expeditions to "WC" turning out to be any more than ho-hum.

In other months and years I hunted more successfully in greener pastures. But that's another story. Or several others.

ADDENDUM

The text above comes from Kern's memoirs-writing period in 2004 and 2005. A much earlier manuscript, from perhaps 1995, tells the same story. It's typed with a manual typewriter on erasable paper before he began to use an electric typewriter, possibly in the late 1980s. He would often say, after the sale of Boylan-Pearce in September 1980, that he wanted to devote more time to writing, and this essay shows he'd begun.

Where the Girls Are
Chapel Hill to Greensboro in 1938

When we were freshmen in the fall of 1938, it was not only a different era; it was a different world. The University had an enrollment of about 3,500, and we thought we were Big. As a rule women did not enter the ranks of the undergraduates until their junior year, and they were scarce indeed. (We called them "co-eds" in those days.) Spencer Hall [also known as Women's Building] and the two sororities housed just about the entire female enrollment. Walking across campus, if we happened to see one, somebody would say, "Look, there goes a girl." In such a monastic existence, one of us observed, "When the co-eds start to look good to you, you know it's time to leave the campus."

Which is just what we decided to do. We knew the solution to our problem was in that school 50 miles up the road—WC [Woman's College of the University of North Carolina, now

UNC-Greensboro]—where 2,000 beautiful, lonely girls were panting for male companionship on Saturday night. So about mid-Saturday afternoon one day in October my two roommates, Dub Martin and Bill Tope, and I, decked out in freshman finery, showed up at the corner of West Franklin Street to hitchhike to Greensboro. "It's always easy to get a ride to Greensboro. There are just dozens of cars going up all afternoon." Only thing was that about fifty guys were already ahead of us on that corner. And the Greensboro cars that went by were already loaded with lusty young bucks. But they waved to us as they went past.

Eventually, though, our turn did come up, and we did get a ride. It was to Hillsboro in a farm truck. We got to Market Street in Greensboro in five easy hops—to Mebane, to Burlington, to Elon, and finally to the promised land.

After a bite of supper we were in high, good humor as we hoofed it up to the WC campus, humming "Three Blind Dates." Because that's what we had—three blind dates, fixed up for us by a friend who went to Oak Ridge, for the Lord's sake. You've all had blind dates, and you know how they turn out. These were no worse—and no better—than what you have experienced. It's enough to say that none of the six of us ever saw one another after that evening. My main recollections of the evening are looking for a boy's rest room on an all-girl campus and wondering how we were going to get back to Chapel Hill.

The trip home was even worse. The cars going back were even more full than they had been coming up. It had gotten cold, and there were no rides. We finally got one as far as Burlington, arriving there about 1:00 AM. By that time traffic had vanished from the highways. Nothing. At 2:00 we gave up and checked into a cheap hotel in downtown Burlington. No toothbrushes, no razors, no pajama—just us. We slept well, though.

We were only mildly disturbed by people checking in and out of the rooms on either side of us—several times during the night.

Sunday morning was better, though. We got back on the highway about church time, and it took us only two more rides to arrive back at Chapel Hill in time for lunch. The cooking at Swain Hall cafeteria had never tasted so good. The beds at Number 9 Steele Dormitory had never felt so soft.

They say you learn a whole lot more at college than what they teach you in the classroom. The three of us got a broad, liberal education that weekend. That's why, when I read not long ago, that the girls outnumber the boys at Chapel Hill now, I cried a little bit—for my lost youth.

October 1940 saw perhaps the major turning point in Kern's life, meeting Katherine Highsmith, whom he would marry in 1943. Chapter 12 presents the essays on Kaye, in more or less chronological order.

❦ 4 ❧

FORT BRAGG AND CAMP WHEELER

(1942)

I

I graduated from Carolina in June, 1942. I had already received my draft notice to report to Fort Bragg in July. The government was kind enough to let me finish college before inducting me. Assembling with other potential draftees in downtown Raleigh, we were transported by bus to Bragg for preliminary in-processing.

These first two or three days were very military, even though we were all wearing our civilian clothes. But we slept on cots in wooden barracks under rigid supervision and were confined to our quarters in and around the building.

The next day was devoted to undergoing our physical examinations. My recollection is that were absurdly simple, though in retrospect I guess they did a pretty good job of finding and rooting out those who were obviously physically unqualified.

Immediately afterwards those of us who had passed the tests were marched off and lined up in an assembly area—I guess there must have been a couple of hundred of us in that group, including several of my friends and acquaintances. The process itself again was absurdly simple. A non-commissioned officer explained to us that we were about to enter a period of active duty in the army which was to last for the duration of the war plus an additional six months. Then we were directed to hold up our right hands and swear—as directed, we repeated the oath—to preserve, protect and defend the Constitution of the United States of America and to obey any lawful orders given to us by higher ranking officers or supervisors. And that was it.

We were each given a card, which we were enjoined not to lose upon pain of death, which stated—by name—that we were now private soldiers in the Army of the United States, and assigned a service number. It has been more than sixty years since I used it, but I still remember it: 34312945.

Just for passing reference, those acquaintances who were in that same cycle with me were: Marion Fuller, a classmate of mine at Broughton High and Carolina; Edwin Penick, a son of an Episcopalian bishop, a couple of years ahead of me at Broughton; Bob Garrison, who had earlier competed with me for the affection of a local girl (she married somebody else); and Walker Smith, who was the son of one of our employees at Boylan-Pearce.

After induction, in those days it was the army practice to immediately give two weeks leave for us to go home and get our personal affairs in order. So we were bussed back to Raleigh and released with orders to report back on the exact date two weeks later. Those two weeks were filled with the usual going-away activities, storing of clothing, filing of textbooks and college papers and other memorabilia. But mostly filled with apprehension for what lay ahead. Kaye and I saw a lot of each other, I guess most every night and lots of days too. Strict gasoline rationing was in effect, so we could not use automobiles to get to each other's houses and had to ride the city buses. They stopped running at eleven o'clock, and that meant an early end to the evenings. When I visited her house we would do our courting in the swing on her side porch. When she came to my house—2123 Woodland Ave., where my father lived alone except when I was around—we used the big, metallic, free-standing swing in the back yard, with a blanket along if it got chilly. One night I stayed out at Kaye's until after the buses had stopped and walked home. But it was a long trek in the darkness, and I didn't try it again.

The most memorable event of those two weeks was a three-day trip that my Dad treated us to. We went to Wrightsville Beach by bus—remember, it was gas-ration time. Kaye went with me, of course, and Dad was accompanied by his secretary, Virginia Barber whom he later married. We stayed at the Ocean Terrace Hotel, a large, resort-type establishment, the finest on the beach, about where the Blockade Runner now stands. (It was run by a Mrs. Snyder, who had previously run "Kitty's Cottage," the mecca of well-to-do Raleigh folks in the between-the-wars days.) We had connecting rooms with a bath in between. Ostensibly Dad and I shared one bedroom, Kaye and Virginia the other. But we were pretty casual about who was in which bedroom and when.

Breakfast was served daily in the big, big-windowed dining room. I remember that I thought then—and for many years later—that it was the most elegant thing to be served by black waiters in white coats. Perhaps the most noticeable thing about this fine resort was that all the windows on the ocean side were painted black. It is hard to believe now that this was war time, and German U-boats were patrolling our coastal waters and actually sinking our merchant ships within full sight sometimes of the seashore. (The dining room had a big, black curtain, which was drawn in the evening.) Still the blackout conditions afforded many dark little nooks and crannies for cuddling and smooching. Daytime activities were about the usual: surf bathing, beach walking, shell hunting and so forth. We ran into a friend of Kaye's who had a sailboat, and he gave us a ride in the lagoon behind the strand. (Kaye and I said many times that the first thing we were going to have after we were married was a sailboat. But one thing and another happened, as it will with young marriages, and we never did get around to having that boat.)

We went fishing one afternoon from the bridge that connects the beach to the mainland. Kaye was wearing an old cast-off pair of my pants plus a ragged terrycloth shirt. Her hair was stringy and she had no make-up on a sunburned face. I remember saying to her "Honey you never looked any worse than you do right now. And I never loved you more."

But the days were all too short, and soon we were back in Raleigh and facing the dread day when I would have to report back. The last morning I was in town we went to Krispy Kreme Doughnuts, and ate them in the car (her mother's car). After that we went to the duck pond at Montlawn Cemetery and fed the waterfowl, where we exchanged vows of everlasting love, daily letters, and phone calls and visits as frequently as we could manage.

Going back to Fort Bragg was a repeat of the deal from two weeks earlier. Except this time a number of our group came in roaring drunk, and the bus ride down was a rowdy one. They were dealt with by the disciplinarian sergeants who greeted us upon our arrival.

Once again we were confined rigidly to our barracks and its immediate vicinity. The next few days—perhaps as much as a week—were devoted to undergoing a multitude of aptitude tests. There were a lot of them. Foremost among these was the so-called "Intelligence Test" to measure how smart or how dumb you are. Your IQ score was entered upon your various military records. (I wonder if they still have IQs these days.) As I recall, everybody was in one of five categories. Category V reflected a score of less than 70 and was considered deficient; those in Category IV had scored between 70 and 90 and were "below average." Category III was for those with scores of 90 to 110 and comprised the huge majority of those tested—"Average." Category II was for those with scores of 110 to 130, and was rated "Above Average." Category I was for the really bright ones, though I don't remember the descriptive word. Your IQ score was no secret and widely known among the testers and the tested. (If you're interested, my IQ score was 122, which I think is a fair assessment of my level. "Smart, but no genius.")

There were a dizzying number of other tests, one right after another. I remember taking one for radio operator and telegrapher. Another one was for criminal investigator. As I have related before, the decision of which Military Occupational Specialty (MOS) you receive depends overwhelmingly on what the army happens to need on the day you come through. Therefore most of the testees were given the number of "Infantry Rifleman," "Artillery Crewman," "Armored Technician," or "Air Corpsman." Remember: the Air Corps was part of the army in those days.

One of my tests turned up the fact that I could type and file, so accordingly I was classified as "Clerk-Typist" and destined to undergo Army Administration training as part of my basic training cycle.

Between the tests our time was occupied in performing on any of a number of work details, of which there is no end around a military camp. It is here that I was first introduced to "KP"—Kitchen Police. Through the ages there have been infinite jokes and jests about KP, but it is no joke when you are on it. It is back-breakingly hard, demeaningly dirty and exhaustively long. I never ceased to dread it from one stint to the next. My first encounter was in a huge dining hall for all the inductees and their supervisors.

Eventually, though, the in-processing and classifying came to an end; and we were divided up into groups according to our respective MOS for transportation to our basic training sites. The navy calls them "Boot Camps," but we just said "Basic Training." Our group, I remember, consisted of several hundred of us. We were given a meal in the late afternoon and then put on a troop train bound for Macon, Georgia. The destination was Camp Wheeler, a World War II facility designated as "IRTC," which stands for "Infantry Replacement Training Center."

The train was crowded and over-heated. We had water and toilet facilities but no sleeping arrangements other than the straight-back passenger seats. And there was no food on the train, which was several hours late in arrival times. So it was pretty much a sleepless night and hungry morning. In my misery I remember saying to myself, "But it's going to get worse than this before it gets better!" Actually, though, I remember it as one of the most miserable nights I ever spent.

But about noon—a Saturday, I think, we arrived and were marched down to our new home for the next three months: Fourth Battalion, Company A, Infantry Replacement Training Center, Camp Wheeler, Georgia.

II

Smiley

Nearly everybody who has ever been through a cycle of basic training or boot camp will tell you about what a mean and rough sergeant he had. I had one too. His name was Sgt. Shoemaker and he was a meanie. We called him "Smiley" because he never did.

I graduated from Carolina in June of '42. I got drafted at Fort Bragg the following month. At the physical examination groups of us stood around stark naked, awaiting our turn. We had numbers painted on our chests in Mercurochrome. Mine was Number 56. After we passed the physical—and nearly everyone did—the processing began. (See *No Time for Sergeants* for details.) We were issued our uniforms and various other articles of military equipment, then classified according to our prospective Military Occupational Specialty, and shortly afterward shipped off to a training center. Don't be misinformed. The classification you receive depends overwhelmingly upon what the army happens to need on the day you pass through.

I ought to tell you about Morris Capps, who was also in our draftee group. Morris was a young Adonis, a real matinee idol in looks and physique, and the object of admiring glances, attention and swoons from the teenage girls and belles of Raleigh. After donning our Government Issue uniforms, frequently ill-fitting—"Do you want it too large or too small?"—we waited to see how bad Morris would look when he was leveled down to the same khaki uniformity as the rest of us. But when Morris put in an appearance, he was still as sharp and as spruce as if he had just stepped out of a band box. The military had not damaged by even one whit his good looks or his aplomb.

A miserable, all-night train ride—one of the worst experiences I can remember—went to Camp Wheeler, Georgia, just outside Macon, to the "Infantry Replacement Training Center" there. They told us that it was a privilege to be selected for the infantry, because the infantry was "The Queen of Battle," and the rest of the army's activity revolved around the infantry. But we weren't that dumb. We knew which branch always had the highest casualty rates in battle. At least, though, our caps could be piped in infantry blue, which happens to be the same as Carolina blue. And so basic training began.

We were divided into platoons (about fifty), and each platoon was assigned to a barracks building: 25 men on the first floor, another 25 on the second. There was a "latrine," and three private "bedrooms," one for the platoon sergeant and one each for his corporals. The platoon commander was a new Second Lieutenant just out of ROTC at Tulane. At the end of the day he would retire to officers' quarters. The day and night supervision of the privates was in the hands of the on-site "non-coms." (More about them later.)

The barracks buildings were arranged into a battalion quadrangle with a flagpole and banner in the center. The day would begin at 5:45 AM, and the day spent in learning to march, physical training, field conditions, military courtesy (that means saluting at the proper time), and all the things that raw recruits have to learn in that basic thirteen-week cycle. We wore fatigue uniforms during the day and sweated them to the skin. Usually the training day ended at 4:30 PM, and we would shower and change into our khaki uniforms for retreat ceremony (pulling down the flag) at 5:30. Usually the evenings were free unless we had scheduled nightly exercises and training maneuvers.

Once a week we had to take out our cots and mattresses—bodily—to let them air in the sunshine while we trained through the day. It was another hygienic measure, and it worked. I think it's surprising that in over forty years of military service I never saw a louse or a flea or any other body vermin.

We took three meals a day in the company "mess hall." Nowadays it's called the "dining facility," but it's about the same. I think the desired intake was about 3,500 calories a day. There were meat and potatoes at every meal. The food was high quality—better than in rationed civilian homes—and generally well-prepared: plain fare, but welcomed by us hungry trainees. Before you went down the "chow line" you were required to take a salt tablet and a large glass of water to replace the sweat and salt you had lost during the previous hours. (This practice has since been discontinued as unhealthy and undesirable.) At meals the by-word was "Take all you want, but eat all you take." When you went to scrape your plate after a meal, a sergeant would stand at the garbage can and give you a hard time if you tried to throw away anything edible. It was the "Clean Plate Club" on a mandatory basis. (Maybe that's why I have regularly continued to gain weight ever since.)

KP (kitchen police) would come to each of us about once a month. KP is no joking matter. We would be awakened about 4:30 in the morning and report for duty to the mess hall. The day was consumed in hard—HARD—and dirty labor. It was worse if you happened to draw the detail of washing the pots and pans for a 200-man company. If you were lucky you were released by about 7:30 or 8:00 PM. Exhausted. I used to dread KP from one month to the next. (Unfortunately I never escaped from that detail until two years later, when I became a sergeant.)

Up the street was a theater that showed first-run movies every day, a branch PX (post exchange, that is) and one pay telephone booth for the entire battalion. The PX sold candy, cigarettes, soft drinks and beer (army beer, 3.2% alcohol). It also sold various sundry items, like shoeshine and brass polish, etc. But no medications of any kind. The army did not approve of self-medication, and you couldn't buy any on post. (Go to the infirmary, and the medics would look at you and prescribe whatever might be necessary—if anything.) In the evenings the PX was jammed with wall-to-wall bodies, all sweating profusely.

The one pay telephone generated horrendous lines of homesick soldiers—like me—all calling home for a word of kindness and love. Sometimes it would take hours before one could finally get through on the limited and crowded telephone lines.

A mile or so away was the post library. It was never crowded, and was a pleasant way to spend quiet hours in the early evening.

But most of all, it was HOT! HOT, HOT, HOT. The Georgia sun of summertime hung over everything like a palpable blanket, humid and insistent. There was no escaping it. None of the buildings were air-conditioned. What cooling we had was done with large electric fans. Our barracks building had a huge ceiling fan which began to make things more bearable after the sun went down—about 8:30 or 9:00 or so.

And then there was "Smiley." Remember Sgt. Shoemaker, our platoon sergeant? He was regular army, and I guess he thought it was his mission in life to show us retread-civilians how rough it could be in the service. And he did a good job at it. Smiley was stockily built, thick set, and perpetually glowering with a hostile frown. The slightest mistake—out of step or a dropped piece of equipment—would bring on a tirade of abuse. Frequently the whole platoon would suffer from an individual's lapse.

Smiley terrified us with predictions of what would happen at our first barracks inspection (Saturday afternoon). If an item were out of place, a ripple in a bed blanket or a speck of dust, punishment would be swift and severe—loss of weekend privileges, extra duties, forced march and the like. "You just wait. You'll see."

When the inspection did finally come, with us lined up at attention beside our bunks, a rather kindly-looking gentleman (wearing an eagle) strolled briefly through our building and was gone again in about a half minute. But Smiley was undaunted. After the colonel left he said, "You guys were lucky. That was Col. Febiger. He don't hardly never look at nothing." (A wonderful example of a quadruple negative.) "Next time you might get Col. Tracy. He's the worst one of all."

One thing that instilled in us an undying hatred of Smiley was uniforms. We had two pairs of khaki summer uniforms (shirt and pants). We would send one pair out on Monday and it would come back spruce and clean on Friday afternoon just ready for Saturday inspection. Then after inspection Smiley would run us double time around the barracks area, so that our newly starched uniforms were sweated through and soggy for the weekend and the rest of the next week. He didn't have to do that. We thought it was just plain mean. And I still think so. Those of us who could afford it went into town and bought a couple more of regulation type summer uniforms.

Some of the more literate of us wrote a little song. In it we expressed how much we hated the military life, how terrible the living conditions were, how much we were abused by our superiors, etc. The sorts of things that would be called insubordination if we were confronted outright. The words went something like this:

> The infantry in Georgia is a hell of a place to be. The temperature in the barracks goes to a hundred and twenty-three (etc.).

We sang it to the tune of "I'm a rambling wreck from Georgia Tech," and we would sing it as we marched along on our daily hikes. Smiley would slog along beside us in his usual way, head down, perpetual scowl on his face.

One day one of our more courageous members called out to him, "Hey, Sarge. How do you like our song?"

Smiley's response is forever emblazoned in my memory: "Ah, you goddamn college kids. You give me a pain in the ass. You think you're so goddamn smart and you don't know a goddamn thing. You come down here and you always write a song. And it's ALWAYS the same goddamn song!"

Sergeant Shoemaker had never been to college. But knew a lot about training draftees.

III

Camp Wheeler

A Visit From Kaye

Camp Wheeler was located about ten miles south of Macon, Georgia. It was named for General Joseph Wheeler, one of Lee's cavalry commanders who operated mostly in the Western sector. (Typically army posts in the South are named after Confederate generals, e. g., Lee, Jackson, Stuart, Head, etc., whereas the Northern ones were named after Union generals: Grant, Meade, Custer and others.[1])

Our group was mixed in with other inductees from various other centers. I think it's interesting that the inductees in the South received fatigue uniforms made of blue denim, whereas those from the North had received the olive green

---

1. The military bases named for Confederate generals were renamed in 2023.

twill ones. We retained our blue denims all through basic training, and did not get the green twill ones until we arrived at our next station. (Of course, we all had the summer khakis for everyday wear.)

The thirteen-week basic training cycle was, I think, a pretty well-rounded one. It included calisthenics and various "hardening" exercises each day. There were also the frequent long hikes. Some underwent twenty-mile hikes, but none of the ones in my group were longer than ten miles—which took a half day. We had training on the rifle range with the old "O-3" Springfield rifle that required manual bolt-action after every shot. I qualified as a "Marksman," which is not as good as "Sharpshooter" or "Expert." But in a short time I received my Marksman badge, the first recognition of any kind that I ever got. (I still have it.) We also were trained in bayonet fighting—hated that—and in hand grenade throwing, which was fun if you'd ever played baseball. Then there was the obstacle course. Until you have actually done it you can't realize how demanding it is. There was also close-order drill and extended-order drill as well as night marches and map reading, tent-pitching and bivouac living. Plus numerous other familiarization experiences that kept our days well filled.

After the first seven weeks those of us who were in specialist training—like me as a "clerk-typist"—had our straight line training cut in half, and we spent the final six weeks with half days in—for me—Army Administration. We learned to fill out all sorts of army forms like Service Records, Pay Rolls, Classification Cards, Morning Reports and Duty Rosters and Military Correspondence, and many others.

While we were going through it all we were concerned with the rigors of what we were experiencing. Looking back on it, after all these years, I remember our basic training as a well-planned, well-executed program. We learned an awful lot in a short three months.

The two things that stand out in my mind are the intense summer heat and the intense, homesick longing for Kaye.

The heat was constant, a physical presence from which there was no escape. Hardly any of the buildings were air-conditioned, and whatever clothes we were wearing were drenched with sweat within a few moments of putting them on, and were still damp the next time we wore them. At meal time a sergeant stood at the head of the chow line and required us to take a salt tablet and a full mug of water before we could eat. Each barracks building had a huge fan in the ceiling. It was useless during daylight hours, but cooled us down a little after dark when the temperature went down. But even that took some time. We heard many horror stories about how many were dying of sunstroke and heatstroke, but everybody in my platoon survived the ordeal.

One form of training that we loved was the many training films—Military Courtesy, Personal Hygiene, Security Measures and many others. They were given in the theater, a big, wooden building that seated a lot of trainees. It was air-conditioned, and when it was on the schedule it provided welcome breaks from the heat outside. In the evenings they showed full length, current movies. The features changed two or three times each week, and I went to all of them. It was there that I first saw *Casablanca,* Bing Crosby's *Holiday Inn,* and a number of others.

The other ever-present, unceasing [sentiment] was my longing for Kaye. We both kept our promises—throughout my service time—of a letter every day. I wrote mine at the post library or the nearby service club or sometimes sitting on the side of my cot. I was the envy of the platoon at Mail Call, with the quantity of letters I received plus a more than occasional box of goodies. But that didn't fill the emptiness.

Long-distance telephone service in 1942 was nothing like it is today. Our battalion of several hundred was serviced by one outdoor pay telephone booth. There was always a line, and the connections were agonizingly slow. The procedure went something like this: You dialed the long-distance operator, gave your name and placed a person-to-person call. Then you would wait outside, along with the others until—eventually—the pay phone would ring, and the operator would tell you that your party was on the line. It was always—always—at least an hour and sometimes much longer. And you'd better have your quarters ready, because she wouldn't make the connection until your coins were in the slot.

We hadn't seen each other in well over a month. And the exchanges were emotional ones, to say the least. After we had said the requisite number of "I love yous," I can remember saying (tearfully), "I think about you all the time." Which was true. And then we began to make pipe-dream plans for the next time we could be together.

I figured that there must be a better way of telephoning than using those night-time toll booths, and I soon found a better one. The guest house up at the far end of the post was not at all busy on Sunday mornings. So I began to take the long hike up there and use their in-house telephone, which was better. Of course it meant Kaye had to miss Sunday School and church. But she never objected.

Before entering the service my father had obtained for me with his wholesale connections a pretty solitaire diamond of a respectable size—about one-third or one-half carat. I had arranged to have it mounted into an engagement ring, and my dad wrote to tell me that it was ready. (Debbie[2] has the ring now.) Then I began to implore Kaye to come down and visit me, so I could give it to her in person. She was not yet eighteen years old, and her mother was opposed to the idea. But her straight-laced father—who shall be ever blest—took the compassionate view and spoke out in favor of it. So the trip was on.

I got a weekend pass from my company from noon Saturday to Sunday evening. So Kaye's time with me was just about 30 hours, not counting her long hours on the train. But we both thought it was worth it.

I rented a car, for the first time I had ever done so, and met her at the railway station. Macon is only on the Central of Georgia, which meant that Kaye had to go to Atlanta and transfer to Macon. She arrived, excited and blooming as ever, wearing a blue herringbone tweed suit and a brown beanie. Perfect!

I checked her—not me—into the best hotel in Macon, and after giving her time to freshen up, we drove together to look at Camp Wheeler. To observe the proprieties we checked her into the guest house there. Although we knew very well that she was not going to remain on post overnight.

For dinner that night Kaye had changed into a dress that she knew was my favorite. It was a red "princess" style with a fitted waist and a square neckline. We had dinner at the elegant dining room of the Hotel Dempsey, but I have no idea of what we ate or what was said, so enraptured were we just to be back together again, if only for a few hours.

I suppose every city or town has its secluded, romantic place, and we managed to find one for our car. It was there that I formally asked her to be my wife—although we already knew it was going to happen. Then I slipped the ring onto her

---

2. Kern's daughter-in-law Deborah Mitchell Holoman, wife of David.

finger, and it was "official" to be in the eyes of everyone. Back at Duke her roommate and the girls at Delta Gamma made a big thing of it. Which was all right with Kaye.

She spent the night in her room at the Dempsey Hotel. I called for her early. The rest of Sunday is in my memory just a blur of tenderness and happiness at being together. We had lunch at a nice country-club-type restaurant. It's odd that I remember so vividly what Kaye was wearing. On that day it was another "princess"-style dress, this one black, with a black-and-white cardigan. But all too soon came the dreaded time when her train had to depart to take her back to Atlanta and Durham. We parted with sadness, but with all kinds of vows to get together again when time and space and the army would allow.

That weekend in Macon remains in my memory one of the high spots of our long relationship, courtship and marriage. I'm sure many couples had similar experiences of snatching a few moments of happiness and satisfaction from the frenzy of war and its madness. But this one was especially ours.

Christmas leave, 1942
832 Wake Forest Road—the Highsmith residence

❦ 5 ❦

CAMP GORDON AND FORT DIX

(1942–43)

I

Our thirteen-week training cycle at Camp Wheeler over, we trainees were all graduated and shipped out to various combat units. So far as I know we were all sent to be replacements in the three regiments of the Fourth (Motorized) Infantry Division training at Camp Gordon, Georgia, about a dozen miles south of Augusta. Fort Gordon was also named after a Confederate General, John B. Gordon, who achieved some prominence during the latter stages of the Civil War. I believe that now, in post-war days, Fort Gordon is the training center for the Military Police.

The Fourth Division was a Regular Army organization with a distinguished history. It had fought in a number of Civil War battles and afterward had participated in subduing the West with campaigns against the Indians. Its shoulder insignia, which I was proud to sew on, depicted four green ivy leaves, a play on words with "I-V," the Roman numeral for "four." It was commanded at that time by Major General Raymond C. Barton. His military career was not distinguished, but he was in command when the Fourth Division stormed ashore at Omaha Beach on D-Day, June 6, 1944. The Fourth was the first division to be motorized, which meant that it could put all its troops in wheeled vehicles at the same time without having to march its infantry soldiers from place to place on foot. (I think my fondest-remembered parade was when everybody rode by the reviewing stand mounted in open-air 2½-ton trucks without the several miles of marching.)

I was assigned to Service Company, 8th Infantry Regiment. It was commanded at that time by Colonel James A. Van Fleet, who had an outstanding career in World War II, and later went on to be a four-star general and, I think, briefly Chief of Staff of the Army. Service Company was responsible for the maintenance of the regiment's many trucks and other wheeled vehicles and also for various supply and transportation missions. The personnel whom I met upon becoming a member of Service Company were mostly not draftees; they were hard-bitten Regular Army enlistees who were making a career of the military life. They were a rough and quarrelsome outfit, many of whom had served—and still occasionally served—in the post stockade for various military offenses: AWOL, insubordination, petty theft and the like. I was secretly afraid of many of the privates and lower-ranking non-coms, but I tried not to let it show, and escaped with only a couple of minor skirmishes.

Service Company was commanded by a fine, effective Regular Army captain named John Spangler. Later on he was killed in battle on Omaha Beach on D-Day. He welcomed his three newly-assigned privates to the company with a good orientation speech. One of us outlined the rigorous basic training that we had just undergone and asked how soon we could hope to have some time off. To our surprise he immediately gave us each two-day passes—Friday afternoon to Sunday bed-check time. I took advantage of this unexpected good fortune by hitchhiking to Columbia, S. C., and then taking a bus late Friday evening to Raleigh. My first visit home, a surprise both to Kaye and to my father. Dad took us, with Virginia and some other friends, to Proescher's Restaurant in Cary, the only place in the area for really fine steaks. I had to leave Sunday afternoon by train into Columbia, and then by bus back to camp. This was a much-appreciated welcome to the Fourth Division.

I was assigned to be Assistant Company Clerk in regimental headquarters, where we did all the paperwork for the companies. It consisted of maintaining Service Records, preparing the monthly payroll, correspondence and similar duties. I was familiar with all of these things from my school at Camp Wheeler and had no trouble fitting in. The clerk to whom I was an assistant was grossly inefficient. From my perspective today he must have had Attention Deficit Disorder. But he couldn't concentrate on anything, and would spend long intervals just staring into space even though there were clearly defined tasks in front of us. In a relatively short time it was learned that I could do the job, and Walsh was demoted and sent to the motor pool. In due time I was given his rating and received my first promotion—to corporal. (I skipped over being a Private First Class—PFC.) I felt sorry for Walsh's misfortunes but was delighted to get some recognition and a raise. At that time corporals made $66 a month, while privates earned only $50.

Work continued in this fashion for the ensuing months of fall and winter. When Col. Van Fleet arrived daily at his headquarter, someone would shout "ATTENTION!" and we would all rise while he made his way to his own office at the end of the building.

The principal drawback of my clerking duties was that it was tedious and required long hours, often into the evening, because we were frequently pulled off of our assigned duties to participate in many training exercises—range firing, motor marches, map exercise and obstacle courses to keep up our physical conditioning. I remember going to Captain Spangler and complaining, "I can either do the required office work, or participate in the training. But I can't do both." Captain Spangler was not sympathetic. He replied, "Well, Holoman, you'll just have to do both. No matter how long it takes." After that it was back to the office until far into the evening, to get the paperwork done.

About the middle of December came the rumor that the Fourth Division was about to move out. It was later substantiated by POM activities (Preparation for Overseas Movement). That meant bringing all forms and records up to date: wills, beneficiaries, powers of attorney and all the rest, at the same time completing all the required training. All very hurried, and at the same time very hush-hush. With wartime security, troop movements were a big secret, and no one of our fifteen thousand troops was supposed to breathe a word of it to anyone else. Final destination was to be North Africa. All leaves were canceled—including my much-anticipated Christmas leave, and individuals put on full-time alert. (In those days leaves were called "furloughs.")

But no secret that big can be closely held for very long. The Fourth Division had been stationed near Augusta for a long time, and was a part of the community. One Sunday evening in late December the biggest civilian movie theater in Augusta staged a big farewell ceremony for the Fourth and expressed their fondest best wishes.

So the cat was out of the bag. I'll never know whether it was because of the widespread break in security or for some other abrupt change in army plans, but early in January it was announced that the whole thing had been called off. The Fourth Division was not moving. And we remained at Fort Gordon until about the middle of March, when we really did move. But this was to Fort Dix, N. J., where the division stayed for nearly a year, until it was moved to England in preparation for the invasion of the continent. By that time I had been transferred out and was studying French at Rutgers.

The training and other activities at Fort Dix were pretty much the same as they had been in Georgia, just more of the same. But transportation was better. We were only a couple of hours away from New York, even less than that from Philadelphia. I got a chance to visit both places plus a couple of quick trips home.

As a corporal I was put in charge of a work detail outside the post of about a dozen privates. I did poorly. But it was my first experience of being in any position of authority in the army.

About the middle of May came the opportunity and the reality of being transferred to Army Specialized Training Program and being sent to Rutgers University for about nine months.

II

In the spring of 1943 the army instituted a program which it called The Army Specialized Training Program (ASTP). The concept was to withdraw a number of promising and educated (read "college grads or students") from the ranks of the combat troops and send them back to colleges and universities for a year or so of intensive training in advanced specialties which the army anticipated it might need at some future time before the war's end or immediately afterward. I don't think the program was a big success, for it folded up after about nine months, and the huge majority of participants returned to combat status with the troops. But for those of us who were chosen and for the few who were rewarded (including me) it was a godsend. It included one of the happiest and most satisfying periods of my life. I can't join with the fabled undergraduate who proclaimed "Willingly would I die for dear old Rutgers," but I affectionately remember my days there.

In May of that year [1943] I was stationed at Fort Dix, N. J., not far from Trenton. I was a corporal and a company clerk in the Fourth (Motorized) Division. (I should mention that my commander [8th Infantry] was Col. James Van Fleet, who then made a name for himself in Normandy and later became a four-star general.) When we learned of the existence of the ASTP program we were starry-eyed with the vision that we might be among the chosen few. What a chance to get away from the drudgery of camp and learn to make a valuable contribution to the war effort. Fortunately the breathless waiting was only a few days.

I don't know what criteria were used to select its candidates. Undoubtedly the college degree, an honor society and four years of French. But I know that I was one of the *very* few who received the blessed order to pack my duds and report for change of station. Out. I had no idea of what the process and the future would bring, but I looked forward to the unfolding of this new experience in my life.

A bus ride to the depot and a short train ride took us to Pennsylvania Station in New York City. From there another bus took us uptown (we were only a handful) and unloaded us at the Hebrew Orphan Asylum. I don't know how long it had been devoid of orphans, but it was ample space to house troops drawn from all over the army area and for the classification and administration activities to get us assigned. By this time there were several hundred of us—maybe more. Our quarters were one very large dormitory room with double-deck cots. The facility is located in Morningside Heights, not far from CCNY, not far from Columbia.

My recollection is that I stayed there for a couple of weeks undergoing processing. There was plenty of free time to explore Grant's Tomb, Riverside Drive and the view of the Hudson River. I took the subway downtown into the Times Square area, gawking, and a trip to Radio City Music Hall (about $1). My brother Boyce came up to New York on a buying trip, and we met in town where he took me to dinner and a stage play. It was Frederick March and Tallulah Bankhead in *The Skin of Our Teeth*. We had bed check every night at eleven, so I had to get special permission to out that late.

On Sunday I went to church at Riverside Baptist. That afternoon I went to an Italian restaurant and was introduced to my first pizza. In those days they were called "pizza pies." Can you believe it was nearly twenty years before you could buy a pizza in Raleigh?

But finally the classification was completed, and I was informed that I was going to Rutgers University to study the French Language and Area.

Another train ride took me (and the other incoming students) some thirty miles down the line to New Brunswick, the home of historic Rutgers, "On Banks of the Old Raritan," as their college song goes. There was a military headquarters on the campus where we were in-processed and assigned a dormitory room. I'll tell more about Rutgers a little later, but glorious happy times seemed just beginning, for after our reception we were immediately given a ten-day leave, or furlough as they were called then. I took advantage of that time to go home and get married to Kaye.

I went first back into New York City and bought a new khaki summer uniform including a billed hat and a matching blouse (jacket) for my wedding attire. Then I took the train to Raleigh, and arrived late Saturday afternoon.

I had told Kaye earlier that I might be available for the wedding on very short notice. When she and her family got the word that I was coming, they got on the telephone to all the friends, relatives and neighbors. (There was no time, of course, course, to send out invitations.) When the wedding day arrived (on Tuesday) there was a very respectable attendance on hand.

For wedding gifts we received a service for twelve in Old Master sterling silver and a service for eight in Lamberton's fine china. We received a few crystal pieces which we never added to or completed. Plus assorted individual gifts from well-wishers, all of which we appreciated. Because of wartime shortages we received no small electric appliances, but lots of cut-glass pieces—which were in vogue at the time. My father gave us a generous check with which we later purchased a nice radio/record-player, which was a joy of our life in New Brunswick. He also opened up a savings account for me at a local S&L where he deposited $25 a week for as long as I was in the service.

Four of Kaye's aunts lived in a house on the corner of Jones and Blount Streets.[1] We called it "The Aunt Hill." They gave us a rehearsal reception on Monday evening. It being summer time, they held it on the broad veranda of their home. (No home air-conditioning in those days.) They served the punch

---

1. 604 N. Blount Street is at the corner of Blount and Peace Streets.

from a great cut-glass bowl. From the weight of the ice, etc., it broke in the middle of the party. But that didn't spoil the merriment and good will, though it spattered the contents all over the porch.

The wedding breakfast was held the next morning at Carolina Pines Hotel out of the city on Tryon Road, a very elegant location at that time.

Kaye and I were married on Tuesday afternoon, June 22, 1943, at Edenton Street Methodist Church—the old one that burned down in 1956. The officiating minister was Dr. John Glenn, a previous pastor. Also in attendance was Dr. Andrew J. Hobbs, the current pastor.

In her wedding gown Kaye was a typical radiantly beautiful bride.

Kaye's maid of honor was her younger sister, Louise. Her bridesmaids were her older half-sister Lula Belle, Minnie Morris (Mickey) Huggins, a friend from childhood, Ginny Totman, a friend from Duke, and Lucille Herring, a cousin from Durham.

My father served as my best man. My groomsmen were my three brothers plus, I think, my cousin Bill Holoman.

There was a lavish reception for us at the Woman's Club over on Hillsboro Street, where the Holiday Inn now stands.

After the reception Kaye and I—she had a navy-blue going-away dress—motored to Chapel Hill in the car borrowed from my father and spent our wedding night at the Carolina Inn.

Next day, returning to Raleigh in the evening, we took the train to New York City and shared a lower Pullman berth for our second night of married life.

In New York we stayed at the Governor Clinton Hotel (always my favorite) for a three-day honeymoon of dining, show-going, sight-seeing and lots of affection.

For the last three days of my leave we honeymooned at the Hotel Roger Smith, New Brunswick's finest. After that I found a room for Kaye in a house about a block from the Rutgers campus and reported for duty and classes.

6

RUTGERS

(1943–44)

Rutgers University[1] is located in New Brunswick, N.J., a brisk ten-minute walk from the Pennsylvania Station. Its campus stretches along Easton Avenue on one side and the Raritan River on the other. It was founded by the Dutch in 1775, and a "Second Reformed Dutch Church" stands diagonally across the avenue from a corner of the campus. The historic early buildings are built around a quadrangle. There is a fine statue of the Dutch ruler, William of Orange, with this inscription on the pedestal beneath: "All his life he was the guiding star of a whole great nation; and when he died, all the little children cried."

It became a branch of the New Jersey college system during the nineteenth century as a land-grant college with an ROTC unit. I don't know if it had closed down during the war for lack of students. I did not see any students while I was there. The

---

1. See also "Living with Kaye in New Brunswick," chapter 12, part III.

gymnasium and athletic fields were not in use and the fraternity houses were empty.

The army had set up an administrative headquarters for the ASTP students in one of the campus buildings. There were a half dozen officers (captains and lieutenants) to maintain morale and discipline, the requisite clerks and several personnel and a dispensary for sick calls. We were fed three meals a day on the large basketball court of the gym, which was catered by a non-military contractor. We had a military retreat formation every afternoon after classes, and were confined to our quarters for study during the evening from 7:30 to 11:00, as I remember.

There were several hundred members in the ASTP student body. We were divided into sub-units and housed separately depending on which course of study we were entering in. We had one large group studying engineering. After the ASTP program folded up, a substantial number of these (we later learned) were transferred to Oak Ridge, Tenn., where they worked on the super-secret A-Bomb project. We language students were divided into groups of Spanish, German, and French speaking. My dormitory was Leupp (pronounced Loop) Hall. My room assignment was a largish one that housed four students on two double-deck bunks. The four of us were a strangely assorted quartet. There were two Jews, one Catholic, and one Protestant (me). The Catholic was Eddie Backzewski, the son of Polish immigrants who spoke both Polish and French fluently. He was not comfortable to be quartered with Jews—and we had many in the program. Howard Rudner was older and more mature. He spoke French poorly and was something of a "loner," usually withdrawing to read the daily paper or a magazine.

My other roommate was Morris Springer, a devout, yeshiva-schooled orthodox Jew, the son of a rabbi. He was a slim six foot four inches tall, sweet-tempered, incredibly naive and un-worldly. About twenty years old, he had attended classes at the University of Chicago, but had not graduated. He was by far the most accomplished French speaker in our group. The first morning as we were dressing for breakfast I noticed that Morris had on his army cap and was bowing his head in a sort of rhythm. "Morris, why have you got your hat on?" I asked. To which he replied in some surprise, "Because I'm praying." Then I noticed the phylacteries on his forehead and the strap around his lower arm. Morris continued this practice each morning as long as we were together at Rutgers. We others became accustomed to it.

More about Morris (he liked to be called "Moishe"): Morris was so very vulnerable that he was frequently (unfairly) the butt of our jokes and ridicule. After the ASTP program was discontinued, on his own initiative and at his own expense he published a periodic newsletter for his Rutgers friends. It was not enthusiastically received, and he dropped it after a few issues. Then some 45 years later (in early 1990, I think), he got back in touch with me. He had seen my son Kern's name in a music publication and had obtained my address from him. He was at that time teaching French and English at Hebrew University in Jerusalem. He was also art and music critic for a Jerusalem newspaper. We corresponded a little, and then in early 1992 when Kaye and I visited the Holy Land, we made a point of getting together with him for reunion and old-time reminiscences. We had a really delightful dinner at a nice restaurant with him and his wife. She was a Jew from Eastern Europe and had survived the concentration camps. Both her mother and two sisters had been gassed there, and she was very bitter. But our spirits and camaraderie were not dampened, even though it was snowing outside for the first time in Jerusalem for many years. Later on they divorced and Morris returned to his home town, Chicago, and set up housekeeping with several other devoutly orthodox Jewish males. On two of our trips to Chicago (to visit Chris and Connie) we had lunch with him. Morris passed away several years later toward the turn of the century.

Back, now, at Rutgers, the other members of our French-speaking group were a mixed lot. For some reason (I don't know which) it was heavily Jewish. Some of us were accomplished linguists. (I was about in the middle.) Others were so little accomplished that they could not speak much more French than "Bon Jour" and "Merci." But no matter; all were exposed to the same courses of study. And for them it was a matter of "sink or swim." We were encouraged and urged to speak French among ourselves at all times. And we made a sincere stab at doing this, but we had to make major concessions for those in the "non comprendre" group.

The curriculum that Rutgers provided us was excellent, and it was intense. We had classes every morning and every afternoon plus frequent course-related seminars in the evenings. In addition to the French language there were also classes in French geography and economics and in the history of France. There was also a course in American history. There were even classes in French military terms and expressions, like *camion* (truck), *fusil* (rifle), *mitrailleuse* (machine gun) and many more. There were homework assignments for every night, and we were to turn them in on time. There was mandatory organized athletics in the late afternoon and swimming pool activities. There was a requirement that everyone should swim a mile, but I don't think this was ever enforced.

The teachers were capable and high-quality, most from the Rutgers faculty, but also from qualified locals. We were not infrequently asked to evenings in the homes of some of our teachers. There was one in particular, Marguerite Richards,[2] who after the ASTP program was discontinued, took a job with the US Information Service in Europe. We happened to be assigned in London and Paris at the same time, and we continued a warm and lasting friendship. The courses of instruction that I received at Rutgers were superior to any of those that I ever encountered in college or in the military or elsewhere. I learned a lot there; it opened up doors and opportunities that would not have been available to me otherwise. I will always be grateful for the months that the army sent me to Rutgers.

Those who were unqualified or incapable of improving were eventually returned to troop assignments, as were those who were eliminated for disciplinary problems.

One of the many exercises that we were given was to translate the Gettysburg Address (on Lincoln's birthday) and deliver it orally in class.[3] We learned to sing French patriotic and folk songs and also to translate and sing the Swiss national anthem. I had previously read (in English) the first four books of Proust's *Remembrance of Things Past*. In my leisure time I was able to read in French the fifth and sixth books, *La Captive* and *Albertine Disparue*. I also read *Cyrano de Bergerac* in French, although in these courses the emphasis was much heavier on language than literature.

Rutgers followed a traditional academic schedule, so we had leave time in the early fall and again at Christmas and New Years.

As the winter of 1944 wore on we became aware that there was something in the wind that was not right. And so we were

---

2. See also the mention of Prof. Richards near the beginning of chapter 11.

3. He would recite his version every year as part of the holiday ritual. In about 2005 he typed it out, though with no accents and plenty of errors. The manuscript is in his archive.

disappointed but not really surprised when at the end of third trimester were told that the program was at an end. Each of us was given our orders for another week's leave and then to report to a new assignment. Mine was to Camp Shenango for POM (Preparation for Overseas Movement).

⚜ 7 ⚜

OVERSEAS TO ENGLAND

(1944)

When the ASTP (Army Specialized Training Program) folded up and was discontinued the vast majority of its participants were reassigned and generally sent back to combat units preparing for the invasion of the European continent, certain to take place that year (1944). A substantial number, however, from colleges across the country, were designated to be assigned to the European Civil Affairs Division (ECAD) being organized in England to staff the many—many—detachments to administer justice, law and order to communities on the continent after they had been liberated from Nazi German occupation. I was one of this selected group.

Civil Affairs / Military Government was basically two names for the same type of operation. Civil Affairs were to go into friendly areas and communities like France, Belgium and Holland. Military Government was to go into Germany and Austria, formerly hostile, to accomplish the same purpose. It was assumed by our planners—rightly so—that after four years of German occupation and exploitation, even friendly communities would be unable to care adequately for their needs without assistance, particularly if there had been battle damage. In Germany and Austria the problem was intensified by the fact that, in addition to wartime shortages and destruction, the populace was presumed to be hostile to conquerors.

In a word the mission of ECAD was to keep the problem of conducting a non-battle campaign off the backs of the military commanders so that they could devote their full attention to defeating the enemy without being diverted by the problems of the indigenous civilians. The various detachments were given this duty. Some detachments were tiny, as few as four or five; some extremely large—dozens of personnel, depending on the size and severity of the occupied communities. Cherbourg, Le Havre, Paris and later Antwerp were crucial cities in that they also had to serve as bases of supply for Allied troops. All of the above was in the planning stage in the early spring. ECAD was the only American division ever activated on foreign soil. Of course it wasn't really a division in the strictest military sense, but it was so called. It had its own shoulder patch and insignia.

Those of us designated to be a part of this emerging force were given a few days leave and then ordered to report to Camp Shenango, Pennsylvania, for POM (Preparation for Overseas Movement). My days during that leave time were devoted to getting Kaye re-established back in Raleigh with her family, of goodbyes with friends and family back home, and an emotional farewell with Kaye. It was the first time we had been separated, even for a night, since we had been married the previous June.

A series of bus rides took me to Camp Shenango, which was somewhere in the Pittsburgh area. In the short time we were there the soldiers were counseled and aided in getting their personal affairs in order: wills, insurance policies, immunizations, dental work, bringing service records up-to-date, and the like. All very helpful and necessary, I'm sure, but a little tedious for us awaiting transportation to an unknown future.

One other thing I remember about Camp Shenango was that we were all required to experience simulated enemy fire before going overseas. This consisted of crawling on our bellies for a hundred or so yards while machine guns fired live ammunition a few feet above us. I'm sure it was rendered safe by the supervisors, but still it felt pretty scary. The worst part about it was that it was a particularly rainy day and the field was extremely muddy. Even today I shudder to think how many uniforms were completely ruined by that exercise, because we were all issued new uniforms before we left the camp.

A train ride took us to Camp Miles Standish, which was some twenty miles outside of Boston. This was the final staging area before actually boarding the ship for Europe. The only thing I remember about it is that this is where we packed our belongings for the trip. One evening we were assembled in our barracks, and a lieutenant came in and instructed us on how to put it all in one large, green duffle bag, piece by piece. And this was no small task, for EVERYTHING had to go into that one piece of impedimenta. If you couldn't get it in, it had to be left behind. Or sent home. The only exception was musical instruments. If you had an instrument of any kind, you were allowed to take it along outside the bag. I suppose this was with the thought in mind of some morale-building in the future.

One night a half-dozen or so of us took the bus into Boston. But we didn't know anything about the city and after a subdued dinner we walked around forlornly for a few minutes and returned early to camp.

Next morning, under the weight of our packed duffle bags, we struggled aboard the ship that was to take us to our new adventure. The date was March 23, 1944.

The ship we were on merits a considerable description. It was a converted ocean liner. I never did find out its original name. It had been converted for troop transportation and carried several thousand soldiers. I don't know how many, but it was a lot. By no means were all of them designated for ECAD; many of them were being sent as fillers to the combat troops already in England and training for the invasion. There were even some WACs (Women's Army Corps) on board, but we didn't see much of them, as you can imagine.

Our quarters were divided into compartments, and they were cramped and crowded. A small compartment would house several dozen; a large one many more. Our sleeping facilities—bunks—were canvas stretched tightly across steel pipes. They were tiered with several bunks mounted in layers. I seem to recall that mine was in the middle with two bunks above me and two more below. Our duffle bags were stood up haphazardly against the sides of the walls—bulkheads. There was a large, galvanized iron garbage can in each compartment for us to vomit in when we were seasick, which most of us were for the first few days.

Bathroom and bathing facilities were adequate, but for most compartments they were not very close by, and you had to take a considerable walk to get to them. The principal drawback was that the water in the taps and showers was salt water, which didn't lather, and even after you had washed and bathed as best you could, you still felt sticky and not really clean. Drinking water was available from tanks conveniently located around the ship. Despite the unpleasant living quarters we still spent a fair amount of time in our bunks, because there wasn't anywhere else to go. No recreational facilities and no organized activities. And no planned supervised diversionary programs. We were allowed to go on deck at our discretion, but it was usually pretty chilly up there. Nevertheless there were some fine days, and many of us would spend hours up there, weather permitting.

We were fed two meals a day, rigidly scheduled so as to accommodate the many soldiers who had to be fed in limited space and limited cooking facilities. I think my feeding time was in the late morning and again in the early evening, about twilight. There were no chairs; we ate standing up at long benches about waist high, and were urged along to get out as quickly as possible to make room for the next contingent.

The principal worry on everyone's mind was whether we would be attacked and sunk by a German submarine—U-boats, as they were called. Our ship was not travelling in a convoy. When we were out on deck we could see no other ship than our own in all that vast expanse of Atlantic Ocean. We were assured that there were ample destroyers on all sides out beyond the horizon to protect us. We had to take it for granted that they were out there. I suppose it was effective, because we did not experience any attacks or alarms for the entire voyage. We did not have any lifeboat drills as is mandated on all ships in these post-war days. Maybe they just didn't do it on troop ships. I don't know.

The voyage lasted, I guess, for about ten days or so. The days were filled with nothing more than boredom and ennui. As we neared the coast of England we went through a calm bay of some sort where we were told we could see the coasts of England, Scotland, Ireland and Wales from the deck of our ship. But all of us were eager to get off the ship and press on to new assignments and adventures, whatever they might be.

We disembarked on the Mersey Docks in Liverpool, spent the night there in some makeshift quarters, and the next day, after a short train ride, we arrived in the area of Manchester, where the just-being-organized ECAD was assigned.

The various companies of ECAD were settled in a number of small communities on the outskirts of Manchester. My company was in a pretty little village called West Didsbury, about five miles out from the center of the city via the Kings Way, the main thoroughfare. Our company headquarter was on the corner of Parr's Wood Road and Fog Lane, about two blocks off from Kings Way. Company headquarters consisted of two large Quonset huts. One of them housed the company office and supply room; the other held the company kitchen and dining hall. (By that time we were being discouraged from calling it a "mess hall," though many still did.) The large city of Manchester had received its share of bombing during the German blitz, but that was a couple of years before. I don't think the village communities had undergone much if any bomb damage.

The quartering of our troops—"billets"—was something I had never experienced before or since. All of our enlisted personnel were quartered in private homes. Of course, in the United States that's a "no-no," forbidden in the Bill of Rights. But it is very much permissible in England, and that is what was done in West Didsbury. A representative from the civilian housing authority had previously made a survey of all the homes in the area, and told each of the homeowners, based on the amount of space they had, "you must quarter two or four—or more—soldiers in your house until further notice." One home had a large, open top floor, and it was required to furnish quarters for ten or perhaps twelve of our troops, converted into a sort of barracks area. We were polled to volunteer for which of these spaces were desired—buddy-system and friend-system, and generally given the spaces we asked for. There was one second-floor single room available, and after the crowded conditions on the troop ship, I thought I would like the privacy of a single. So I volunteered for it.

Unfortunately the owner of my designated house was most unenthusiastic about having a foreign soldier living in his home. So when I went to take up my new quarters, I found myself locked out and the proprietor not answering the doorbell. I went back to company headquarters for help and was given temporary shelter overnight. Then, the next morning, accompanied by a uniformed policeman, I went back to my house, where the bobby explained to the homeowner—gently—that yes, he was required to furnish the designated room. So I moved in that same morning.

My decision to "remain single" was not the wisest choice. After the day's duties were completed I would retire to my room with only myself for company. I was quite lonely during the several weeks I lived there.

At 5:45 each morning the first sergeant or his henchman would come racing through the street of Parr's Wood Road, loudly blowing his whistle to arouse us to the morning reveille. We would all come pouring out of our respective houses for a company formation right there in the village street, then repair to the dining hall for breakfast and beginning of the day's regime.

There really wasn't a lot to do in those early days. Calisthenics, of course, and close-order drill and hikes through the countryside. A lot of that. There was some desultory review of our language specialties. Remember ASTP? We were all classified trained linguists, and some of us really were. Later on we went to some organized classes—investigative, map reading, communications and others. One time I looked up in a crowded class and was surprised to see that the instructor was

Lt. James H. Pou Bailey from Raleigh. I knew him as a senator's son and a rising politician in our area, but I had never met him, and did not introduce myself.

Our enlisted personnel was headed by two master sergeants, each jealously vying for supremacy. They had interesting names; one was named "Pentecost," the other "Bibleheimer." Pentecost stayed indoors and administered the company headquarters. Bibleheimer served as drill sergeant for our open-air activities. But it was a situation that could not be allowed to last, so when our contingent was pulled out and sent away, Pentecost was tabbed to go with us.

Discipline was not rigorous, and living conditions were pleasant. Because of England's long-time need for soldiers there was a shortage of eligible men in the area, and the local young womenfolk welcomed the influx of "Yanks" with enthusiasm. And our men responded with equal enthusiasm. Dating and socializing of all kinds was widespread. The only disciplinary problem I recall was when one of our soldiers was punished for his negligence on guard duty—which consisted of patrolling around the two Quonset huts in the evening. There was a fish and chips shop up on the corner of Kings Way, and our man was caught in the act of eating fish and chips while on patrol duty.

I became quite close and friendly with the family in whose home I was quartered. They were a middle-aged couple named Moss, and an elderly mother living with them. After early reservations were dissolved they would frequently invite me to have (late) afternoon tea with them, and I usually accepted. My acceptance, I think, was enhanced by the fact that we soldiers were given a weekly army ration of seven packs of cigarettes, plus cigars and assorted candies and gums. Since I did not smoke, I gave my cigarette ration—most of it—to my landlords. This was a godsend to them, as there were no other tobacco products readily available to them. Their social life consisted in going to the pub several blocks down the street. They did so almost nightly. It was just the kind you see in the movies, with dart games, wall posters, an affable bartender and lots of flowing (warm) beer from the taps. They invited me to accompany them, and I did so a couple of times. But it was very, very British and not particularly appealing to me, although many of our soldiers did frequent the pubs.

Our letters home were rigorously censored before being allowed to go forth. But British mail was not censored, and Mrs. Moss wrote several letters home to Kaye, my wife, and told her where I was and how I was living. I doubt that this breach of security had any lasting negative effects on the outcome of the war.

Easter Sunday fell on one of the days I was stationed in West Didsbury. I went to the morning service at a local Episcopal church. Even on Easter it was very poorly attended.

Across Kings Way at the village of Heaton Moor several miles away was the theater which showed—for free—current movies to the troops. It was a long, dark walk, but not having anything else to do, I regularly made the evening hike over there each time a new movie was scheduled.

I took the bus into Manchester one Saturday afternoon. It is a large city, but a commercial and industrial one, which I found uninteresting. The only thing I recall that caught my attention was a statue of General Gordon, the martyred hero of the Battle of Khartoum. He was wearing a fez and mounted on a camel.

It was rumored that General George S. Patton was quartered in our area. But this was only a few months after the soldier-slapping incident in Sicily, and no one had any desire to run into him unexpectedly.

I don't remember how long I was in the Manchester area. We must have arrived in early April. My time there until about early May seems longer. But in London, Theater Headquarters (ETOUSA) was organizing the G-5 Section for Civil Affairs / Military Government. So consequently several dozen of us were pulled out of ECAD and sent to London to staff the G-5 Section. I was selected to be one of that group, and lived and worked there until our headquarters was moved to France in August.

❧ 8 ❧

LONDON TO PARIS

(1944)

I was stationed in London from May until late July in the summer of 1944. My assignment was in HQ ETOUSA (Headquarters European Theater of Operations, United States Army). I was a corporal in those days. ETOUSA was the large administrative command that looked after logistics and the other myriad items of support of our army in Europe. The big headquarters that did the tactical and strategic planning for all the allied troops was SHAEF (Supreme Headquarters Allied Expeditionary Force). This is where Eisenhower, Montgomery, Bradley and all the other REALLY bigwigs were located, outside the city at a place called, I believe, "Checkers." Command at ETOUSA was wielded as Eisenhower's deputy by Lt. Gen. John C. H. Lee, a martinet who—although we never saw him—we learned to hate cordially because of his stern and rigid enforcement of his powers. Owing to his initials he was referred to affectionately as "Jesus Christ Himself" or "Court House Lee" because of his penchant for court martial charges.

The headquarters of ETOUSA was in a series of buildings around Grosvenor Square, a number of buildings, a lot of soldiers. (Since the end of the war it is now the location of the American Embassy and contains a large standing statue of President Roosevelt.) My section of the headquarters was G-5 (Civil Affairs / Military Government). You called it the one when you were dealing with friendly governments, the other if dealing with the enemy. This branch of the military exists for the purpose of keeping civilian matters off the backs of the tactical commanders. Our section operated out of the building with the address of 33 Grosvenor Square. It was a five-story mansion which had been the residence of one of the Rothschild families.

I was initially assigned as a mail clerk, handling incoming communications. Subsequently I was transferred to the Information Sub-Section, which was in charge of funneling information—public relations stuff—to and from the local French and English newspapers. My immediate superior was Major Thomas Headen,[1] to whom I owe a very great deal. Tom had been a reporter on the Kansas City *Star* and later a city editor of the New York *Sun*. Tom was one of several people in my life who saw something in me that I could not see in myself, bringing me along in several directions and spurring me to things that I might not have otherwise undertaken. It is principally to him that I owe my commissioning as an officer.

Our G-5 Section of the headquarters was headed by Brigadier General Cuthbert Stearns, a sensitive and compassionate man. More about him at some subsequent time.

---

1. Thomas P. Headen (1903–77). He is mentioned with virtually identical language below, in the account of WKH's commissioning in 1945. After the defeat of Germany, Headen became the civilian media director for the entire American sector and in that capacity was the subject of an international political incident when he was captured and jailed by the Russians for allegedly crossing into East Berlin.

The very large contingent of enlisted men staffing the headquarters was billeted in re-worked apartment houses along Green Street, which runs from Hyde Park Lane to North Audley Street, about a block from Grosvenor Square. The officers were quartered at locations somewhere else in the city. I don't know where.

We lived in large rooms, about ten or twelve to a room as I remember. We slept on bunk beds, but like no other bunk beds you ever saw. The lower berth was about four inches above the floor, just enough room to accommodate our under-bed shoes. The upper berth was about three feet above, so we could either crawl down into bed or else jump spryly up into the higher one.

We had bed-check every night to make sure we had not strayed off into the city. And we had reveille every morning. We would line up in formation in the street outside our houses for another attendance check. The thing I particularly remember is that usually while we were in reveille formation, overhead immense quantities of B17 bombers flew in seemingly endless squadrons on their way to the daily daylight bombing of the enemy on the continent. Each plane would generate a long vapor trail across the sky. A REALLY MOVING AND IMPRESSIVE SIGHT. And reassuring that we headquarters paper-shufflers were somehow adding up to something meaningful.

Administration of all these enlisted soldiers was in the hands of Second Lieutenant Israel Noodleman—wonderful name that. Lt. Noodleman had a tough job. Because in trying to put together a comprehensible duty roster—KP, barracks orderly, Charge of Quarters, etc. his charges worked for officers whose ranks were a country mile higher than Noodleman's. It was routine for him to receive a note from a Lt. Col., a Col., or even a Gen.: "Excuse Pvt. Jenks from KP today; I need him for a job in my office." And what would that do to the KP roster? Who would wash the pots and pans? The situation got so onerous that Noodleman in desperation went to see JCH Lee himself. The outcome was that Gen. Lee issued an order that company duties took PRECEDENCE OVER ALL OTHER REGULAR DUTIES. You stood KP even if your colonel might be bothered. Leaving a complacent Lt. Noodleman, but a bunch of disgruntled field grade officers.

The offices operated seven days a week, but the duties were staggered so that nearly everyone got about one or two days off each week. I made the best of my free times by exploring that wonderful old city to the maximum. (I was a major in English literature, remember?) The big statue of Eros in Piccadilly Circus had been taken up and stored away, but Nelson was still standing on his column erect, though it had been badly scarred in the blitz bombing of London. Westminster Abbey and Buckingham Palace were still undamaged. Closer to where I lived, only a block away from vast Hyde Park, were other landmarks. There was Selfridge's huge department store, Marble Arch, an execution site in the old days, now a monument to free speech where any would-be orator with a cause could mount his own soap box and declaim on anything without fear of arrest or reprisal. There was Sherlock Holmes's Baker Street—the old address is now an office building—St. Marylebone Church where Elizabeth Barrett secretly married Robert Browning. And deep in the heart of Kensington Gardens was the utterly charming statue of Peter Pan, surrounded by fairies and woodland creatures.

There were several USO Clubs and Red Cross service clubs available for our pleasure. They were usually not too crowded; they served doughnuts and coffee and lots of hospitality and TLC. They provided, too, a quiet place for letter-writing. I wrote a letter to Kaye every day, one to my Dad every week, and kept up a pretty good correspondence with my friends back home and at places around the world.

We had our own theater which showed both current movies and amateur musical theatricals organized by some of our own people.

The fish and chips houses and particularly the many "pubs" were popular with 'most everyone. We learned to order the various kinds of beer ('arf and 'arf), but never got to liking the fact that British beer is warm—served without ice or refrigeration.

And the very efficient British subways were always a blessing. They were called officially "The Underground" but usually referred to as "The Tube." They were deep under ground—much deeper than the American subways—and had served as bomb shelters during the height of the German blitz bombing. They went everywhere, and were, of course, free to service personnel. As were the fabulous red double-decker buses.

Meanwhile everyone knew that the invasion of the continent was imminent. We knew where the various invasion forces were situated, poised and ready to strike. Sometimes it seemed that the entire British Isles might sink into the sea under the weight of so much military might. Expectation and tension were high, both among the British civilians and the military. Some of our people knew when and where the planned invasion would take place. Most others did not know; and those who didn't know didn't want to know. Everyone was afraid that some inadvertent utterance or slip of the tongue might give away the priceless secret and imperil the lives of thousands.

Then on the morning of June 6 [1944], General Stearns assembled his entire section and announced to us all, "This morning at daybreak allied forces began a large-scale landing on the coast of Normandy. General Montgomery (the ground commander) is very confident and reports that rapid progress is being made." This, of course, was the historic Operation Overlord, the beginning of our conquest of Normandy, and the beginning of the end of the war.

After that we got our news of the progress of battle just like everyone else did: from the newspapers and the BBC (British Broadcasting Corporation).

The night after the invasion began we experienced our first air raid. Just after midnight heavy bombs began falling upon London in various spots around the city. The British anti-aircraft artillery in Hyde Park and elsewhere opened up with a thunderous response. It was very noisy and very frightening to us who hadn't been through one before.

We learned the next morning that what we had encountered was not a German air raid of the conventional kind, but the first of the "buzz-bombs" that were to plague the metropolitan areas for the next three months.

The buzz-bombs were basically flying rockets that had been developed by Werner von Braun and his crew at Peenemunde. They were equipped with a thousand-pound warhead (a big bomb), had side fins and a rudder and were propelled by a rocket at the back. The Germans established a large number of rocket-launching pads along the coast of France, would aim them toward England and let them go, day and night, in dismal, determined succession. They would fly until they ran out of fuel, making a sound like a low-pitched trombone, and then drop on the city below wherever they might have arrived, and explode with a terrifying and damaging blast.

The Germans called them V-1s, short for "Revenge Weapons." (The V-2s, even more terrifying, came along later, after I had left London.) The Germans used these weapons in answer to the heavy night-time saturation bombings of their cities by the British. (The Americans employed daylight precision bombing.) The buzz-bombs had no tactical or strategic value. They were used solely for the purpose of inspiring terror into the hearts of the civilian population. And they succeeded admirably. The people were in what was effectively a continual air-raid warning, constantly on the alert for the ominous drone of the rockets. And then when the noise would shut off, a silence of some twenty seconds would ensue, with heart-in-mouth waiting for where the explosion would occur.

They did not fly particularly rapidly. A British Spitfire or Hurricane plane at 150 MPH could easily catch up with one and destroy it in the air. And they did. But there were so many of them that many did get through and would wreak damage when they struck.

We soldiers were not immune to the terror. We were just as fearful as the civilians; we had no defense against them. At night I had a hard time sleeping, with an ear cocked to hear the ominous drone. Frequently I would take my mattress (as would several others) and go to the lowest inside sub-basement to spend the night. This was not a defense against damage, but simply repairing to a place where we couldn't hear the drone.

The closest that one of the buzz-bombs crashed to me was some fifty yards away. When it did, the walls of the old building literally swayed back and forth for a number of seconds, and we wondered if the whole thing would collapse. (I worked on the fourth floor.)

Meanwhile the battle in Normandy went on. After several weeks our headquarters divided into two sections. One half moved over into Normandy and became "FECOMX" (Forward Echelon, Communications Zone) awaiting the move into Paris as soon as it should fall. I was one of the rear group that stayed back to keep the home fires burning and endure the buzz bombing. Lord Haw-Haw, the German propagandist, broadcasted boasting of all the damage being done and threatening even worse weapons to come. He added, "And don't think we've forgotten about you Yanks on Green Street. We have something special for you." An empty threat, but nevertheless the cause of some conversation here.

One thing I remember distinctly from London was a large map posted on our office wall depicting the planned partition and occupation of Germany after the war. This was almost a year before V-E Day, but the lines were clearly drawn even then. I heard one officer say cynically, "It looks like the Russians got the greenery (the Eastern farmlands), the British got the machinery (the industrial North) and the Americans got the scenery (beautiful Southern Germany and the Alps)." The French were to get the long-disputed land along the Rhine (the Black Forest, etc.). Berlin, the capital city, was to become a separate enclave administered cooperatively by the four powers.

Just about this time General Patton's Third Army conducted its historic and spectacular drive across France, right up to the German border. It was evident that the Germans were going to evacuate Paris, and our headquarters decided to move right in on the space they were leaving. Everybody was to pack up bag and baggage and make straight for Paris.

As I was the most recently promoted NCO (to sergeant), I was given the task of escorting our files to the new headquarters in Paris. I was given one assistant, a corporal named Dale something or other whose last name I have forgotten. The files consisted of a number of heavy steel four-drawer cabinets, all securely locked—there weren't any microfilms in those days—and a small safe. I supervised a work detail in loading the files onto a 2½-ton truck. Our office chief admonished me, "Don't let these files get out of your sight for a single instant"—an order that turned out to be manifestly impossible. But we did our best.

Our truck moved across London to become part of a convoy heading for the coast at Southampton. We spent the first night sleeping under the truck and the next morning proceeded to the coast. There we were loaded onto a small cargo ship which turned out to be our home for the next week.

The truck with the files was loaded into the darkness of the lowest hold. The best I could do was to visit it several times a day to make sure it had not been tampered with.

Our ship anchored just off the Isle of Wight, and waited there for over six days for our turn to enter the (artificial) port at Carentan to unload.

Life aboard ship was a mish-mash of idleness. There was no organization, no discipline, no command or routine. We passengers were simply a group of disorganized bodies from a number of military sources. One soldier said to me, "You know how when you go on a picnic you always throw in a bottle of olives just in case? Well, I'm one of the olives." And the ship's crew didn't care.

Boredom was acute. We each had a bunk, space for our duffle bags, and an adequate latrine. Fortunately there was a big supply of paperback books on board; and I think I read more books in a week than I ever did the rest of my life.

The eating arrangements are worth telling about. It was army C-Rations. All day, every day. Now a C-Ration comes in two cans. One can contains crackers, a candy bar, four cigarettes, a fork and spoon and a small roll of toilet paper. The other contains one of a variety of lunch meals, corned-beef hash, beef stew, pork and beans and similar dishes. Really rather tasty. But all the lunch cans were dumped haphazardly into a large pot amidships which was constantly filled with hot water. We could go to it any time of day or night and pull out a hot meal whenever we wanted. It was really not a bad arrangement, and we certainly never starved. But the lack of variety got old in a hurry.

I must confess that during this time, without supervision I let myself go. I didn't shave or wash very much and never changed into fresh clothes or uniform. Why should I? Nobody cared.

Eventually, however, our time in limbo on the ship came to an end, and we took our turn unloading at the dock. Another night under the truck, and the next morning we joined a Quartermaster company heading for Paris. I should relate that this company had recently overrun an abandoned German buzz-bomb launching site. Several of their men had sickened and one had died from drinking the liquid propellant of the rockets, a mixture, I believe, containing ethyl alcohol. The First Sergeant said to me, "The trouble with these guys is they don't know how to cut it. If you, mix it with a little pineapple juice, it goes down just as smooth."

Anyway, the next day our convoy was off to Paris. It occupied the better part of the day, as we got lost several times. The maps and road signs were confusing and misleading. My first day of sightseeing in France was out of the back end of a 2½-ton truck. I can remember my first view of Chartres Cathedral was up close and receding in the distance as we left the town.

Our truck arrived in Paris about mid-afternoon. Our convoy commander had his orders and directions, and we arrived at our destination without mishap. Our headquarters was a large hotel in mid-town Paris. I supervised the unloading of the truck and escorted my charges to their new location, already decided upon by those who had arrived earlier.

The hotel contained an army dining hall where any "casuals" could eat at any time. I was so embarrassed to find myself among those clean and neatly dressed soldiers. With a filthy uniform, a week-old growth of beard, matted hair and face literally caked with dirt, I vowed that afternoon that I would never go again a day without washing and shaving. It's a vow that I have never broken in the sixty years since then.

Paris, 1944

❦ 9 ❦

PARIS

(1944–45)

I

The headquarters for the Theater of Operations (ETOUSA) was established in the Majestic Hotel on Avenue Victor Hugo, just about a block from the Arc de Triomphe. It was a very spacious facility, about eight stories high, as I remember it, and plenty ample to house our numerous offices. (The big operational headquarters [Supreme Headquarters, Allied Expeditionary Forces—SHAEF] was located in the palace of Versailles some miles out of town.) The Germans had occupied the Majestic Hotel as their administrative headquarters for occupied France. And when they moved out we moved right in on their former space. Despite Hitler's desire and command (*Is Paris Burning?*), the Germans left it intact when they left, and so we had no problems of destruction to cope with upon our arrival.

The rooms and desks that we took over had many vestiges of the German occupation—office equipment and personal belongings. On the first floor was an elaborate communications center and a highly sophisticated telephone switchboard. Some of our early arrivals were preparing to rip it all out and replace it with our own stuff. Then the Signal Corps people showed up and said it would take a year to duplicate anything like that. And so the German switchboard remained in place. There was a problem in connecting up the lines and determining which plug connected with which offices. When I left Paris nine months later they still had some lines where the recipient on the other end was unknown. Perhaps to Hitler or Goering in Berlin?

Many of the directional signs in the hallways were still in place. It was a little chilling to read the arrow pointing toward "Geheime Staatspolizei"—GESTAPO.

For the first few days we slept on the office room floors and used the hotel bathrooms. After things got organized we were moved into an abandoned schoolhouse called Lycée Claude Bernard. The classrooms were large and easily accommodated a dozen or so classic army cots in each, although bathroom facilities were severely limited. But we remembered how much better off we were than the troops in combat, so we didn't complain. Well, not much.

Our school was located at Porte de St.-Cloud, about three miles from the center of Paris and our hotel. To get to and from work we were transported in 2½-ton cargo trucks. They departed in time for work, 7:30, I think, and brought us back right at the end of the day. Some of us would occasionally stay in town for the bars and bistros, and walk home late in the evenings. But that meant a dark, dreary walk, and most didn't do it. I don't remember just when the Paris subway, called the Métro, began to run again, but it was very soon. It was extensive, convenient and free to soldiers in uniform, so that's what we used for our transportation the rest of our time. It was always very crowded.

The officers were quartered in various hotels around the city. The very high ranks had suites in luxurious hotels like the George V and the Prince de Galles just off the Champs-Elysées.

One of the things that we enlisted men did grumble about was that we were not allowed to use the elevators in the hotel. The officers rode, but we were required to use the stairs. This was only an annoyance to those who worked on the fourth floor (like me), but it was a genuine hardship to those who had to climb up to the eighth floor. We thought that was unnecessary discrimination.

The Arc de Triomphe is surprisingly big, about seven stories tall. On the ground beneath the arch is the tomb of the French Unknown Soldier with its eternal flame. The Arc is situated in the middle of a large circle called the Étoile, from which twelve magnificent avenues radiate out in spokes to the rest of Paris. On one side runs the Avenue de la Grande Armée, which leads to the gorgeous Bois de Boulogne park. From the other side runs the Avenue des Champs-Elysées, about a mile and a half long, running past the most fashionable and expensive shops and couturiers. It ends at the huge Place de la Concorde, flanked with twelve statues at the periphery, each a monument to the great cities of France. (From the Franco-Prussian War to World War I the statue to Strasbourg was draped in black because it was in the hands of the Germans.) The square holds Cleopatra's needle and two lovely fountains. This is the place where the guillotine was sited during the Reign of Terror, where Marie Antoinette, Louis XVI and the other aristocrats met their fate.

The square butts up onto the river Seine, and many of the tourist attractions are stretched out along its banks—the Louvre Museum, the Tuileries Garden, the Ile de la Cité with Notre Dame Cathedral, the Sainte Chapelle and many others. Through history Paris has never been sacked or razed, and it is very proud of its preservation of dignity and beauty. It was and is well-deserving of its enduring reputation.

The civilian population of Paris was pretty close to starvation when the allies arrived there. The reception and distribution of foodstuffs had come to a standstill. The farmers and the meat producers had stopped bringing their wares into the markets, and nothing was coming into the city. Nothing. This was an immediate problem for Civil Affairs. We solved this out of our C/A office by organizing what we called The Red Ball Express. By this we supplied Paris with our own army supplies from our base in Cherbourg. The 2½-ton trucks were identified with a big, red ball painted on the sides of each cab so they would not be diverted or stopped, and rushed the 200 miles or so down the highway to feed our French friends. This lasted for a number of days until the city of Paris could get back on its feet; but while it went on, the people in the countryside stared with mouths agape at the seemingly endless procession of American trucks speeding past them.

While the crisis went on we military personnel had our daily rations cut in half. It wasn't a starvation affair, but it wasn't any fun either. In Paris we were fed three meals a day in a rather nice restaurant within easy walking distance of our hotel. Very civilized, but it was still army B-Rations (no fresh fruit or vegetables, fresh meats or dairy products). The big meat staple was Spam, which many of our troops learned to hate. I rather liked it, but even I saw it too often.

This was about the time when pictures were being shown in the newsreels and newspapers of French women being seized by their fellow citizens and having their heads shaved. Lots of conversations and satisfaction about it. I had cleaned up pretty well after my sojourn in the boon-docks, but still felt the need of a good professional barber. My professional barber turned out to be an attractive young French woman, and conversation flowed freely along, as it does with most barbers. I asked—all this following conversation in French—why the girls were getting their hair cut and scalps shaved. "Because they had gone to bed with the Boches." (The liberated French always referred to the Germans as "Boches." It is their slang word for pigs.) I asked "Only for that?" meaning, was that the only offense for which they were so punished. "Yes," she replied. "It is a small thing, of course. But not with the Boche."

While we were getting settled in Paris, General Patton and his Third Army was completing its spectacular drive across France and was knocking at the door of the German homeland. He stopped (or many say he was stopped by our higher ups) just west of the city of Aachen. For what seemed to be weeks we read stories daily of our battle to seize Aachen. One of my duties was to read the French daily newspapers and brief our officers on what the French were saying about us. I read daily that the allies were fighting to take "Aix la Chapelle." It was some days before I finally came to realize that these were two names for the same city. Aix la Chapelle is a historic place. It was the capital of Charlemagne as well as his tomb. It was also the capital of the Holy Roman Empire which he founded.

Not far from our hotel / headquarters was an Episcopal church that called itself The American Cathedral. It conducted services in English at various times during the day, including early mornings before our work began.

My friend John Jernigan (a fellow Tar-Heel) was a devout Episcopalian, and he regularly attended the short morning sessions. It was also attended by a few—a very few—American soldiers. But one other also was Lt. Gen. John C. H. Lee, the much feared, much reviled commander of ETOUSA.

It happened that during the winter months at the conclusion of the service General Lee would make it a point to come over and help John with his heavy service overcoat. Among our friends it became a talking subject that a ranking general would perform this service for a lowly corporal. Some satisfaction, as you can imagine.

One day John made his regular visit, but this day General Lee was not present. At the end of the service a major came bustling up to help John with his coat and said, "I hope you'll be willing to accept valet service today from a mere major." I'm sure others had been noticing General Lee's kind attention.

There was a big movie place on the main street where our troops were shown first-run movies—for free of course. Then farther down town was another posh theater which our troops returning on leave from combat must have found like heaven. In addition to showing the movie it would also show always a genuine, first-rate live floor show *a la* Radio City. The crowning climax of every show was always "The Avila Girls," who would deliver a flamboyant Can-Can. Even after all these years I never see a Can-Can without remembering my affection for the Avila Girls.

Downtown there was also a rather low-key USO Club. They didn't do much other than serve the traditional doughnuts and coffee. I guess they figured that there was too much competition from Paris's other attractions. But there was always a quiet lounge where one could write letters home.

Our work at theater headquarters was mostly routine office work. We did work six—or was it seven?—days a week, but we were seldom called upon to work at night or in the evenings. And we were allowed frequent time off.

Hardly anybody returned to our schoolhouse-quarters at the end of the day. There simply wasn't anything to do in the quiet suburb around St.-Cloud. Most everybody chose to stay downtown to visit the many interesting places and ride a late-night subway back. I don't remember that we had bed checks in Paris. I think the only requirement was to show up at the proper spot for our assignments.

One of the places that we would like to frequent was a little dimly-lit bistro behind the Place de l'Opéra called Le Manoir. I whiled away many an evening there with some of my close friends (John Jernigan, Bill Mann, Jim Kelly and others). We would talk about everything from triviality to philosophy, but mostly we just enjoyed watching the semi-mondaine world go by and the comings and goings of the customers. The management didn't care as long as we continued to buy its watered-down drinks.

When the American army arrived in Paris things had come to something of a standstill at the departure of the Germans. But one by one the theaters, night spots and cafes began to open up until they reached something like post-occupation normalcy.

Even though there was a war going on, the fall and winter of 1944–45 was probably the best period of my life for attendance at cultural and entertainment locales. I went to the opening of the first legitimate stage play after the Germans left, a gorgeously costumed play called *Louise de Lavallière*, one of the mistresses of Louis XIV. I was privileged to attend the first performance in post-occupation Paris of the Conservatory of Music Orchestra directed by Charles Munch. I saw a production of Jean-Paul Sartre's existentialist work called *Huis Clos* (English title, "No Exit") and went two or three times to the famous Folies Bergère on Montmartre. Very raucous and naked in places, but beautifully staged and well-done. Had seats down front in overstuffed divans.

One Sunday afternoon I went to a performance—in French—of the American play *Arsenic and Old Lace*. It was interrupted in the middle by a genuine "claque" from the balcony with lots of foot stomping, seatback pounding and loud shouts of "Le théâtre pour les Français! A bas les Americans!" It was not violent, only loud, but it was a kind of electric moment that I had never experienced before in the theater.

The theaters in Paris were not heated, and when the weather was cold—which it frequently was—we would watch the performance with overcoats on and hands in pockets. When the audience was large our body heat would warm us a little, but when the curtains would go up there would be a surge of cold air from the stage. I remember that a blast came out from the vast stage of the Opéra at a performance of *Boris Godunov*, enough to make us think we were really on the steppes of Russia.

Other operas attended included *Faust, Carmen, Thaïs* and more. The French theaters offered free admissions to Americans in uniform. Seats were available if not previously sold out, and I don't remember ever being turned away.

The USO entertainment groups of Hollywood-type singers and dancers with shows for the combat troops always made visits to Paris on their way to the battle lines. But well-known companies from the US and the UK also made their appearances. Katherine Cornell arrived in her signature role of *The Barretts of Wimpole Street*. The Sadlers' Wells Ballet came from London with Robert Helpman and Moira Shearer as the stars. At that time Margot Fonteyn was still a promising ballerina in the chorus line. And Donald Wolfit came with his Shakespeare company for a three-day tour de force as Hamlet, Shylock and Benedict.

On Christmas Eve we were suddenly and unexpectedly told to pack our duffle bags to prepare for a move. We learned later that our school building was being evacuated to be turned into an emergency hospital for the large number of troops being wounded in the Battle of the Bulge.[1] Well after dark we were loaded onto trucks and transported to the Petit Palais, a museum built just off the Champs-Elysées, whose art works had been stored for safekeeping during the war years. We were under cover, all right, but other than that field conditions prevailed. Water, lights, latrines, etc., all had to be brought in. We lived in this environment for about three weeks. There were rumors that the Germans might be planning a stab at Paris, but I don't think they were anything more than normal uncertainty and apprehension.

Early in January we were reassigned to facilities at a genuine college campus of the Cité Universitaire with actual dormitory rooms—four to a room—and genuine bunk beds. And honest-to-god bathrooms down the hall. The campus was on the South side of the city and right much farther from the center of town. But it was still served by the Métro system, and we continued to commute to work as long as we were stationed there. These arrangements were the best I had encountered since leaving Rutgers.

Life continued in this mode for the winter months and until I had a drastic change in my status in early April.

While stationed in Paris I had gotten into a pattern of writing and distributing every week or so descriptions of my current life there. These letters have survived in a manila folder for the last sixty years, and are also included as a part of my "memoirs," to be read, perhaps, in conjunction with these latter-day accounts.

The next—and last—chapter of my Paris writings [ch. 11] will be an account of how I received a commission and was sent to school again, and then assigned to Germany.

---

1. See also "Joyeux Noël in Paris" in "Other Writings," below.

II

Stearns

The chief of our G-5 Section (Civil Affairs / Military Government) of the headquarters was Brigadier General Cuthbert Stearns. Somewhere in his past career General Stearns had become entangled in military bureaucracy and had not advanced as rapidly as others and was assigned to a relatively minor position in the command and staff structure of the army. Marshall, Arnold, and Bradley were among his contemporaries.

To us underlings he was a much-revered person, intelligent and efficient in his duties; and yet compassionate and approachable in his personal relationships. Those of us who worked for/with him considered him something of a father figure.

We learned that General Stearns had a son who was the apple of his eye, an upperclassman at West Point and a graduate of the class of 1944. I think his name was Cuthbert, Jr. After the normal post-graduate training and processing he was assigned as a Second Lieutenant of infantry to one of the combat units fighting on the border of Germany.

He had arrived in the early months of 1945, and our general was most gratified that his son was in place so close to him. Naturally he was eager to pay a visit at the first opportunity to his son in the field.

So early one Sunday morning General Stearns obtained a command vehicle and had himself driven the hundred or so miles to the front for a first greeting with his son since graduation. Unfortunately he got the word, "Lt. Stearns is out on patrol." General Stearns awaited all day the return of his son. To no avail. Finally, as twilight was falling he gave up and had himself driven back to Paris to resume his duties there. "Sorry I missed you. We'll get together another time."

A message was waiting for him on his desk back in Paris. "Lt. Stearns was killed in action today while he was out on patrol."

So he went back to the command vehicle and travelled the route for the third time that day. He made his way to the Graves Registration tent and was directed to the body bag. There by the light of a kerosene lantern the bag was opened for him, and he identified the body as indeed that of his son.

As he was contemplating this great personal tragedy, he felt a hand on his shoulder. It was the hand of his friend, Lt. Gen. Patch, the commander of the 7th Army, beating up from the south. They had been classmates at West Point.

"Your son?" said Patch. Stearns nodded. And then Gen. Patch murmured sadly, "*My* son was killed last week. In the South Pacific."

And then those two old soldiers and old friends in that darkened tent sat down together and reminisced and shared their grief.

General Stearns had his son's body brought back to Paris, and in an unusual event held a funeral service for him in the American Cathedral there. All of us in the G-5 Section attended to pay our respects and express our sympathy to this saddened soldier and father.[2]

---

2. The archive of Kern's wartime correspondence includes a letter of thanks from General Stearns to his men for attending the funeral at the American cathedral.

10

LETTERS FROM PARIS

(1944–45)

Shortly after I arrived in Paris in August, 1944, the writing bug got a hold of me, and I began to send home enthusiastic letters about what it was like in Paris at that time. I thought they were pretty good, so I made (carbon) copies of them and mailed them to Kaye and my Dad and various friends that I thought would be interested. There was about one every week or so.

I think Kaye disliked the letters. She preferred the more personal and intimate ones with lots of loving sentiments. My Dad, though, was enthusiastic. He began to take them to his friend, Carl Goerch, publisher of *The State* magazine. Carl liked them too and began to run them (gratis, I might add) in his weekly publication. When I received my stories in two successive issues, I decided that I didn't want them published like that, and told Dad to get them stopped. Which he did; I'm sure it was one of the many ways in which I disappointed him.

After those first two issues the letters have languished in a manila file for the past sixty years, to be exhumed now for the pleasure (?) of another generation.

Letters from Paris

This first letter was actually written from Paris, which everybody knew, but we were still trying to preserve the fiction that we shouldn't reveal our location during combat times. I attach it now as an introduction to the other letters to follow.

This is the first of the two letters published in The State *magazine (S/Sgt. Kern Holoman, "A Tar Heel in France," 9 December 1944, pp. 1, 20).*

Wednesday, September 13, 1944

DER MILITARBEFEHLSHABER
IN FRANKREICH
KOMMANDOSTAB   ABT III
PARIS

Somewhere in France

I've visited France's Paris as you can see by this German letterhead stationery which I scrounged. The Germans cleared out from here a couple of weeks ago, seemed pretty much in a hurry, and left quantities of their material and equipment behind. Including this stationery.

I'm writing to you on this stuff partly to impress you and partly because paper is just as hard to find here as 'most everything else. I've "scrounged" this paper just as I have scrounged practically everything I've had for the past weeks. The word "scrounge" is a British term which we have adopted. You might say it means plain stealing. You don't scrounge from individuals in the service nor from civilians, but you sometimes scrounge from other army units. No one dares to leave a jeep on the streets unattended, because if he does, some other army unit will take it. Jeeps are very scarce, and Paris had no transportation except for bicycles (and the streets were black with them) and a few horse-drawn vehicles.

Well anyway, I've visited Paris, and what a trip it was! I still can't believe that all this is happening to me. But during those few hours in Paris, I was thrilled. The city is perfectly beautiful. I've never seen another that can even begin to compare with it. Outwardly, at least, it's hardly battle-scarred at all, inasmuch as "le Boche" in '40 and we in '44 didn't have to fight too hard to get it.

I won't try to describe it you; too many Americans before me have tried to do that. But in the flesh it's more than one could believe from any of its descriptions. It's laid out like the World Fair, and in many places it looks like a World Fair—green parkways, the Eiffel Tower (still standing, contrary to rumors), the Trocadero, the avenues running spoke-like off the Arc de Triomphe, the Arc itself, like Natural Bridge, turning out to be about five times as big as I had expected. I can see why the French shed such copious tears over Paris and why everyone who has visited it wants to return (as they say in the proverb).

Paris was dressed up for its liberation. Of course the fighting had completely stopped by the time I got there (you know me) and the celebration had subsided quite a bit. Not a single Frenchman—male or female—rushed out to kiss me, although I did get a couple of babies handed up to me.

The city looked just as if a parade had passed through a few hours earlier. Flags and bunting were flown, hung, draped and swirled from windows trees and buildings: the Tricolore, the Union Jack, the Stars and Stripes, and here and there a flag of Belgium or Holland, and even one of Italy.

The streets were full of people, all with a smile for every American. How long that will last is problematical, but they were still welcoming us when I got there.

The much-vaunted French smartness among the women seemed a little bizarre to me; a little overdone, but awfully nice to look at. Red shoes (wooden for the most part), plastic earrings, extreme dresses, a ribbon around the hair, a bright kerchief, short, tight skirts and obviously few girdles and brassieres—that is the raiment for the most part.

In the afternoon and evening I saw those go-to-hell hats [presumably the French dragoon helmet, with red plume] that mount and mount and end in a flower pot. Bicycles were everywhere, and unlike the English women who ride with one hand and constantly tug at their skirts to keep them decently lowered, the Parisiennes just ride with their skirts in full bloom like the sails of "Old Ironsides." English women on bikes sit on their skirts. French women don't! Their skirts ride somewhere between the upper thigh and the waist, depending upon the speed, wind velocity and direction. Some wear pants; some don't. Lots of men ride bicycles too, but that exhausts this subject.

American army vehicles comprise most of the motor traffic; but there are a number of German cars with their characteristic green and yellow camouflage markings, now bearing "FFI" in large chalked letters.

The French drive like the devil, honking constantly, swerving in and out. Miracles of escape are to be seen on every side. The cyclists just ride anywhere at all, without looking at what may be coming. Apparently they take the position that the motorists must assume the responsibility for their safety, while the motorists take the other point of view.

When an American car pulls up to the curb, it is immediately surrounded by civilians of both sexes and all ages. The adult French no longer shake hands with every American, although they are extremely friendly and approachable. Now it is just the children or perhaps a Frenchman still hysterical from liberation. The children come up, shake your hand and ask shyly (as yet) "Avez-vous de gum?" The French love to shake hands and I think they feel offended if you don't love it with them.

Naturally I had a big time talking with the civilians. In the first place they want to be friendly, and in the second place they just like to be able to talk to some of us in something else other than baby-talk and Indian sign language. My French gets me by quite well.

Everybody is anxious to talk about what happened while the Germans were here. So far as I can make out, they were pretty well-behaved—so far as breaking up things is concerned. They didn't know they were leaving until a day or two before they were told to evacuate. For the most part they had no idea they were losing the war, so effective was their censorship. So when the news came that Paris was to be evacuated, it came as a bolt. They couldn't believe it, and the French say that they were very scared. But they believed that it was just a strategic move and that they would be back within a few weeks.

On the whole, I gather that the Germans acted like anyone else away from home. They were homesick, especially the German civilians who had been brought into Paris to work. The latter were looked down upon by both the German army and the Parisians. German discipline was strict on their own soldiers as well as upon the French. Apparently the women who had their heads shaved after the Germans left were guilty of collaborating with them in the bed.

October 1944

This is the second and last of my letters that got published.[1] I have copied it verbatim from the way it appeared in *The State* magazine. The temptation to edit my sixty-year-old writing was almost overwhelming. I would have said something different—and sometimes more, sometimes less. But for the sake authenticity it is rendered here just as I wrote it.

A Tar Heel in France, II

It struck me that in London—on the subways, in the streets, in the restaurants—it was the men you noticed. In Paris, you invariably notice the women. And, thinking a little further, I decided that the cities themselves are essentially like that. London is undeniably masculine. It's sturdy, a little plodding, built for use, and self-conscious. Paris is just as undeniably feminine. Paris is pretty and gay and charming. Paris is anxious to please. Its shops are full of smart little things that make you wonder, "What will they think of next?" And they sell myriad flowers in the flower shops and on the streets. The statuary that so freely adorns everything is white and dainty, and invariably gracefully feminine.

Paris makes a minor concession to the male of the species. It comes in the form of little metal hutments that adorn the great sidewalks and promenades at not-too-great intervals. In outward shape they are circular and the sides are gray-painted aprons, well filigreed, as much for ventilation, I suppose, as for illumination. These sides extend from a man's shoulder to his knees, so that both head and feet are plainly visible all the time he's inside. If a Frenchman should happen to be with a young

---

1. S/Sgt. Kern Holoman, "A Tar Heel in France," *The State*, 30 December 1944, pp. 5, 17.

lady, he sees no reason to cease their conversation, so that they continue over the top of the apron, she waiting outside, and he standing inside. It seems to be SOP [Standard Operating Procedure] to button the trousers after coming out, though I suppose one could tarry inside if he felt any reason to do so. The benefits of these little buildings are only potential, though, for it has been my observation that when a Frenchman wants to go, he just goes, and doesn't concern himself with walking more than a few steps away.

The Male is a Drab Creature

The Paris male is a pretty dreary sort of creature anyway. He is smaller than the American, frequently moustached, more frequently clean-shaven. He dresses soberly and usually carries a package or a portmanteau. And in the evening when he walks with his wife or lady friend, you say to yourself, "How did he get that babe?" She is usually superbly dressed, despite the enormous prices quoted in the shop windows. Prices in France run to astronomical figures. When the Germans were here they deflated the mark to a great extent so that it was worth about forty francs (three times its pre-war value on the market). When paydays came around the German soldiers were paid off in bushel baskets full of francs. The American doughboy takes a beating in exchanging his dollar for fifty francs. Consequently a cloth handbag costs $30, a very cheap (man's) suit $125, or a bowl of those flowers I've been telling you about (lilies and dahlias) $40. That last is a month's salary for me.

The French would rush to the banks to exchange the German-printed franc for the French-printed one, and the banks would pay the Germans the costs of occupation in their own money.

ATTITUDE OF THE WACS

As yet I've seen no fraternization whatever between the French natives and our WACs [Women's Army Corps]. I noticed the same thing in London. The GI (I think more and more that he is wonderful) was gregarious with all the English, men and women, especially the latter, but it was very seldom that one saw a WAC out with an English soldier or civilian. They were always with several others of their kind, or, if they dated, with a dogface. The WACs are looking good in Paris. A lot of them have been out in the pastures and fields of western France for several weeks, and when they finally got to town they rushed to have facials and permanents and whatever else women have done to be more appealing. After the first few days, they really looked cute wearing trousers, combat jackets, helmet liners, but otherwise very feminine and pretty.

The other night I walked out to Notre Dame, but by the time I got there it was deep twilight and I couldn't see enough about it to say I had really visited it. I'm convinced now that one should always see great things like that in half darkness, for I know that all those great sights of nature and those man-made which have impressed me most were those which I couldn't see quite well enough to analyze. The sensation is more one of feeling than of seeing.

Notre Dame is on a kind of square and it sits flat on the ground, without steps. Across the square it loomed out of the dusk at me, and it brought a feeling of its overwhelming might. The feeling left as I approached more closely, and it was merely drab and conglomerate and a little trite. It isn't a pretty building. I guess it's rather ugly really, but I like it a great deal for no good reason. Walking around it, I was thrilled again by the platoons of gargoyles that leered down from every corner. And the flying buttresses at the back have a nice, soaring effect in complete contrast to the stolidity of the front. I'm through with Notre Dame now. If you want to read any more about it get a guide book. The above was not copied from one, but I'm sure it must sound as though it was.

In Defense of "Dog-face"

(Let me pause for a brief classical allusion to a previous paragraph. Lest you should feel a pang that your own particular soldier should be a member of that class known as "dog-face," I'd like to point out that one of the greatest commanders of all times was called by that name. Agamemnon was called "thou dog-face" by Achilles in the first book of the Iliad. I think you'll find it on page two.)

Today I saw an interesting souvenir that one of the boys picked up. I hope to find a similar one to send to you for the sake of interest. It was a rather well-printed counterfeit American dollar, made in Germany. Both front and back were quite good imitations of the real thing. But it opened up like a book, and inside was printed in French such sentences as, "This American dollar is Jewish." "It is covered with Jewish symbols, the star, the eye of Jehovah, the triangle, the thirteen arrows." "This dollar is not good without the Jewish signature of Morgenthau." "This Jewish dollar is financing the war." "This money has no odor, but it smells of the Jew." You hear about such things as that—the lengths and the devious means to which the Germans go to achieve their aims, but you never believe it emotionally until you actually see it. It's a lot easier to believe something intellectually than to believe it emotionally. Cases of shell-shock and combat-exhaustion come from men learning through their feelings rather than their brains what battle is like. That's why, when the flying bombs came over our house in London, we could believe it with our emotions and cower on the floor. But an instant later, after they had passed, we could insipidly say "bang!" as if a buzz bomb were the most impotent trifle in the mind of man. That's also the reason, I suppose, for a boy I heard of who wept when he read the binomial theorem, because he found it so perfect, and algebra so beautiful.

October 1944

The school building which the army has ordained that I should call home has a long room which is filled up with chairs that used to be desks, and nightly gives forth with movies for the GI's. There is a beautiful theatre on the Champs-Elysées which also shows free movies for us; and anyone with any sense would go to the theatre, but they keep this one running for the benefit of the inmates who haven't the energy to take the Métro (subway to you) into town. The other night, though, the long room of the school was the scene of our latest course in Sex Morality and the Horrors of VD.

At about 8:30 that night they cranked the siren, and we all came tumbling out of the building and down to the interior court which is the delight of the company officers. The system approved by Good Housekeeping was for all of us to crowd around the single door to the movie room and listen (above the B-17 drone of a hundred conversations) to a Lithuanian sergeant trying to pronounce our honest, non-Lithuanian names. As each name was called, the man in question was supposed to sound off and pass into the room. At the door stood a first lieutenant of the Medical Corps—in other words a doctor—who fulfilled the supreme task of the army doctor as we passed through the door. (As it happened, I didn't know the SOP, and had already passed the doc without performing the desired ritual before I knew what was expected of me. But he didn't see me pass, and not being overcome with fear at the moment, I didn't bother to remind him of his omission.) After an hour or so of waiting within, the rest of our little population was properly processed into the room and the show began.

The first speaker of the evening was a chaplain, a youngish sort of person with metal-rimmed glasses, wavy hair and a pulpit voice. He was unquestionably anti-sexual promiscuity. No, sir, there was no doubt in his mind about it. It was wrong and he'd have none of it. He argued logically from the point of view that we shouldn't hit Johnny over the head with a stick because we wouldn't want Johnny to hit us over the head with a stick. And he reminded us that we wouldn't want some soldier to do wrong by our little sister. He warned us, too, that germs are no respecters of rank and anyone was liable. Apparently we had been deluding ourselves that any self-respecting germ was class conscious enough to draw up to a full halt as soon as he found himself about to invade the domain of a chevron or a bar.

The chaplain was followed on the podium by the medical officer—the one who had presided so ably at the box office. With all respect for the cloth I must confess that the medic was considerably more broadminded about the whole thing than was the chaplain. He recognized the beast that dwells in each of us. He was aware of the demands of the flesh, the call of the wild. With the exception of a few Latin terms which he dropped in order to spice up the affair, he confined himself to the Saxon monosyllables so we'd know what he was talking about. (One must always approach the men from their own level.) In précis his speech was "Don't. But if you do, be careful." He had some form of constructive advice, then, to add to the chaplain's negation. I was forcefully reminded of the speechmaking scene in the Hall of Demons. You'll find it in the second book of *Paradise Lost.*

The preliminaries finally ended, and they prepared for the main bout of the evening—the movie. You have to have been in the army for at least a year to know how the GI feels about that movie. At least once every three months it is before every man like Christmas turkey served cold on the 29th of December. The cinema part of the program ran into difficulty. All the lights in the room were on the same switch, and in order to turn out the ceiling lights, they had to turn out the bulb in the projector too. The only thing to do then was to get a ladder from somewhere and unscrew each bulb in the ceiling—about twelve of them. The ladder turned out to be a single-strand affair, so two bruisers held it perpendicular while a bantam-weight scampered to the top for the mission. It looked like something out of Barnum and Bailey. But you can't beat the army for efficiency, even though it moves in devious ways. The lights did go off, like morning stars blinking successively out.

The movie turned out not to be the hoary old epic so dear to our hearts, but a relatively new release which will gain at least honorable mention when the Academy Award is handed out. I had only seen it twice before. It had a star-studded cast (no pun intended) including Ward Bond, Samuel S. Hinds, Tim Holt and Joseph Cotten, and, seriously, contained a very nice treatment of the delicate subject. Just as most of the boys had decided not to sleep through this one, the camera light snapped off. It seemed that a fuse had blown out. The Lithuanian sergeant rushed around frantically trying to find the fuse box in the dark, but he failed dismally. Eventually the whole thing had to be called off. Or, to be exact, it had to be postponed, for I'm sure we'll see the rest of it soon. I don't know whether we'll just see the part we missed, or whether they'll send for the chaplain and the doctor again. That just about ends the story. The anti-climax came the next morning when the daily newspaper ran a banner headline saying RAF WRECKS EMS CANAL. We felt that we had been lied to and cheated. The medical officer had told us that VD was responsible.

October 1944

Probably I have told you before that it is the responsibility of my boss—and therefore of myself—to see that the lower echelons get whatever information they need in order to run their little Civil Affairs detachments. Consequently he is the "Information Officer," and such is his title on the door of our office. But the sign on the door has led to the understanding that we are a combination encyclopedia and clearing house for general information on any subject that happens to be troubling anyone who comes by. Every day characters of all shapes and ideas make little pilgrimages to our door expecting the "Information Officer" to solve whatever problem confronts their war-torn minds. And we get some grotesque situations to answer. Today a woman—a French woman—was afraid the French were going to requisition her automobile for its own use. Would the American army officer please give her a paper to keep them from doing it? The other day a captain wanted to know where he could get his raincoat re-rubberized. A soldier lost his wristwatch. Would we be sure that an announcement of it got put in *Stars and Stripes?* The French "League of Patriotic Young Women" is putting on a benefit show for the families of dead FFI soldiers. Would we get an American jazz band to play for it?

Now in all these things we don't have the slightest authority to do anything at all. All we can do is to be kind enough to direct them to the proper place. So in addition to the regular duties that we have, another job has come into being, simply because of an unfortunate sign on the door. And we don't really discourage it, because it is far more interesting than the regular line of duties. Many of them, partly out of some sense of gratefulness, partly because they want to be nice to friendly soldiers, sometimes ask me, sometimes the major, to come to a meal at their house. These are uniformly refused for three reasons: first for policy, second because they don't look prosperous enough to patronize the black market, and any food we ate would be food out of their own rations; and third because they usually say it won't affect their meat points because a neighbor just gave them a fine rabbit from the country, which they are going to serve for dinner. Rabbits, as far as I am concerned, are merely fine examples of Mendelian fecundity, but are not eating meat.

Sometimes their requests are amusing, like that of the dapper little man who wanted the names of American soldiers who would sell their weekly cigarette ration cheap. Sometimes they are bewildering, like that of the impatient, ascetic looking person who had some "important" information to give about the Sinai Peninsula. Sometimes they are pathetic, like that of the woman whose daughter was dying, and who wanted to know how she could get her husband released from a German Prisoner of War camp.

The most common request, though, is for permission to travel somewhere. A woman had a daughter who went to visit a little town south of Paris. Then the liberation broke out, and they lost track of each other. Could the army give her transportation to this town? (It couldn't.) But one thing they all ask for is a "paper." By "paper" they mean some sort of written permission to do something or other. Four years of living under the German rule has bred a great deal of respect in the French mind on the powers of a "paper," to get things accomplished, and almost instinctively he turns to the military authorities when he wants to do a little something apart from his day-to-day existence. And they find it awfully hard to understand that the American army is not here to enmesh itself in their way of life. It seems inconceivable to them that the Allies *want* them to manage their own affairs. Time and again they come to the Allied Military in matters which are strictly and unquestionably French in nature. And I have heard the Frenchman wonder aloud—in the streets, not in the office—whether the Americans were going to go away and let the French Communists take over their land. As if we have the intention of deciding what shall be the form of France's government. If the presence of the live military has done this to France in four years, what must it have done to Germany in 12?—or 112, depending on your own opinion of Germany.

Nearly all the inquirers speak a little English; and unless they can't get along at all, we let them use English. When English is the language, we appear to be the smart ones and they are dumb, whereas in French we are the dumb ones. Besides, when French is the language I find myself saying "yes" when I don't mean to at all—probably the result of trying to appear that I understand more than I do. It's a mildly funny sight to see the visitors staring blankly ahead of them, thinking in French and translating into English as rapidly as possible, which is a very slow gait. Try saying a few sentences in French, and you'll find yourself doing the same thing. Thinking in your own language and then speaking in a foreign tongue is like wrapping a knife in cotton, and then trying to cut with it.

Not long ago—so Major Headen tells me—a man was demanding to know why the Americans hadn't wiped out all the Germans in France before pushing on to Germany. Why were there still outlying bands of them in France which had not yet been mopped up. "I don't understand how you could do it," he said. "I want to go to my estate in Cannes, and it is impossible. I can do nozzing until they are gone. But nozzing."

To the office of Civilian Affairs at _____

Dear Sirs,

We shall be very indebted to you if you could interfere by the Military authorities, who are concerned, so as to obtain for us, as i loan for two days, some military films representing as show of about two and a half hours.

These films will be (abbe) shown so families, members of which have been slot by the *Boches*.

We triwst you will be abbe to help us and thanking you before hand we are

Yours very Truly.

October 1944

The French tell me that October is always cold and rainy. This one, anyway, has lived up to its advance publicity. The gay little sidewalk cafes with their wicker chairs and bright awnings have all been pulled inside one by one, leaving in their wake only the bare concrete blankness of the sterile sidewalks. Not long ago I was shivering outside over a glass of wine pretending desperately that I was being fashionable. A lone die-hard French couple was at a neighboring table with a good deal more fortitude than I, and were discussing the practical aspects of marriage such as whether so-and-so is going to marry such-and such or just go on sleeping with him. The woman of the couple was a dainty dish with large brown eyes, a large mouth, a red fox jacket, and lots of style and all in all the sort that holds up traffic. Speaking of a third party she offered the most delightful vitriolic comment I've heard on this side of the Atlantic. "She is the sort of woman," she said, "who goes to bed when you ask her to sit down." It sounded awfully smooth in French.

But my essay for today is not on eavesdropping from the French tables, but on food. I had intended to call it "I EAT—THREE TIMES A DAY."

Everyone knows that soldiers in combat don't live in barracks. But I believe lots of people would be surprised to learn that England is not dotted with army camps of the American variety. Even back there the GI's lived in whatever was available, without waiting for the carpenters to erect two-story white frame buildings. Instead they were billeted in private houses, or quartered in tent cities or in warehouses or empty buildings. In London, for instance, our dining hall was a little building in the heart of the city which had formerly been a retail store for horse equipment. All remembrances of Seabiscuit and his friends had been ground away with the persistent passing of the days and the unending procession of hungry soldiers. Somehow, though, I could never quite escape from the thought that one day a little man in a red coat would ride into the room and ask to buy a saddle.

In Paris, by way of contrast, we dine at an ex-restaurant that was designed for no other purpose than to feed people. It is the glory of our soldiers. The favorite threat these days (to make us do what we ought to do, or not do what we oughtn't do) is to speak of turning us away from our beloved restaurant. Morale is an elusive little item, but an establishment that can serve C-rations as often as our little restaurant, getting as few protests in return, deserves to rank somewhere between the chaplain and the USO as a morale builder.

Our café—even the most uncouth of us cannot bring ourselves to call it a mess hall—is situated near the middle of town, less than a block off of the main drag. The front is of black glazed tile with a wide glass window occupying most of the facade. Inside it is like the eating places that you pass on every block of midtown Broadway—high ceiling, whole walls paneled in mirrors, red topped tables, red leather seats and chairs, gold light fixtures, and red and gold cloak racks. There is upstairs service for the rush hour (which is all the time), and the double circular stair case is of marble with gold hand railings. The wall at the top of the stairs is adorned with a huge Chinese mosaic. From the ceiling a skylight looks all the way down to the diners on the ground floor. A balcony on the second floor is green with palm trees and other potted plants. From this balcony I hear dinner music.

The dinner music is furnished usually by phonograph records of pre-1940 vintage, but periodically we hear the Com Z Quartette. This musical organization is composed of olive drab gentlemen playing an accordion, a bass fiddle, a clarinet and a guitar. The guitarist is the original for Milton Caniff's Terry of comic strip fame, and he looks it. I'm not sure whether the quartette has a repertoire of eleven or twelve numbers; but I know that if you gobble your food and leave immediately, you won't hear the same song more than once. Even if you don't care for this type of music that they grind out, it still adds tone to the establishment. On occasions we have volunteer local talent such as a violinist or a soprano, but that doesn't happen often enough to mention really.

Over in one corner is the bar. Don't get excited; it only used to be a bar. At present it doesn't dispense anything more powerful than water and an occasional fruit juice. The wall above the bar has a mural jungle scene of a python just on the point of devouring a great leopard. To my mind a picture of a snake above a bar is the epitome of poor salesmanship, but maybe the French know better.

We are served—get this—by a squadron of girls in neat black uniforms with neat white aprons. They are as prompt, cheerful and courteous as if we were going to leave dollar bills beside our plates instead of gravy spots. They speak about the same amount of English as our lads do of French, and the two groups have great difficulty in getting together—linguistically speaking. The Americans, I might remark, are being surprisingly slow about catching on to the language. Most of them learn indelibly the French slang for sexual intercourse within two days of getting to Paris, but after two months they still struggle to remember the French for such words as bread and coffee. It's all a matter of essentials, I suppose.

There is a mess sergeant, of course, an unpleasant person with a ladder of hash marks running up to his elbow. He has more decorations that I've ever seen on any other enlisted man, probably including some for meritorious work on pots and pans. But with no KPs and a semi-civilian kitchen, I don't see how he keeps busy all day long now. In addition to the mess sergeant we have a head waiter who makes a real attempt to smile at each GI who enters and direct him to his place. He wears a blue suit for breakfast and lunch, but at dinner he shows up in a tuxedo—with service ribbons. On occasions I have seen him help a soldier put on his coat, but that is something of an exception to the general practice. All of this, I have no doubt, sounds utterly fantastic to you, and I agree that it is. That's why I think it's worth telling about. I'm reminded of the episode in a recent moving picture in which the soldiers get on the boat to go overseas. They see the ship being loaded with champagne, caviar, and finally a bevy of beautiful Goldwyn girls. One old timer shakes his head and says, "Well, it wasn't like this in the last war." To which the answer is, "Don't worry, Buddy. It ain't like it in this war either."

I don't know what the moral to this story is. Spam is Spam no matter how you slice it, and I don't think C-rations will take the place of roast beef on American tables for Sunday dinner. But when you go into an army mess and find pretty girls handing you your Spam on a flowered plate you immediately begin to make sure there are no tacks in your chair. It just isn't military.

October 1944

I TAKE A WALK HOME

My two and a half years in the army have been characterized by not living in an army barracks. In past months I have lived in an orphan asylum, a fraternity house, a college dormitory, and now in a French lycée. Phi Beta Kappa seems to have had its effect, for the educational aura as you see still hangs about me. My sojourn in Paris, though, is the first time that I have had to commute to and from work. Living in the suburbs in the most fashionable tradition as I do, each morning I dash to the Métro, fight the crowd to get on, and scan the headlines while hanging by one arm from the straps along with the Gallic breadwinners. The Paris subway is built for carrying large numbers of people, and is not concerned with comfort. About 25 people can sit down in a single car, and about 100 can stand.

There are as many windows inside as if it were a sight-seeing bus, although the view is no more thrilling than that from a subway in New York. Profuse signs on the windows inform those of us who can read French that it is absolutely forbidden to smoke, to spit, to touch the doors, to get off while the train is moving or to use profanity. The European list of "don'ts" in public places seems to be much longer than our own. The trains amble along the track leisurely, and there is a long time between each one. And the crowds that wait for them in each station are simply terrific. When the trains pull into a station they are so full that the people are jammed against the doors and windows. The doors open and one or two ooze out, and immediately an even greater number tries to get on—and eventually succeeds in doing so. The other night I was riding the Métro when the push began, and one of the last to get on was a neat, dapper little Frenchman who just managed get an elbow and one foot inside. Without any expression of annoyance or impatience he pushed against the crowd with all his might, and finally got both feet, his head and most of his body on the desirable side of the door. The doors closed on his arm and shoulder and the train pulled out of the station while he casually struggled to free himself. He eventually did, about halfway to the next stop. French subways stop running at 10:00, and that statement is the only item about subways that my story really needs for a preface.

One of my French friends here is a student of literature and so is his wife. I met them a week or so ago because I happened to stop on a street corner and look puzzled, and they were the first to come to my assistance. (That trick is always good for one drink.) They had asked me to dinner at their home, which I refused, but I did agree to call on them after dinner one night. And so I boarded the Métro which crossed the Seine, changed lines two or three times, walked a brisk ten blocks, and I was at their house—which is an apartment. It turned out that they are students of literature in the same sense that I am: that is to say they studied it in college. At the moment he is a librarian and she works in a little fur shop. They carry the rather historic name of Valmy, and a very nice pair they are, she small, dark and restless, he, larger, blondish and reposed. The both had learned English in college which is where I learned French, and all of us considered ourselves pleasantly bilingual. They had a big bottle of red wine which they said was very good, and we killed it during the course of several hours. The conversation was on a pleasantly high level and we lapsed into English or French, trying not to look impressed with ourselves when we said something right. But we did keep the French-English dictionary close by, ready to shuttle it back and forth in case of difficulty. About eleven o'clock, though, I realized that I'd be turning into a pumpkin at twelve (bed-check time) and prepared to walk home. They insisted that I couldn't possibly find my way back all that distance, so I whipped out my map and showed them my proposed route back, and seeing that I knew what I was doing, they agreed to let me go. (Everybody in Paris carries a big map of the city around with him. The trick is not to buy one, but to keep from buying more than one.) We shook hands several times and I stalked out into the night.

Paris' observance of blackout regulations is lax to say the least, but any kind of blackout at all in a lonely suburb is a fearsome thing. Less than a minute after I had left my friends, I had lost my direction completely and was stumbling all over myself without even knowing the direction of the sidewalk, to say nothing of my quarters. I suppose I'd have maimed myself if I hadn't seen a flashlight proceeding down the street. Under the assumption that most flashlights have something behind them, I accosted the owner and asked for aid. The owner was a very tall, very thin girl with a red blouse and shoes that raised her heels a foot off the ground. And the turban on her head reached into the sky nearly as high as her peroxided hair. When I told her my troubles she took me by the arm and pulled me into one inky street after another until we came to some sort of thoroughfare. Her flashlight, by the way, did not run on a dry-cell battery, but on a little generator which you work constantly by squeezing it in and out when you want light. It must develop terrific hand muscles. By its light I could see diamond rings on her finger, which, if they were real, must have cost a fortune. The automobiles went by on the street more or less frequently. When one would pass she would scream to them something that sounded like "Eck!" in a rather grating voice. She spoke not a word of English, but at length one of the cars stopped and she asked the driver to take me with him, but he obviously didn't believe her story. They had a furious argument which ended with both of them pulling out their identification cards, which apparently satisfied him, but just the same he left without giving me a ride. The next five minutes were spent in my telling the girl not to bother any more, and her insisting that it was no trouble. Finally a soldier in a jeep stopped and she said, "It is one of your friends," and let me do the talking. The driver said he was just going a block or two up the road. "Well, take me that far," I said. "Anything to get away from this babe." And I winked knowingly to give him the impression that I was just getting back from a big night. So the girl and I shook hands and we drove off with me shouting "Merci, mademoiselle!" into the darkness.

Two blocks later when the GI let me out, my walk home began, and soon I met another girl who had another GI in tow. They asked me if I knew where some street was, and it just happened that I had passed it a minute or two before. "Certainly," said I, and the map came out. We had to spread it out flat on the sidewalk and get around it on our hands and knee, striking matches to see. Even at this hour of the night such a sight will attract a crowd, and in an instant a half a dozen people were speaking words of advice over our shoulders. And then the cops arrived. A car full of gendarmes screeched to the curb, and its occupants poured over to us to get in their two francs worth. It made quite a little gathering there in addition to a lively discussion, everyone having his own idea on just where the place was. It seems to be a common occurrence in Paris for a person to live years and years in a place without knowing the names of any streets except the big ones in his own neighborhood. Everyone in the present case came to something of an agreement, and we shook hands all the way around; and I left and marched on down the street. The policemen offered me a ride, but I refused because I was having too much fun walking.

For at least a mile I walked on down the road completely by myself and completely without incident. Then I found myself overtaking two men in civilian clothes who were speaking English. My uniform and the late hour immediately led them to think that I was lost, and they asked if they could help me. This time I was able to convince them that I knew my whereabouts, even without unfolding the map. But as I was talking they fell into step on each side of me and began to ask the hackneyed old questions about how did I like Paris and when did I think the war would be over and all that stuff. As the conversation progressed, though, I found that one of them had lived for a great many years in Chicago, which he pronounced Shee-cah-GO, and the other one had been a merchant in England. They were just coming back from a movie—a benefit show for the dead members of the FFI—and the first American movie they had seen in nearly five years. It was an old stinker called *The Old Soak,* but the audience, they said, was in no mood to be critical. In the beginning of the picture when the MGM lion appeared and roared, the audience broke into spontaneous, prolonged applause. He was an old friend who had come back.

These friends didn't last very long either, and soon we found ourselves shaking hands where our paths parted, and dissolving into the darkness. At this point I was still an awfully long way from home, and it was beginning to look as if I wouldn't even "show" in the race against time. All at once, thought, a 2½-ton truck roared to a stop beside me and a sheepish American voice called out from the cab, "Hey, Sarge, do you know how to get to _____ Street?" and fate loves me too much, I guess. That street runs right beside my little red schoolhouse. I got back a good five minutes before midnight, and I was sleeping peacefully when my Lithuanian sergeant came around shining his flashlight in everyone's face. A flashlight is the very first item on my list of things to steal.

I may not know much about Paris in the daytime, but I'm certainly learning it by the Braille system.

---

6 November 1944

If you're really "au courant" to the Paris point of view, you look down on such upstart parfumeries and cosmetic houses as Schiaparelli, Coty, Lelong, Molyneux and Chanel. What are considered tops over here are Guerlain, Caron, and one other whose name I can't make out from my notes. Even Guerlain exported to America only those scents which are not in demand over here. Tabu is on the market in jumbo-sized bottles, but it too is pretty well ignored by the cognoscenti. Either they can't meet its well-ignored challenge, or they can and just don't give a damn. Perfume and liquor are two of the few commodities which are allowed us by the prohibitive rate of exchange. Of course, the army points out that we don't have to buy anything, since we are fed, clothed and housed at no charge to ourselves, and we are not compelled to buy gadgets, trinkets and baubles. But men are men, and so we do buy them within our limited means. And even the French agree that they are limited. It's a strange sight to see our men in their combat clothing with France's mud and the grime of campaign still hanging from them, walk jauntily into the ultra-smart shops and ask to see or smell some dainty commodity.

Guerlain has a shop about halfway down the Champs-Elysées where a uniformed doorman salutes as you go in, and a distinguished-looking gentleman bows to you when you are inside. The sales room has no merchandise in view, but only sample packaging and long rows of atomizing bottles containing the various products. The whole shop is a study in marble formality. Floor, steps, pillars, and even the sales counters are severely classic. Quite a number of chic women employees are ready to wait on you. Since the language is still a barrier, the general procedure is to point questioningly at a bottle—any bottle. One of the women picks it up, grabs your hand, and enthusiastically squirts the stuff on it for several seconds. Then she rubs it in vigorously and motions for you to smell. You inhale and all the opium dreams of Samarcand are yours. Before you return to complete consciousness she has the other hand and is going through the same procedure there, only with another scent. At this point you run out of hands and you naturally think the game is over, but the lady keeps on alternating and motioning you to smell. But by this time you don't want to smell anything but fresh air. You point to one of the bottles—any bottle—and nod. You fight to make your head stop reeling while she goes to find a ready-packaged supply. Box under arm (the sizes are that big) you stumble into the street realizing with a shudder that you smell perfectly heavenly for all the strollers on the Champs-Elysées. You keep glancing over your shoulder to see if any of the boys are following you down the street.

The Parisiennes take their perfume much more casually. The day I was in Guerlain's a lady dressed in purple and fine raiment strolled in, picked up the most expensive bottle in sight, sprayed it literally all over herself, put the bottle down and strolled out, having spoken no word to anyone. On another occasion in a little cocktail bar, a woman groped into her handbag and eventually dug out a vial of perfume about the size of a man's after-shaving lotion. She poured generously into her hand and splashed it on her neck and arms and bosom, bird-bath style. Thus far, this woman is one of my favorite pictures of Paris. The shops, by the way, make a standard allowance of fifty francs for each pack of American cigarettes, and woe to the hapless GI who gets caught disposing of his in this manner.

The Paris street scene has altered in that the number of civilian automobiles on the street has tripled since the first days of my stay here. Hence the number of miraculous escapes that I once mentioned has quintupled. The French autos go honking furiously through the streets, the drivers shouting unintelligible things to those who don't jump out of their way with sufficient promptness. Frenchmen don't blow their horns with the ball of the thumb, in the American tradition; they use the entire palm of the hand, and they are convinced that the harder they push, the louder will be the resultant noise. And volume, of course, is the primary objective. The standard price of American gasoline on the black market is 60 francs per litre or about $5 a gallon. I make no accusations about where it comes from or how much is obtainable, but it does exist.

Those who are not in the income bracket which permits buying real gasoline (which they call "essence") use "producer gas." This is a mixture of carbon monoxide and something else which is formed by nothing more than burning a live fire in a built-in furnace. Most automobiles carry these furnaces in back in place of a trunk, and they are genuine fireplaces whose only gas exhaust is the pipeline to the motor. The gas is only about 60% combustible in the cylinders, and as you can imagine, that remaining old 40% cakes all over the motor in the form of carbon. Naturally this ruins the motor in a relatively short time, but they're going to get a new car anyway as soon as they are available. Outwardly the cars seem to run as well as any other; the incongruity is when the owner comes out of his house and carefully stokes up before beginning his journey.

A form of transportation that I haven't told you about is the velo-taxi, the occidental version of the jinricksha. This machine is a little boxlike wicker chariot mounted on two bicycle wheels. The top is made of green or red awning cloth, the windshield a sheet of eisenglass. There is a space within for one person, and this person must duck low to get inside, for the body of the machine rides only about two inches above the ground. The whole affair is attached to the tail of a bicycle, which is ridden on by the velo-taxi driver, who supposedly earns his living by pedaling people from place to place in this manner. This innovation is offspring of the notorious velo-taxi of Paris in the days of its occupation by the Germans. In those days it was pulled by a bicycle built for two—and the two were underworld characters who would trundle their passenger off to some deserted spot and demand gigantic sums of money in return for (a) not leaving him there to walk back to civilization, (b) not giving him a terrible beating, (c) not turning him over to German authorities on some pretext or other. These practices have apparently stopped now, and so far as I know, the only sinister thing about the industry is the prices that the chauffeurs charge for their services. They charge 100 francs ($2) to haul you from the Arc de Triomphe to the Place de la Concorde, a distance roughly the same distance as from Times Square to Columbus Circle—and a downhill run at that. "Velo," I might remark, is the French colloquialism for bicycle, and the six-day bike arena near where I live is called the Velodrome. The real word for bicycle is "bicyclette."

12 November 1944

Even for an old soldier and hardened traveler like me it was a thrill to see Churchill, Anthony Eden, General de Gaulle, and General Koenig in one five-minute period.[2] Not a big thrill like seeing the Grand Canyon or dodging robot bombs, but a little one like a thirty-yard run in a football game. That quartet showed up as something of a surprise to the French on

---

2. On November 11, 1944, Armistice Day.

Armistice Day yesterday, but the real interest of the day to me was in the way the French celebrated the occasion. Even forgetting for a moment what a farce it is to celebrate that peace at this time, the Armistice Day was one of the most amazing things I have ever seen, and I suppose it was entirely French in its nature. I'm sure it could never happen in the United States in just the way it was observed here. These people are Latins, I kept telling myself, and they are more suited temperamentally to screaming their heads off and raising more ceremonious hell than we are. Then, too, I suppose the fact that this was their first Armistice Day in five years helps to explain it.

The Arc de Triomphe is taller than an eight-story building, and when we passed under it on our way to work that morning, we saw it flying a tricolor flag big enough to wrap Boylan-Pearce in. The blue end was fastened to the top of the arch, and the red end anchored to a big knob at the head of the Unknown Soldier's tomb. On every one of the twelve great avenues that angle off of the circle which encloses the Arc were assembled formations of soldiers detailed to march three and a half hours later. The mile and a half length of the Champs-Elysées was roped off from the streets; soldiers with rifles and policemen with white batons were stationed outside the ropes ready to martial the crowds into their proper places. And at 7:30 a thin tight line of people already had begun to press against the ropes, waiting for the parade to begin at eleven.

You've never seen anything like the Champs-Elysées looked at 10:30. You've probably seen people packed closer together, because that street is wide and so are its sidewalks. But there were people—grown men and women—in the trees, sitting on the lamp-posts, climbing on the vehicles, standing on window ledges, or on chairs or stools or ladders. By this time the policemen had locked hands and were standing as a barrier to keep the mass from surging out into the avenue. Then from away down the avenue a wild screaming swept over the crowd and kept coming closer and closer. When we were engulfed in noise, a shiny, open car rolled past briskly. In the back seat were Churchill and de Gaulle, the latter acting as composed and stolid as ever, the former bare-headed and looking like a cherub, pleased as punch, making the V-sign to the right and to the left in turn. The crowd was so thrilled by these two that they nearly missed the second shiny black car, which held Anthony Eden and some French dignitary. Eden looked as dapper and smooth as was to be expected, and a whole ripple of "Qu'il est beau!" fluttered through the noise. We had known the night before that the two Britishers had arrived, but I'm sure it was a pretty little surprise for the French.

Let me say at this point that I was only a spectator at this affair, and not one of the performers. I was doing it clandestinely while supposedly at lunch—it was surprising that it took all the office personnel so long to eat yesterday. A little blonde girl stood on a stool directly me in front of me, and I was on my toes so much I felt like Vera Zorina.

Only a few minutes after the party had passed up toward the Arc, a terrific explosion came from that direction. It was the canon at eleven o'clock to commence the one-minute silence, but we thought for a moment that the Germans had picked this opportune moment to throw V2s at Paris, with Teutonic thoughtfulness. The French knew what it was, though. Their screaming and chatter stopped as if someone had pushed a button to shut it off. We Americans stood at attention, not knowing whether to salute or not, and on about the forty-fifth second decided that we should. When the second canon shot came, the noise started again, but gradually, not all at once.

And then Churchill, de Gaulle and Eden came back down the avenue, only they were walking this time with a sprinkling of bodyguards around them and photographers backing down the street just ahead of them. The pictures of none of them do them justice. They are all much better looking in the flesh. Yesterday there was nothing of the bulldog about Churchill, and nothing birdlike about de Gaulle. The general was very formal as he marched, but Churchill, wearing an RAF officer's overcoat was as affable as if he were receiving guests in his own home. And the crowd went into a frenzy this time, screaming over and over again "Vive Shursheel! Vive Shursheel!"

The military part of the parade began after they had passed, and this was not much different from any parade. The Republican Guard passed first, wearing red and black uniforms, looking like traditional 17th century. Then came Koenig, the leader of the FFI, a big man who marched confidently alone, several companies of French troops behind. The Americans furnished a band and two platoons of soldiers, plus a naval platoon. The British sent about the same number in addition to a company of RAF. Mostly, though, it was a French affair, and it took more than an hour for the French troops to pass by—regular army, FFI, Zouaves, Spahis, Chasseurs, Senegalese, all wearing the insignia and gadgets of their units; but all wearing American field jackets. During practically the whole time they marched by the crowd chanted "Vive la France! Vive la France! Vive la France!" much as we used to yell "hold that line!" All except one little fellow about five years old, who was perched up on his father's shoulder. He didn't concern himself with issues, but just clapped his hands and chanted "Beep, beep, beep!"

The last of the troops to pass by were the mounted Republican Guard, with shiny silver helmets and horsehair plumes that fell all the way down their backs. They wore black boots and white trousers and red and black coats. On magnificent horses they rode knee to knee and flank to flank, stretching across the entire street. File after file of them passed, and the spectators subsided into a proud respectful silence which I imagine is traditional.

After that the parade turned into a drab procession of armored cars and fire trucks and ambulances, etc. The crowd lost interest and dispersed over a period of several hours. From nowhere men appeared, selling post cards with de Gaulle's picture for three francs each. Newspapers were offered for sale, printed in red, white and blue, with flags of all nations and pictures of Churchill, de Gaulle and Eden. The cinema marquis soon showed "Welcome Churchill" signs. Flags and colors to be worn were on sale as if it were outside a football stadium.

As soon as the parade was over, bands of civilians, mostly children, began to form themselves into little groups behind various banners. Each banner, followed by a solid phalanx of humanity, marched with measured precision to the Arc de Triomphe, and with a ceremony, laid a wreath on the tomb of the Unknown Soldier. This wasn't something that lasted just for a few minutes. When at dusk I again crossed the Champs-Elysées bands of them were still fighting their way toward the Arc with their flowers, while some of their number directed the traffic around them. There were hundreds of thousands of people on the streets yesterday, and all of them must have belonged to at least one of these groups. I dropped by the tomb of the Unknown Soldier this morning. There was a solid rectangle of wreathes, mostly chrysanthemums, extending thirty yards away from his tomb. They were from such organizations as Society of Chinese Dead for France, 1914–1918, Society of Women of Saint Denis, Committee for the Liberation of the French Cinema, and hundreds of others.

One of the boys who works with me came in very excited yesterday, that he had seen Churchill's daughter, Mary. "She's a pretty woman," he said. "She's a captain of something in the ATS (British WACs). I could tell she was a captain, because she had three pimps [pips] on each shoulder."

Paris

21 November 1944

The working class of France is represented in my little world by the two young women who come into my office nearly every morning to empty the waste-paper basket and stir up the dust. They knock at the door sometime between eleven and twelve, usually at the precise moment I decide that it is now time to lock up and go and eat lunch, but they never stay long enough to retard my going. They give the room a good deal more promises than licks. When they enter they are as bashful and coquettish as if they were overly bold young ladies calling imprudently at the apartment of the young gentleman of their choice. They hesitate at the door, skittish and shy, even now, though I have never once chased them around the room. While they muster up their courage before beginning their chores we usually have a bright little chit-chat. The three of us flit through the office—my flitting is purely for broom-dodging purposes—and the morning is radiant with our conversational gems. We make an amiable little sight, should any of the higher brass decide to peep in at one of these sessions.

I have seen these girls daily for a couple of months, but both are nameless to me. I differentiate between them mentally as "The Pretty One" and "The Ugly One." The distinction is most unfair, for both these adjectives are comparative. The Pretty One isn't very pretty, and the Ugly One isn't very ugly. Spiritually, however, they are Mike and Ike; there just isn't any difference. The American army is to them a great and solemn mystery, just as it seems to be to most of the French. They are visibly awestruck at the deep thoughts and mighty plans that spring from the bowels of the headquarters which employs them. One of the first days I was here the Ugly One wanted to know what grade my stripes represented, "Capitaine? Lieuténant?" I told her that I'm a sergeant-chef, an ambiguous grade that I'm not sure exists. Neither was she. Both these young ladies are rather petite and just a wee bit ethereal, but they go about their work with a stolidness and devotion that is inspirational to us less conscientious GI's.

The first night I arrived in Paris I was homeless except for the back half of a 2½-ton truck that I had inhabited for several days. My back was already well-tortured by that corduroy feeling, and rather than brave it for another night I decided to curl up in my blanket here on the office floor. I remember thinking as I dozed off that it was the softest floor I had ever slept on. I was awakened the next morning by the two little chambermaids groping around and stumbling over me in the darkness, looking for the keys to some other offices. This whole incident of our meeting struck them as being very funny indeed, even though I was fully dressed at the time, in addition to my blanket which I was wearing army-fashion. Ever since, that has been our little joke, and we have fun giggling together over it.

These girls apparently come with the building, for they worked here first for the French, and then for the Germans, our predecessors, and now for us. Like all good Frenchmen they hate the Boche. One day I asked Pretty what they did when the Boche left. The corners of her mouth turned down and she looked quite fierce as she stormed, "We cleaned and deloused (dépouillé) from top to bottom!" Maybe they did and maybe they didn't, though I must say it was in a very orderly condition when we took over. They don't speak any English except what they have picked up here; and after discovering that I understood French, they used to converse with each other in German. One day I swung out with "Ach, sie sprechen Deutsch, Fraulein?" "Wie geht es Ihnen?" and "Sie konnen eingehen," which are three of the four German sentences that I had learned from my phrase book before the army decided that the book had too friendly a tone and withdrew it. The fourth sentence was "Wo kann ich etwas zu essen bekommen?" which didn't seem very applicable. (I'm not guaranteeing any of this spelling, by the way). The girls were surprised. "Ja," I said. "I speak German ein bischen." After that episode the girls wait until they are cleaning someone else's room before talking and secret stuff.

One day when they entered I was reading the newspaper following my usual practice of relaxation during working hours. After we had had our daily giggle over something, I asked them if the German office soldiers worked as hard as the Americans. "Yes," said Ugly. "They are unhappy if they are not working. If they have nothing to do, they make work for themselves." To me that is one of the most damning things that have yet been said about the Boche.

Back in London the housework was done by more settled women of the English biddy type. They insisted on being called charladies, but they were more than glad to do our weekly washing for us in return for a couple of shillings and an occasional pack of cigarettes. The maids in Paris, I thought, would take in washing at the same price and with the same spirit as the English women. So I gave my laundry to Pretty, along with a cake of soap, which was unobtainable here. It was a medium-sized wash, ten or fifteen pieces, nothing heavy. A week and a half later it came back—done beautifully—with a neat French laundry mark on each piece. Price: $2.16.

Both the girls showed a lot of interest in our helmets. We were wearing only the plastic inner lining without the tin hat arrangements when we moved in. One of the first mornings they summoned their courage and scampered over to my liner on the table and thumped it ever so lightly. Then they shook their heads. It wasn't nearly heavy enough to give any protection. I tried to explain, but it's surprisingly difficult to explain a mechanical operation in a foreign language. Later in the day I was able to show them a helmet complete, and they understood, but were still uncertain in their acceptance. They don't seem to think it's very practical, which just goes to show you how wrong a French chambermaid can be.

At some time in our association, they have conceived the idea that I have a deep, smoldering hatred for the major who is my boss. It probably comes from the fact that I sit in his cushioned chair when he is not here. At one of the daily sessions Ugly came to me and put her hand on my shoulder as if she were going to congratulate me for being promoted to major general. "You don't get things very dirty," she said proudly. "Not nearly as much as the blond gentleman," nodding toward the major's chair. And with that she smiled and tiptoed out of the room, going I suppose, to pose for one of Mr. Corot's nymph paintings. I'm very glad that the language barrier exists, or I don't know what sort of damaging statements she would make to the major about me.

"Oh vanitas vanitatem," sayeth the prophet, and the world choruses, "Amen." But only the French and Earl Moran would put vanity in the scullery and sex behind the broom.

Paris

4 December 1944

One day last week the Parisiennes celebrated the continental version of Sadie Hawkins Day, only they dignified it with the title of "Saint Catherine's Day." Historically and traditionally, though, it shapes up to about the same thing, for on this day all the unmarried girls of eligible age are supposed to roam the city looking for their man, trap him, and make him say "yes" before the stroke of midnight. The logical question to ask at this point is wherein is this day different from any other day in Paris, but the answer is, of course, that on this fête day the whole proceeding is more festive, more open, and more organized. All the girls wore pink carnations apparently for no other purpose than to warn the males that they were on the prowl. Funny hats seemed to be quite in order also, because St. Catherine was a dressmaker by trade. Generally speaking the hats looked like permanent editions of New Year's Eve party hats, with streamers, tassels and pom-poms, and done up in garish, flashing colors. One unconcerned looking young lady was wearing a yellow beret which sported a fine aluminum model of a high-speed continental steam engine. A far-fetched wheel motif was the only explanation I could think of for it, but it looked kind of nice. Most of the fun came after dark, when the girls would run around in groups of fifteen or twenty, singing frolicsome songs (St. Catherine's singing, if I remember the poem, drew an angel down) and frequently surrounding some passerby, dancing and shouting things which were doubtlessly hilarious, to judge from the accompanying giggles. Sometimes they would kiss the trapped wretch if he looked bashful enough. Lots of American soldiers slunk through the streets trying to look bashful, and a few succeeded, but in general the girls kept their man-hunting on a love-at-home basis. I don't mean to suggest anything naughty by all these goings-on. These were just nice girls having a good time on an occasion which has no equivalent in America. The girls, by the way, were called "midinettes," which means dressmaker, but it is given now to any St. Catherine's Day reveler.

Most of Paris's night clubs are up in the Montmartre district, lying in a rough semicircle around the Church of the Sacre-Cœur. The great majority of them are closed at the moment, but one by one they are beginning to turn on the lights and open the bottles. The Moulin-Rouge is operating now; and though it is little more than a movie house, it can still afford to keep a troupe of Can-Can girls bouncing every night. The Chat Noir is only a couple of blocks down the street from it. "Chat Noir" means "Black Cat," but it is also a very nasty pun, which is the only real reason I have for mentioning it. The Folies Bergère opened several weeks ago and has been playing ever since to a capacity house composed mostly of allied soldiers. It is quite nude when the occasion demands it, and those who are in a position to know inform me that it is better than the best American burlesque. The Folies' box office has a cute trick of selling more tickets than it has seats, which frequently leads to some interesting complications. One night our mimeographing expert (T/5) was sitting in a box overlooking the goings-on and the takings-off when a major general came in with a ticket to the same box. There were no other available seats. So the general sat on the floor and rested his elbows on the railings while the GI enjoyed the show—somewhat gingerly—from his chair. I believe the general was pretty wise to make that move. It would have looked mighty bad if he had ranked the kid out of his seat, which he unquestionably could have done.

Closer into town is the Tyrol, a little place much frequented by the Germans because, I suppose, of the beer and the friendly little floor show. There is also the Bœuf sur le Toit, whose name is another dirty pun, but is a respectable night club nonetheless. Georges Carpentier, the patriarch of French boxing, runs a bare-breasted, be-G-stringed club called the Lido. Returning palmers tell me that a glass of beer costs a hundred francs there. (I haven't made it yet.) The smart thing to do, they say, is to order a bottle of champagne (800 francs) and nurse it along for a whole evening whose show lasts from 9:30 to 12. That way the whole evening shouldn't cost more than fifteen or twenty dollars, and that is the way the French work—only it isn't even fifteen dollars by French standards. The Americans—and I suppose the Germans too—found they couldn't let it go at that. One bottle leads naturally to another, and a month's pay is gone while they were still sober enough to bother about it. Charpentier was accused of collaborating with the Germans, but some committee which rules on such things decided that he really didn't after all. Probably he hates the Boche too, and after all it is a pretty fine distinction between trading with them and collaborating with them. No doubt it was a matter of choosing between the Nazis for customers and no customers at all. At any rate he has been forgiven, and his Lido Club has found high favor among those of the allies who can afford it.

The French are crazy about American popular songs—and so are the English. There are innumerable quantities of four- and five-piece rhythm bands around Paris which do exclusively things like "Beat Me, Daddy," "In the Mood," and "Shoo Shoo, Baby." The majority of them are pretty good. They have something appealing about them, but whatever it be, it is not American. Since we have been here we have seen "le Jazz hot" give way to "su weeng," and "booGEE," but aside from the name, it is all the same thing. They dance to it, but even their jitterbugging has an acute accent. They kick their legs out, and some of the brawnier Frenchmen even toss their partners up in the air from time to time, but it's a studied sort of gaiety that needs saddle shoes, chewing gum and bobby socks to make it really authentic. It's like playing bridge and riding horseback, not because you enjoy it, but it's just the thing to do here. The British are even worse than the French in this respect, for some English swing bands can play Shaw's "Begin the Beguine" and Miller's "In the Mood" in a flawless note-for-note imitation without making you want to tap your foot even once. The French like different effects, and they love elaborate instruments like white pianos, electric guitars, drum sets complete to the last tom-toms, etc. They also like to set French words to our songs, but their translations don't mean nearly the same things. Nevertheless there is something satisfying about hearing familiar songs in another language.

Charlie Chaplain (Charlot here) in *The Gold Rush* is playing in a nearby movie house. He is a great favorite here, and I'm sure more people have been to that theater than went to the Yukon in '98. More than any other American film the French are anticipating Charlot in *Le Dictateur*.

TRANSCRIBED 2 MARCH 2005

PARIS

11 DECEMBER 1944

I went to a party not so very long ago at the home of Madame S. (name withheld for obvious reasons). This lady lives in a little apartment just off the Place Victor Hugo, which suggests that she is moderately well-fixed. It was my first visit, and when I walked into her living room, I had mouth open, ready to compliment the first thing that struck my eye. But I didn't see a thing in the room worthy of the trouble of opening my mouth. Everything in sight was commonplace; the chairs were to be sat upon, the carpet to be walked upon, the lamps to give light, the tables to hold the lamps. It was just anybody's sitting room from anywhere in the world. I was told later that the "secrétaire" was a Louis XVI piece, but you might have found it anywhere between here and Cheyenne.

Mme S. looked exactly like her apartment, for she is the sort of person one meets everywhere and is never surprised to find. She is pushing fifty, bulges in the wrong places, is short and dumpy and has restless black eyes that dart around constantly as if she were afraid someone will lose attention and that she will miss anything. She speaks in an animated tone just above a whisper, and her sentences usually climb up and end in a giggle that reminds you of Billie Burke. Mme S. is a type, and while I don't imply that all Frenchwomen are like her, there are many of her kind.

I don't know how Cpl. Jernigan found her. Jernigan meets everyone eventually. He and Lady Cavendish were the best of friends in London, and the Lord Mayor and his wife had the experience one night at the theater. Jernigan is wonderful, and when I start on the neighbors he will be my first character sketch. The genesis of our soirée is that one of our friends had a birthday, and we had scraped together four bottles of champagne, but found no suitably festive place to drink it. It's a real problem for soldiers to find a nice spot in which to drink their own liquor. "I'll find us a place," said Jernigan, and the next morning he came in saying that he had met a very nice lady who wanted us to come to her place for a party. This nice lady, said Jernigan, had entered into the spirit of the occasion with gusto, and she had offered to make sandwiches for us. Then she had counted off on her fingers things to eat that we could bring that would make the party really a success. That fruit cake from home, she thought would be just the thing. Also a few cans of meat or of cheese from our K-rations would be exactly right to put between that bread that she was going to furnish. (I might mention at this point that every citizen of Paris knows exactly the contents of a K-ration box, and you are likely to get dirty looks if you hold out that stick of gum or those three cigarettes). Mme S. also said she would invite a friend of hers to help entertain us and make us all have a better time.

At eight o'clock on the appointed night three of us GI's showed up at her house, along with a captain friend of ours who goes out with us from time to time—the result of a peculiar chain of irrelevant circumstances. We sat around her living room for a short eternity, grasping at straws of conversation and enduring those momentary silences in which everyone's mind spins like a roulette wheel, hoping it will stop on the right thing to say. Mme S., we found out, is a native Parisienne; she married an American businessman many years ago, and once he took her to the U. S. on a visit. It was there that she had learned her English, which sounds at first to be ever so fluent. Soon I noticed, however, that whenever the conversation rose above the one-syllable level, she would smile and answer, "Yes," a little bit uncertainly—just as I do in French. Her speech also had little anachronisms in it like "flapper" and "so's your old man," and I expected her to give out with "23 skidoo" at any minute, but she never did. Her husband had died twenty years ago, and left her with only a moderate amount of money, which seems to have been dwindling ever since. High up on one of her shelves I saw an ancient china beer mug with an escutcheon on it and "Harvard" printed underneath in red, gothic letters. Mme S. got her heat from an old-fashion kerosene burner in her living room, and she fed a block of wood into it every few minutes. The room got so full of wood smoke that we could have used a blanket and sent up signals. Monique, the friend she had invited, would arrive about nine o'clock. But by that time one bottle of champagne was already gone.

Monique (the spelling is phonetic) was a rather nice-looking girl about 25 or so. She had wavy reddish hair, a long nose, a nice complexion, and not too much make-up or perfume—which is mildly surprising. Mme S.'s position in our party was pretty obvious all the way, but I couldn't figure out just what Monique's angle was. She is a pretty astute person, though, and doubtless she had one. But at any rate she ate and drank practically nothing, was obviously not interested in men, and in the conversation she turned out to be the best informed French citizen whom I have met. She had had an English nanny when she was a child, and she speaks English as well as you do. The party livened up immensely after her arrival, as it usually does when a pretty girl is in the midst of a bunch of men.

That was a peculiar conversation, because during the whole evening there was not a single reference to sex, to bodily functions, to the bathroom or to anything even remotely suggestive. We talked about the war, which is pretty safe ground, and about what a fabulous place America is. And of course the black market came in for its share of discussion, as it does when Frenchmen meet. Neither of the women have a lot of money, and their only objection to the black market is that it is so expensive. They can't afford to pay the prices for what they need. (We shouldn't judge them too severely, though, because for four years the black market was practically the only market; and until just a few months ago it was a highly patriotic thing to do, because it supposedly made the Germans mad. I doubt the latter statement; it seems to me that a black market always favors the privileged class. But that's the theory.) Mme S., though, would have willingly turned cartwheels down the Champs-Elysées if she thought she could get a pound of butter at the end; and she said that since we worked for Civil Affairs she was sure we could get her a little something extra. I squelched that idea by waving the French flag, the American flag and the Christian flag in a five-minute speech. (I have since had this mimeographed, and plan to send it to all my friends on V-Day.) We also talked about Communism, but neither of the ladies expressed much concern over that, which made me wonder if they are nearly as well off as they seem to be. All good bourgeoisie fear Communism as they fear hell.

Well, we drank champagne and ate fruit cake and cheese and cheese sandwiches—Mme S. really did come across with some bread—and drank champagne, and the evening turned into a relative success. The captain had two packs of cigarettes which he passed around rather frequently, making everybody happy, for this was at the depths of the cigarette famine, when there just weren't any to be had anywhere. The first one that Mme S. took she smoked so far down that she had to use Unguentine after each inhale. After that she took one each time they were offered, but she always put it away, saying that she would smoke it later.

When we finally had to leave, there was still an unopened bottle of champagne. "Why don't you just leave it here, and you won't have to bother to bring it next time you come," said Mme S. And surprisingly we really did leave it, though we sent Jernigan back to pick it up a few days later, saying that we had to have it in a hurry. You are probably telling yourself that I was a cad to accept the hospitality of the lady's home and then break her on the wheel, but I really don't think we owed her anything.

The next night some older and better friends gave a real birthday party for our friends. There were 18 people at an all-black-market affair, and only three of us were soldiers. For dessert they brought in a three-tiered white cake. Written across the top in letters of pink icing were the following words: HAPPY MANNY RETURNS. But that's another story.

TRANSCRIBED 25 JANUARY 2005

Paris

1 January 1945

Today is the day after New Year's Eve and it is unquestionably the day after last night. The war makes progress and the shoulders of headquarters strain under the burden; but the toil proceeds in a subdued fashion today and the dance to victory today accompanied by the lingering notes of last night's melody. Faces are pallid and drawn, the greetings of the day and year are decidedly glum, and here and there I notice a wince when one more typewriter begins its diurnal clatter. The office is filled with cosmic repentance and Weltschmerz.

If for no other reason than to keep my wings spotless, I must affirm at this point that I was cold sober all night, and I feel wonderful today. But from all I remember of last night I might as well have been roaring. I started going at seven in the evening, and from then on I visited so many places and met so many people that everything has blended in my memory as one big handshake and one big smile. The faces and a few incidents come back like chit-chat in a reception line. The peculiar thing is that I had planned to go home early and write a few letters, but when I broke this news to my friend Jernigan, he was so shocked at the idea-of-going-to-bed-on-New-Year's-Eve that I was afraid I would really lose a lot of face if I didn't get in on some festivities.

So we went visiting. All of us had myriad invitations to go everywhere, and three of us decided to check the rounds. Every family in Paris gives an all-night party (called a "reveillon") on New Year's Eve. Every family invites ten or twelve other families to come and spend it with them—which raises the problem of where the other families come from, a question that I can't answer. Each invited family brings several friends along, and by the time the evening has well begun, not even the hostess knows who her guests are. But the champagne and white wine flows and ebbs like the tide, and the New Year should look more like the White Rock girl than like the precious little infant with license-plate plants. At the first place we went we met a girl named Jeannine, an old friend of Jernigan whom he has had his eye on for some weeks, and she decided that she wanted to come with us—only she wanted to go to her friends' homes. Eventually we compromised and did a splotchy job of visiting everyone. Only from then on I didn't see a single person I ever recall seeing before. Each house served either white wine or champagne to all comers, and one place was handing out something they called orangeade, but it wasn't NEHI. Nobody was doing anything anywhere. They just sat and talked—multiple conversations, not a group discussion—for conversing is a real art over here. At intervals something would make you feel that the dialogue was terminated, and you'd move on to the next person. I must have talked to a hundred people, and with a little knowledge of French I managed to hit it off fairly well. Once I heard a GI not too far away ask a boy "Comment allez-vous?" four times. I thought he must have been a doctor.

For a while I talked to a girl named Frances. She studies English at the Berlitz school, and speaks it quite fluently. Since the Americans came to town she has become very interested in American slang, and we spent the entire time teaching each other expressions of argot that neither of us will ever have the opportunity to use. You should have heard me trying to explain to her the meaning of "What's up, chum?" She had talked to a lot of Americans before me, and some of them had obviously taught her a lot of wrong things to say. Once she called over to a friend of hers "Gettin' much?" This, she explained to me, means "Are you having a good time?" Another time she said something that sent the English-speaking soldiers into hysteria, but I'll have to wait until I see you to tell you that one. I tried to explain both sentences to her, and she really felt quite deeply that she had been duped. After that she thought that every new English word she heard was something dirty, and I thought she was going to slap a boy when he said, "You're joking with me." Several months ago an American said to her, "Oh, my aching back" (a uniquely American expression of dismay), and she went to get him an aspirin. A little weazened French boy was sitting in the corner wearing a French uniform and a deadly-looking knife. He hadn't begun to shave yet, and he was just beginning to need it, and he looked as if he'd run away if anyone spoke to him. Frances told me that he was in the FFI—"but not the real FFI," she assured me. "I was in that." And she had a hair-lifting story about the time when Paris was liberated, when she told her family she was going to visit a friend, and went for five days to live in a barracks with fifty policemen. "It was very disagreeable," she admitted, "but for France everything is necessary."

Only a few minutes before I met Frances, I talked to a young lady named Anite, our hostess, I think. She was about 20, had beyond a doubt the most beautiful face I've ever seen on any human. She had a nice figure too, and she limped along—permanently—with the help of two canes. She told me she was sad at Glenn Miller's death, because he could not more make such music belle for to dance with.

At one place an old gentleman with Father Time whiskers showed me how the French play backgammon; at another a stout woman of 50 with blondined hair took me aside and showed me the family jewels or a part of them. A little bouncy girl of 16 or so with crackling black eyes wanted me to translate into French, "Hold tight, hold tight, foodley-yacky-sacky, want some seafood, Mama" [a contemporary song]. I confess with downcast eyes that I tried to do it.

One house we visited was the home of a family named Noel. There were lots and lots of aunts and cousins married brothers, etc. all named Noel, including a young woman who was run over last August by a Frenchman on a bicycle, and who still has her leg in a cast. She whispered in my ear "I am going to make everyone laugh now." And then she said in a loud voice, pointing to her father (gaffer-type Frenchman) "Papa, lui est Père Noel," and then practically everyone in the room rolled on the floor with laughter. That's a pun sentence. It means Daddy is head of the Noel family, but it also means Daddy is Santa Claus. It is a family joke that is so old that no one remembers just when it started but it gets dragged out every year with a greater laugh each time, presumably because it makes everyone think of happy days in the past.

At midnight we were in an apartment on the ninth floor of some building, and there were so many people there that the walls were bulging. For us Americans with our Anglo-Saxon inhibitions, Midnight New Year's Eve is one of the most self-conscious moments of the year. But not in France. In an instant the entire mob was kissing one another with a frenzy that made you think they wouldn't get everybody kissed within the next sixty seconds. Women kissed each other, women kissed men, and men kissed each other—in the French manner, on each cheek with a flourish. The room was fairly sticky with mass osculation. There were smiles on every face, and a hum of many murmured greetings, but not much screaming, and no mechanical noise makers. It gives you the impression of being very tender and sincere in its way, but not nearly so forced as an American celebration of the same sort. They are Latins, as I've said so many times before, and their emotions run much closer to the surface than we allow our artesian feelings.

This hasn't been a complete or a coherent account, but the night strikes me as having been that way. The incidents and faces have all blended in my mind, and probably the few occurrences I've told you about will soon slip back into their normal position and New Year's Eve 1945 will have a feeling all its own just as the others have. Somewhere along the way I lost both Jernigan and Jeannine, but the other GI and I left early and got in at a fairly respectable hour. The exponents of the military life had taken a bed check where I live a little after midnight, but I'm sure there'll be a mutiny if they try to gig every man in headquarters.

TRANSCRIBED 14 JANUARY 2005

Paris

17 January 1945

FUN IN THE SNOW

The mercury is frozen in the thermometer around here and the snow that fell a week or more ago is entirely unmelted, so that it is still a fine, white powder, without the crust of ice that usually forms on top of snowfalls. Even on the busy avenues and boulevards the passing of automobiles and the plodding of many feet have done nothing more in a week's time than to turn the snow to a dirty gray color that looks like wet sand in the streets. This snowfall has been the signal for renewed hostilities in Paris, and street fighting has broken out all over again. So far as I know, none of us is going to get sent home on account of wounds, for the ammunition is good old American-type snowballs served with cheerful violence around the most fashionable streets in the world.

The French—especially the demoiselles, toward whom the Americans always turn their best side—have found in our soldiers a certain streak of playfulness which I think is something new for them in adult warriors. In their lighter moments it is a sort of puppyish attitude which I imagine is not altogether pleasant to foreign onlookers; but it certainly is not present in the British or the French soldier—and probably not in the Germans either, although the only ones of them I have seen were all prisoners and not much in the mood for lighter moments. Anyway, the French girls have taken advantage of this playfulness to declare an open season on Americans, and it's a rare thing for any of us to come off the streets these days without looking like King Winter himself. It isn't an organized sort of thing among the girls. They simply go out in groups of twos and threes, snowballs in hand, ready to pound any prospects; and they invariably choose the Americans because they respond so cheerfully.

The usual procedure is to saunter down the streets (hands behind backs) and smile invitingly at the passing soldiers. And then, as soon as they have passed, the soldier turns around to look and the girls turn around to smash the snow-balls into surprised faces. (You'd be surprised at how long it took our men to catch on to that gag.) After that the whole battle is impromptu, and everybody throws snow all around till both sides are tired and continue the original line of march. Only in a lot of cases the Americans don't respond at all, because when it comes to grappling with young ladies, they prefer closer quarters than ten or fifteen feet. Hand-to-hand combat is where they excel.

One corner of the Champs-Elysées has snowballs flying through the air so thick that you could climb up on them like a ladder. It has already been christened Purple Heart Corner. One day I was passing there, and a young lady whom I vaguely recalled having met on New Year's Eve recognized me and we stopped to shake hands. This was fatal, as one or two of her friends—or accomplices—opened up a reasonably good imitation of the Balaclavian barrage. Fortunately they don't throw much better than girls anywhere else, and the female Judas who was shaking my hand got it about as many times as I. Both of us plastered in Paris, as the boys say, but much quicker and less pleasantly than the usual way.

A couple of days ago I had done a little extra work, and out of compensation I had the afternoon off. On my way to the nearest open movie house I passed through the little round park of Marbeuf, and rounding a corner I found myself face to face with three high-school-aged Amazons, all giggling and holding great globs of snow in their mittened hands. "Oui?" they asked invitingly, which I gathered was their French way of saying "Wanna play rough?" "Non" was the only possible answer I could think of to this one, and I said it. But it wouldn't have made any difference if I had said "Oui." They insisted and I had to submit to another youthful avalanche. "All right," I said, "If you act like that, I won't liberate you any more." And they looked a little pensive as I left them with that.

All this, of course, is conducted on an impersonal basis. Wealth or rank or station in life should have nothing to do with it. A major was trotting along recently, dabbing at his snowy face with a handkerchief. Presumably he thought it was a surreptitious mutiny in his own ranks, for he was muttering something about a "goddam court martial." And a little private friend of mine—a nice boy whom I had met in the queue at Guerlain's—happened to slip and fall on the sidewalk. Before he could get to his feet, three passing strangers had paused for a moment to rub snow in his face.

So much for the battle. It's in the best spirit of fun, and everyone takes it that way. We enjoy it certainly, and the travel hardened veterans are surprised to find a new side to the ever-amazing French character. A few people throwing snow-balls is to be expected, but such universal participation is a revelation of something or other. Only one person I've seen has lost his temper. This was a biggest French girl who really had been pretty badly snowed under. She was screaming unintelligible and volcanic French, every sentence of which seemed to end with the English phrase, "Ees too moch!"

A couple of nights ago I was on my way home early, and having a few extra minutes, I decided to get off the Métro at a different stop and walk the rest of the way in. The snow had covered all the landmarks, and so I took the wrong turn somewhere. In a half an hour I was completely lost. I suppose I looked it too, because a little boy with a book-satchel stepped up and asked me in the worst English imaginable where I was going. When I told him; he offered to show me the way, saying he lived near there himself. It was lucky for me, for I found as he led me along through the little dark streets that I would never have found my way through all those turnings. He was a talkative little fellow, about 15 or 16, and he is studying for his "Bachaud" at a little school near Luxembourg Gardens. He has been studying English for three years now, and he can hardly speak it all. This doesn't bother him in the least. He isn't the slightest bit interested in English, but he is crazy to learn to speak American slang. (All of the French speak of American slang as though it were a separate language, and they make a sharp distinction between speaking English and speaking American. I think they have quite a lot of justification on both grounds.) My guide, whose name is Jean-Paul Valery, in the few minutes I was with him uttered some of the most fantastic archaisms of slang—which I suppose his teachers had picked up when they visited America 20 years ago. He asked me if all Americans call each other "cake eater." If Jean-Paul didn't like it it was the "bee's eyebrow." He likes the classics of literature, though. Charles Dickens is his favorite American author; and he said that he had just finished reading "Oliver Toots."

TRANSCRIBED 9 JANUARY 2005

Paris

20 March 1945

BIRTHDAY SUPPER

In the few months since Christmas it has been my good fortune to have been accepted into the bosom of a real French family. Our relationship is something more than the usual greediness with which our soldiers generally eat their illegal meals and saunter out with hands in pockets. In this case we (my two buddies, John Jernigan and Bill Mann, buck sergeants in G-5, and myself) feel that we are accepted as friends, as people who are liked for themselves, and not just because they are anonymities in a liberating army. They invite us out two or three times a week, and we accept perhaps once in two weeks. Our friends are what the French call *moyenne bourgeoisie,* and they are rich as the top part of a milk bottle. This family, like most families, is closely knit and composed of several sub-divisions headed by three brothers. Between them they own a shop specializing in laces and linens, an Oriental art shop, an accounting firm, and the apartment in which they live, in addition to several other buildings. The French temperament, you see, is to inherit a certain amount of property from the parents, to add to its assets all during their lives, and to leave to their children a little more than had been left to themselves. Our family is the heir of a long line of such philosophers, and they have been left enough pies to hold comfortably the grasp of many fingers. Their income enables them all to live extremely well (at a time when France is really suffering) while they hardly lift a finger; and a large part of their time is spent in the enjoyment of the graceful pleasures of life. At least one of them has a birthday every week, and a sumptuous supper is invariably given for the occasion.

Not so very long ago it was the turn of Jeannine, the baby of the brood, to have a birthday—her eighteenth—and we were all invited around to get in on the festivities. For our birthday present we dug into our rations and produced about a dozen packs of cigarettes, several cakes of soap, some toothpaste, some shampoo, a deck of cards, a nail file, and a set of American picture postcards. We found a box big enough to hold all these items and packed them in neatly. Then we rooted out the office draftsman, pulled our ranks on him, and made him design us a birthday card, featuring the Army Service Forces shoulder-flash, and our names in gaudy script. We washed and dressed and made our uniforms as presentable as possible and then safaried to the apartment house of Jeannine, who lives a brisk fifteen-minute walk from our office. We wound up in the Statue-of-Liberty stairway to the sixth floor, which is occupied by Jeannine's family. (The rest of the house is occupied by lesser peoples who pay rent, thereby financing black-market meals for American soldiers.)

We walked [up, instead of taking the elevator] because there still isn't enough electricity functioning in Paris to service individual houses. And when we finally puffed to the top of the stairs, Jeannine's father and brother were waiting to greet us. After we had taken off our overcoats and draped them over various articles of clothing in somebody's bedroom, we were ushered into the living room to meet the assembled multitudes, and there really was a multitude. All of the guests were dressed to kill and smoking American cigarettes. We were immediately pushed into chairs and handed cigarettes and aperitifs; and in no time at all the conversation was trickling down a dozen little tributaries. I had Jeannine on one side of me and her father on the other. Both are highly skilled conversation pushers, and we all did exceedingly well at finding a little common ground to converse on.

It was fitting that this party should be for Jeannine, because she was our original entry into the family. Jernigan met her, and she introduced him to the family, and then he introduced them to us. Which is how the whole deal got started. On this night she was wearing a short blue dress, diamond earbobs and a naive hairdo. Jeannine is quite pretty, but she has a sticky-sweet personality which I find a little cloying. She has tiny features and shallow eyes to match. She is very tall for a girl, and possesses a figure that one would be extremely kind to call willowy. Little bird legs and stubby-heeled shoes are at the bottom. Still she has a lovely complexion, pretty hands, and is as graceful as a whippet. Besides this, she has had manner bred into her for years, so that she is never at a loss as to the proper thing to do or say, and she has the perfect hostess's trick of making everyone feel that he is quite important to the gathering. Somehow I get the feeling that she does it like a wind-up doll, and that if a marble statue were sitting in one of the chairs, she'd turn that cultured voice on it and make it feel welcome in Paris.

Jeannine attends one of the best schools for young ladies in Paris. It is staffed entirely by Carmelite nuns. They specialize in languages, the students taking English, German, Latin and Spanish simultaneously. Jeannine is having quite a bit of trouble in her English classes these days, for when she has finished translating, she is invariably told to cease translating it into American and do it in proper English. (The French idea of speaking English properly is to sound like an empire-builder straight out of Kipling. Normally most wealthy French women spend a couple of years in an English convent, and the people who speak English really well do so with a broad English accent.)

Having just turned eighteen, Jeannine is in the throes of the being-ashamed-of-her-parents stage. She tries to keep her father quiet as much as possible, tries to smooth over any remark that he might make, and makes a fetish of rescuing any guest whom he engages in casual conversation. (At present this is occasioned by the fact that Papa is quite browned-off with the role the allies are playing in France, and she is afraid he will say something to offend the Americans. It happens, however, that Papa is about three times as smart as Jeannine gives promise of ever being. He has been to America half a dozen times, and to Burma, Siam and China so many times that he has lost count. He is the Oriental art specialist of the family.) He speaks English perfectly, converses with intelligence on any subject and is absolutely flawless in manners and dress. Also he is smart enough to clothe Jeannine in the finest that can be bought on the black market, and to stuff her esophagus with the most expensive foods. Jeannine considers none of these things. She is ashamed of him just the same. I can't tell whether Papa is aware of the pain his existence is causing his youngest chick. If so, his calm remains pretty unruffled.

Well, so much for Jeannine and her father. Next time I'll tell you about some other members of the family, what we ate, and what we did. Meanwhile you might send me something to eat while I sweat over this hot typewriter.

TRANSCRIBED 3 JANUARY 2005

Paris

5 April 1945

I believe the last chapter ended with the question of whether I would or would not be rescued from the hideous fate of conversation with Papa. I was duly saved by Jeannine, galloping up on her white charger.

Papa is very upset over the fact that neither of his sons is interested in working in his Oriental art shop. He fears that when he passes on, the boys will quickly sell his treasures to the highest bidder and use the money to buy champagne and vacations on the Cote d'Azur. He is probably right. Neither of his sons, as a matter of fact, is interested in working anywhere (which I don't hold against them). I don't know much about the elder except that he has a white-collar job in an office, and speaks perfect English with a British accent, just as his father does. The younger brother is John, or rather Jean, who is about my age. He has an extremely keen mind, and is a genius in his own line of endeavor. His number 1 hobby is learning English, and he has learned it entirely free from American moving pictures. He is a wonderful example of the never-had-a-lesson-in-my-life philosophy, but he gets away with it surprisingly gracefully. He listens attentively, understands almost everything. As is to be expected he speaks it much worse than he hears it, and when he speaks it is entirely conversational idiom. We took him and Jeannine to an American musical stage show several weeks ago. It was packed with Americanisms, but Jean understood them very well. At least he laughed at the proper places. Jean is tall, very thin, dark and pallid at the same time, wears heavy horn-rimmed glasses and a head of wiry, kinky hair. He is tubercular, I think, for he stays in bed most of the day, rising only for the supper meal and the evenings. He was discharged from the French army several years ago. When he is out of bed, though, he is a dynamo. Next to learning English, photography is his hobby. He has an exquisite German camera (which he probably collaborated like hell to get), and it's hard to be in a room with him for five minutes at a time without hearing his call to someone "Tenez!" simultaneously flooding them with light and exposing them to posterity.

Then there is Françoise, called Frances by us Americans. She is not one of the family, but as Jeannine's amie du cœur she gets invited to all the parties. She has about as much poise as Martha Raye. I have yet to see her go through an evening without dropping something, spilling something, tripping up somebody or burning a cigarette hole in someone's clothing or some article of furniture. Once when we had tea at her apartment, she spread marmalade on her hand instead of on the biscuit she had. Frances is very big, very blonde (natural), and is possessed of a raucous laugh that frequently makes you think you have said something dirty without meaning to. She is built like a government privy, as the boys say. Recently she has set her cap for Bill Mann, who is young, handsome, unmarried and unattached. Nowadays when we enter the apartment, we hear her shouting from the depths of the rooms, "Beeeel!" as she rushes to shake his hand, trampling over intermediate persons like the Duke backfield. During the evening she frequently takes Bill to one side and offers him slices of cake and surreptitious goodies filched from the snack table in the dining room. She looks sullen for a while after anyone breaks on Bill while he is dancing with her. (Sgt. Mann, who has 20/20 vision with no rose-colored glasses, refuses to get swept off his feet by prospects of an overseas courtship. He rather thinks he'll still be a bachelor when he returns.) Frances's grandmother died several months ago; and in accordance with the French customs, Frances and the rest of her family went into mourning for a specified length of time. The mores of the country allowed her to go to parties during the time, but they didn't let her dance while she was there. During this awkward time, she had to content herself with sitting on the couch and bouncing up and down in time to the music. Between dances she grumbled over the fact that she had to wear black stockings, and she didn't think they were becoming.

These people whom I have described are perhaps a third or a fourth of the crowd which usually congregated when a party is in the offing. Maybe in some future letter I'll tell you about some more of them, but now to get on with the story. After one or maybe two aperitifs and a lot of graceful conversation that flowed along as slick as a swallow, we all went into the dining room. The room was set with gorgeous silver, china and crystal and a magnificent lace tablecloth straight from their own shop. The dinner was served by two maids, in the French manner, one item of food to a course, and a different plate for each course. Each course was a little better than the one before, and we willingly sacrificed our comfort to our sense of taste—and there was plenty of red wine to help it go down. I was seated between Jeannine's mother, a nice lady with blue hair, the only one in the group who doesn't speak any English at all; and Jeannine's Uncle Robert, a slick apple who is the brains of the outfit. In the course of a couple of hours we finally finished the last lingering dish, drank a thimbleful of cognac, and settled back into some quiet talk-talk. There was a gentle glow of friendship around the table, and Papa told a joke that had references in it to such alimentary processes that I never thought could be mentioned at a dinner table in mixed company. But he told it with no sign of embarrassment either from himself, his daughter, or her friends; everybody laughed, though we Americans didn't think it was a very good joke.

And then they brought on the birthday cake. It wasn't a cake at all, but had a big, hollow cone made up of about a hundred tiny cream puffs (about the size of ping-pong balls).[3] It was held together by honey poured over the mass, and it had a single candle on the top. Each guest received an initial allowance of five cream-puffs when Jeannine had piffed out the single candle and taken the cake apart. They brought in two quart-bottles of champagne and each of us had a goblet full of it. We all toasted Jeannine, the men standing, the ladies sitting. Jeannine was very pretty, and shy and flustered. Immediately afterward Jean jumped up and turned photo-flood bulbs on all over the room. Jeannine was then forced to go around the table to the guests and give each of them a birthday kiss, while Jean stood by relentlessly with each kiss. Jeannine's kisses were just wispy touches on the cheek. French girls don't kiss on the mouth unless they really mean business. A couple of days later Jean gave a picture to each guest, showing him as a co-star with Jeannine. Later on we sang and danced, but that will have to wait until another letter.

TRANSCRIBED 1 JANUARY 2005

---

3. A *croquembouche,* that is.

Weinheim, April 1945
with Bob Mayer
questioning a German policeman

❦ 11 ❦

GERMANY

(1945)

I

COMMISSION
PARIS: APRIL 1945

The long, cold winter of 1944–45 dragged to an end. Our troops who had suffered terribly—many of us think unnecessarily—on the French-German border had crossed the Rhine and were steadily gaining significant victories. It was evident to all that the fighting would soon come to an end. One of the problems now facing the army was a shortage of officers to administer the Military Government detachments for the numerous small local populaces.

For a solution the army turned to the ranks of non-commissioned officers, seeking promising young candidates to fill the existing vacancies. It issued a publication announcing that qualified sergeants who could pass the requirements of a written test and approval by an examination board would be awarded the commission of second lieutenant, with the understanding that they would remain on active duty for at least one year after the cessation of hostilities.

My boss in the Civil Affairs section of Theater Headquarters learned about this program before I did and urged me to apply. Major Thomas Headen, to whom I owe a great deal, had discovered some sort of ability in me and had developed it to good use in our conduct of our part of the war effort. It was there that he lighted a spark of ambition in me which beforehand had remained dormant. (I had been like the millions of others, whose main ambition was to do our duty, serve our time, and return to civilian life.)

Tom found the necessary forms for me and guided me in filling them out. "Now," he said. "Write yourself a letter of recommendation, and I'll sign it." So I wrote the said letter. When he saw it, he said, "All you have said here is that you have been in the army for two and a half years and have never been court-martialed. Here, I'll write you a better one than that." So he wrote me a glowing letter and took it to a general officer friend of his—who didn't know me from Adam—who signed it.

The written test was a breeze. No problem at all, really. So was my appearance before the examining board. It turned out that one of the board members was an officer who spoke French. He was anxious to show off his French before the other board members, and we carried on an animated conversation while the others looked on. I mentioned—casually, of course—that I was a Phi Beta Kappa from the University of North Carolina, and I am sure that helped.

In a word, I passed. It was only a day or two later that I received an official-looking paper decorated with eagle, flag and drum declaring that since he had great confidence in my character and ability the President of the United States was appointing me a Second Lieutenant in the Army of the United States without military branch. (There was no branch for Military Government in those days.)

Observing my success, a number of the others in our Civil Affairs office also made similar applications. Not all of them were accepted, but three others made it. They were Frank Maestrone, Don Schmidt and Art Stone.[1] As we were relieved of our duties we were received by kindly General Stearns who congratulated us and wished us well. I remember that in telling us to do our best, he said "It's not that there aren't enough $10,000 jobs in the world. There just aren't enough $10,000 men." To General Stearns in 1945, ten thousand dollars was the pinnacle of success.

Somewhere in my file of military records I still have that first commission document. I believe the date is April 7, 1945.[2] One of the first things I had to do was to turn in all of my military equipment to the supply room. Then it was a trip to the Officers' Supply Store in Paris to buy new uniforms. (Newly commissioned officers received an initial clothing allowance.) Imagine! Low quarter oxford shoes, an "Eisenhower" jacket—waist length—beautiful "pink" trousers and a forest green blouse with a built-in belt. Officer's insignia with shiny, gold second lieutenant's bars and a gold eagle to wear on my billed hat. I was sure, as I surveyed myself in the mirror there, that nobody in the world was quite as handsome as Second Lieutenant William K. Holoman (new serial number for an officer: 02015900).

I had to bid goodbye to all of my enlisted friends at the office and at Cité Universitaire. It would never do for an officer to continue to be quartered with enlisted men, so I was assigned

---

1. They are pictured together in Kern's photographs from France.
2. April 9, 1945.

to a hotel room in downtown Paris while awaiting orders that would send me to Military Government School.

I summoned up the courage to call and ask a WAC captain with whom I had had some line-of-duty dealings to join me in a cocktail drink, which she accepted. It was nice to realize that the rigid bar which separates officer from enlisted was no longer a barrier for me. And we enjoyed a pleasant half-hour.

I also enjoyed a farewell dinner with my friend, Marguerite Richards,[3] formerly one of my teachers at Rutgers, now an employee of the United States Information Service. It was she who had earlier introduced me to the blessings of the martini—still my favorite drink. (The next time I saw Marguerite was after the war was over. She was back teaching in New Brunswick and I was on a business trip to New York City.)

It was on the second morning of my hotel stay in Paris that I woke up to a gloomy Friday.[4] Gloomy indeed. Because the word was already going around that President Roosevelt had died. It was rainy, and it seemed that all of Paris and all the services were mourning the loss of this gallant leader who had so surely led us to victory and yet had died on the very threshold of his success. I truly mourned too, along with all the others.

I was in a highly emotional state, what with my new rank, parting from my friends and associates, leaving Paris which I had come to love, and concern over the new way of life that I was to face. All day I could hardly hold back the tears. And at times didn't hold them back.

---

3. Marguerite Richards (1904–70) was professor of French and eventually chair of Romance Languages at Douglass College of Rutgers University. She worked for the USIS in Paris, 1944–46, later was active in providing language services for Hungarian refugees arriving at Camp Kilmer and in leading an early summer-abroad program in Strasbourg, where she died.

4. April 13, 1945.

Next day[5] the other three new lieutenants and I took the train to the little town of Romilly-sur-Seine which was where our Military Government training would take place. Romilly is about a hundred miles from Paris and is about five miles down the road from the city of Tours, which was the headquarters of the parent unit for all of Civil Affairs / Military Government in Europe—European Civil Affairs Division, "ECAD."

We were welcomed at a cocktail party reception by the personnel at the school; though I think they were just as interested in the liquor, which flowed freely, as in the new arrivals.

Next morning, following the advice of a staff member, we hiked a mile or so down to road to a farmhouse where a nice French peasant-type lady made a good country breakfast for us, including fresh eggs, the first that we had seen since leaving the US over a year ago.

The church service that Sunday morning[6] was a memorable and poignant event. It was held in a country schoolhouse—not in a church—on our grounds. All the little children of the surrounding countryside had gone out into the fields and had picked and bedecked the room with huge amounts of springtime wild flowers. "In honor and memory," they said, "of your President Roosevelt whom we too love."

The chaplain's service was a eulogy of Roosevelt, and a moving one. He quoted from Walt Whitman's poem:

O Captain! my Captain! our fearful trip is done;
The ship has weathered ev'ry rack, the prize we sought is won.
The port is near! the bells I hear, but O the bleeding drops of red
Where on the deck my Captain lies. Fallen cold and dead.

---

5. Saturday, April 14, 1945. The archive contains his dated train ticket.
6. April 15, 1945.

The following day[7] our Military Government schooling began. We were joined by two or three dozen other newly commissioned second lieutenants culled from all over the army. It was a crash course lasting for two weeks on the rudiments of administering American-style government to a conquered and probably hostile people. I guess it was a good course. I am sure they did the best they could, considering that our teachers had never themselves experienced the situations about which they were teaching. I think that the students, like me, were just overwhelmed at what we were facing. I can't remember anything I learned there. All I ever learned about Military Government I learned on the job and from the experiences of my colleagues.

Anyway, though, at the conclusion of our two weeks, we were given our certificates of completion, congratulated and kissed good-bye—figuratively—and sent on our way by truck and jeep to our various new assignments. I think all of us were assigned to small detachments in Germany, as I was.[8]

I spent two nights on the road in makeshift quarters and on the third day arrived in beautiful Heidelberg, the location of the company headquarters of my detachment.

For a summary of his movements from March 1944 in New Jersey to V-E Day, see the Addendum at the close of this chapter.

---

7. Monday, April 16, 1945. Thus the two-week course in Romilly was April 16–28.

8. The orders to proceed to Germany are dated April 26, 1945. On May 16, censorship of troop location having been lifted after V-E Day on May 8, he wrote Kaye a long letter from Germany outlining his story from the time they'd last seen each other in 1944.

II

Weinheim

When World War II came to an end in early May of 1945—we called it V-E Day—I was stationed with a small Military Government Detachment in Weinheim, Germany.

One of the early tasks with which we were confronted was the repatriation of foreign nationals who had been brought into Germany to assist in their war effort. These were not—necessarily—slave laborers but ordinary civilians who had no choice in the matter, but were ordered to come at the behest of the Nazis. Generally they were housed in cantonments or barracks-type buildings and were fed in government community kitchens. Their work was mostly in manufacturing jobs. They were called "DPs"—Displaced Persons—and the job was to get them back to their home countries as swiftly and efficiently as possible.

Very quickly after peace had been established, we began to receive representatives from foreign countries—from France, from Belgium, from Poland, from Russia and others—whose tasks were to locate their people in our area and make arrangements to transport them back home. This was not easy, as they came from numerous towns and villages. And not all of them wanted to go home. These representatives would make a number of visits to our areas, and we established a warm personal relationship with them. (I remember well Major Perigoudov and Lt. Tchernakovsky from Russia, who became quite good friends.)

Of course we would always invite them to take the noon-day meal with us when they visited. One of the reasons these representatives had been picked was because of their ability to speak

German to the natives here. I found it interesting to note that the language spoken around the dinner table was—German. The common enemy made for us a common language. Everybody spoke German. Except me. My specialty (from Civil Affairs) was French. But you learn fast when you have to, and soon I was speaking the language passably, although I never learned to read it well.

One of the first significant German words I learned was "Fragebogen." It means "questionnaire," and it was the standard device the allies used to "de-Nazify" Germany, that is, to get all of the Nazis out of influential positions in the government and elsewhere. The Fragebogen was a four-page-long sheet which everybody—EVERYBODY—who was anybody was required to fill out, with threats of imprisonment and punishment if they answered any questions falsely.

After the required name and addresses, etc., the first question was easy. "Were you ever a member of the N. S. D. A. P.?" (the Nazi Party). If he answered "yes" he was out. Gone. Disqualified from public office of any kind. Actually there weren't as many as you might think. The important Nazis had either been arrested earlier or had fled from the area.

After the first question the answers got to be debatable and dicier: "Were you ever a member of any of the following organizations? If so, when? Give dates." And there were a lot of them: the Deutscher Lehrerbund (the Teachers' Union), the Association of Financial Officers (the bankers), the Hitler Jugend (Youth, the Nazi Boy Scouts). Most of these people insisted that they had simply been mailed a membership card by the government, and that they had never been associated with the Nazi movement. Did we believe them? Not always. But we didn't usually really know. Besides that, if we removed all those with questionable pasts; the entire infra-structure of local German life would come to a standstill: the schools, the banks, the police, the town administrations would have to cease functioning. Furthermore, since the rise of Hitler the entire country was tainted with Nazi-ism. So mostly we let the minor participants in the structure remain in place and eliminated only the most glaring examples of Nazi activities. Sometimes I thought that instead of de-Nazifying the country, we were only de-Nazifying individuals. The Fragebogen were useful tools in gathering information, but mostly we depended upon our own judgments—sometimes faulty.

I remember that we got rid of the police chief who seemed to us an enthusiastic supporter of Nazi doctrine, and replaced him with the manager of a store that made and sold ice cream. He loved the job and performed his duties in a creditable manner.

One of the regulations that we posted early on was that no one was allowed to circulate (travel) more than five kilometers from his home. This was completely unenforceable, as (after the fighting stopped) the roads were jam-packed with people going somewhere else, to visit relatives or return to earlier abodes or for dozens of other reasons. Always on foot—there was no gasoline available for civilian use. We did the best we could to control it by making arrests, collecting fines, scheduling trials, calling for bail money. Our own Military Government office was inundated with paperwork. But all to no avail. The road traffic continued. The word got around that Military Government was collecting toll money to allow to pass.

Meanwhile the larger movements through our area continued unabated. Not only the Displaced Persons being re-patriated, but also the concentration camp survivors. The army would notify us of their coming and would then send in cots and blankets and rations for the times when they would be with us, usually for just one day or two. It was up to us to find them a lodging place and see that the food was equitably distributed.

From the concentration camps—Buchenwald as I remember—I did not see any of the emaciated living corpses as were shown in the newsreels; but there was ample evidence that they had been mistreated and abused. Some of them were still desperately hungry. I can recall some of the women holding up their skirts to catch the raw potatoes and other vegetables shoveled off the back of a truck.

My principal problem was to find a building—the army did not issue me any tents—to lodge them overnight. Usually I would settle on a school building, since the schools had not been reopened. I designated large rooms as male dormitories or female dormitories with adjacent toilet facilities. The smaller rooms, I said, could be occupied by families and married couples.

One time, at the end of a harrowing day, three couples approached me hand in hand and said they wanted to get married. Of course, I understood immediately what they wanted: they wanted the much more desirable smaller rooms. And there wasn't a preacher or a chaplain within miles. So I said "All right. Join hands," and gabbled "By authority of the Supreme Commander, Allied Forces in Europe, I pronounce that you are husbands and wives." Sometimes I wonder if those marriages endured, or if they dissolved in the cold light of day.

With the local German civilians the idea was to keep them informed of what the American army wanted and to see that they conformed. This was not difficult, as the populace was generally law-abiding and—as a defeated people—anxious to comply. Also, they were so grateful that they were being occupied by the Americans rather than by the Russian army, about which horror stories were already beginning to seep through from the East.

One interesting example of this is an event that occurred to another MG detachment near ours. (This was before the cease-fires had been effected.) The plan of advancement was for the tanks and trucks and vehicles to roll through the towns, to be followed by the MG detachments which would then give the German civilians their directions of what they should expect and what they must do.

In this particular event our detachment arrived in the town fairly late in the evening. The Burgomeister and the town officials were summoned to the City Hall (the Rathaus) and being read their order. As the meeting progressed a rumble was heard in the streets outside. It was the combat troops making their way through the area an hour or so behind the Military Government.

But no harm was done. The troops, the MG and the populace all behaved just as if everything had gone according to schedule.

III

When I first arrived in Germany in late April of 1945, I checked in at company headquarters in Heidelberg. The war was winding down, but the cease-fires and truces had not yet been negotiated out at the higher levels. There was no fighting going on in our area and we were, de facto, already at peace.

Heidelberg is a beautiful city, the home of a famous university that had been untouched by the war's destruction. We suspected, as was rumored, that because of a very secret memo of agreement between the two countries that Oxford and Cambridge in England and Heidelberg in Germany had been exempted from bombing. Be that as it may (or may not be), the only destruction in Heidelberg was that the three (historic) bridges across the Neckar River had been destroyed by the Germans themselves, and the only river crossing there was by a pontoon bridge erected by the American engineers.

A wonderful medieval red castle dominated the city from its heights above. (It was later made to serve as an officers' club for Seventh Army Headquarters.) The spring flowers were in bloom and the almond trees were in full blossom along the banks of the Neckar. After the destruction I had seen in other German cities, this one seemed like a little spot of paradise.

Company Headquarters which administered and served all the small Military Government detachments in the area told me that I was assigned to the detachment at Weinheim, about twelve miles due north of Heidelberg. It is located on the Bergstrasse, along an old Roman road that had served their invasion of "Germania." Today after it leaves Weinheim it progresses north through Darmstadt, Frankfurt and then places north into the British zone of occupation.

Weinheim is a small town of several thousand inhabitants. (I don't remember the exact population.) But it was a prosperous place, the location of several small industries and of a very large leather tannery, the Freudenberg Lederwerke. It was also the seat of government for the numerous small towns and villages in the vicinity of the big city of Mannheim (Stadtkreis Mannheim).

In Germany a unit of government is called a "Kreis." A large city (Stadt) is then a "Stadtkreis." The rural area in its vicinity is governed by a separate unit called a "Landkreis," much like the counties in our country. Each of the communities, no matter how small, is led by a "Burgomeister," and all of them are collectively governed by a "Landrat." His office is located in the "Rathaus." Sometimes a Rathaus would have a "Rathauskeller" (or "Rathskeller") (beer hall) in the basement, but ours did not have one, at least not while we were there.

The Landkreis which our Military Government was to govern, Landkreis Mannheim, included 22 communities, some as much as 20 miles away. Two of them (Hockenheim and Schweigen) were of some size, but the rest were tiny villages, some not much more than crossroads. But we were careful to go to each one and formally post our "Proclamations" outside the town hall, or more usually on a kiosk which every community seemed to have. The MG Proclamations announced our authority and designated the many "dos" and "don'ts" that were expected of them. Usually our rules were not severe and were pretty well observed by the populace. Governing these rural communities was quite orderly.

Our MG detachment was the smallest unit in the army's repertoire. It consisted of three officers (all lieutenants, and I was the freshman) and five enlisted men—staff sergeant to private first class. The other two officers and I worked closely together for most of the rest of the year. Guy Wharton was the older, a banker from California, mature, of sound judgment and authoritative. The other was Bob Mayer, a police officer from, I think, Pennsylvania. He was outspoken, decisive and very reliable in times of crisis. The detachment had had a commander, Captain Bill Cassell. But he had driven his jeep back into the hills and been shot and killed by some unknown assailant. I was his replacement.

The various responsibilities of government were divided up among the three of us officers. Guy was the judge of the Military Government Court and the administrator of the businesses and industries. Bob was in charge of public safety and services—the police, fire department, health and sanitation. I was given the schools, the banks, property control and preservation of monuments, fine arts and archives. And there were other areas too, all of which overlapped with one another. The idea was to keep the local infrastructure running on an even keel, while on the national level the sovereignty of Germany changed hands to the allies, the government was de-militarized, and the real Nazi war criminals brought to justice. But those activities were conducted on a level far outside and beyond our authority and influence. While assuring that the welfare of the civilian populace, particularly food and health, did not deteriorate to the point of becoming a problem for the army, MG was authorized to draw upon the civilian economy for its needed items not furnished by its own system. The two areas where this was most evident were in vehicles—our detachment had only one jeep—and housing: lodging for ourselves and whatever allied troops happened to be in the area.

We did this in the form of "Requisitions." The owner or proprietor of a given piece of property or material was given an official document stating that this item was legally taken over for military use and that when no longer needed it would be returned to the owner or compensation duly given. I am sure that both the owner and the requisitioner had only the haziest idea of how this would be accomplished. And I have no idea of whether it was ever accomplished. But that's how it was done in Germany at the conclusion of the war.

As for lodging, when a house was requisitioned, the inhabitants would just have to move out—leaving their household goods behind—and go and stay somewhere else, perhaps with relatives or friends.

Our MG detachment requisitioned and lived in two rather nice houses on the outskirts of Weinheim. They were on opposite sides of the street. Ours had a swimming pool in the backyard. The enlisted men lived in one house and we three lieutenants occupied the other. Both houses had large areas in the back where they raised "victory gardens" of vegetables for home consumption. Both houses hired local civilian women as housekeepers. We had a very fine cook, who performed miracles with army rations and things she traded for on the local economy. Our dining table was one of the blessings of our existence in this assignment. There were always flowers on the table, sometimes overly large. I remember the first German sentence that I ever understood in full was from Guy to our cook: "Wenn wir essen wir brauchen nicht die Blumen" (When we eat, we don't need the flowers).

We knew from the beginning that in addition to having the authority and the muscle provided by the US Army it would be necessary to find some leadership to the people from the German community, someone who already had the admiration and respect of the local civilians. We felt that this person should be the "Landrat," to preside officially over the 22 communities in our area. The old Landrat, a confirmed Nazi, was long gone. Fled. Possibly arrested in some other area.

Examining all the possibilities for the job that we could think of, we finally centered our attention on the head of the Freudenberg family and the manager of the Freudenberg Leather Works. "Anybody you pick," we were told, "is going to be vastly influenced by Richard Freudenberg." Known and admired among all the communities, he was the obvious choice. He had early on (in the 1930s) opposed and spoken against the rise of the Nazi movement. But, of course, after the ascension of Adolf Hitler he had, like the rest of the Germans, gone along with the tide.

We approached Richard Freudenberg with our choice, and after some reluctance he accepted. (He really had no choice.) But after taking on the job he quickly assumed his leadership role and proved himself an able leader and effective administrator. He understood well his interface with our MG detachment, was cheerful and cooperative and helped keep the local affairs moving forward in a constructive way. He even brought over several of his managerial staff to help in his administrative duties.

In fact, it turned out that Freudenberg knew a lot more about government and its ramifications than any of us lieutenants. Many of the constructive actions that our detachment did—and for which we received due credit—were the work of our civilian Landrat.

Very early in his administration Freudenberg sent a message to the local Burgomeisters intended to encourage and inspire them in their new roll of leadership of a conquered people. I am sorry that I have not retained his exact message, but the words went something like this:

> With the coming of spring Germany has seen its grandiose dreams of power and glory crumble into defeat and despair. Those things our country has desired are no longer possible! But still much remains to us. We have our beautiful land and a strong, willing people with the ability to accomplish much. Even amidst our loss, together we can move forward. Together we can make in this glorious spring a new beginning. Together we can create a new society better than the one we have known. Let us, then, start now to make a finer world for ourselves and our children.

Our MG detachment and the people of Landkreis Mannheim owe a debt to Richard Freudenberg for his post-war leadership to bring them out of their despair.

IV

As the war in Germany wound down to its conclusion there was some talk about a resistance movement among the people, a sort of guerilla warfare against the victors. Adolf Hitler urged the Germans to form bands of "Were-wolfs" to wage underground warfare and continue the fight. So far as I know, nothing came of any of this except talk.

But the allies were determined that the German people must be disarmed. So one of the first orders posted in our "Proclamations" was that all the civilians must turn in their weapons—ALL of them. Every rifle and shotgun, every pistol, any knife with a blade more than five inches long. And so the populace obediently brought their weapons to the Military Government office and turned them in in exchange for an official-looking receipt that we issued. (The Germans love to have a piece of paper acknowledging or authorizing them for about anything they do.) I don't know how many reluctant ones hung on to their firearms and secreted them away. But I do know that soon many thousands of them were piled up in the basement of the Rathaus, soon to be carted away to some army post for destruction. Some of them were really beautiful, almost works of art, and we in the MG detachment culled out some to save them from the dismal fate. Mine was a gorgeous double-barreled shotgun with an overshot rifle cartridge stored in the butt end. The metalwork decorations were engraved with images of deer, foxes, pheasants and other wildlife. It had been made in Belgium with a date of 1887. I also retrieved a Mauser small caliber pistol which I carried, loaded in my belt in lieu of my heavy service 45. Lucky I didn't shoot myself somewhere in the pants. Of course it was all loot, but at least it served its disarmament purpose. Some weeks later army trucks did come by to confiscate all this weaponry and take it away. I suppose it eventually did get destroyed or else came to rest in some storage.

One result of this operations is that the Germans came back to MG complaining that the deer and rabbits would come in out of the woods and hills and ravage their crops. And without weapons they had to way to get rid of them and control their burgeoning population. They pleaded with us to organize deer hunts from the troops. And we did indeed sponsor a few hunts—our detachment even participated in a few ourselves. But it was very sporadic and, I am sure, it was not very effective.

After the fighting ended, the troops wanted to go back home. And the army wanted to get them there as quickly as possible. One new burden that this imposed on our MG detachment was the large organizations—the 84th Division and later the 82nd Division—which took up residence in our towns while waiting for transportation back to the U.S. Their presence imposed myriad demands of all kinds upon the populace as well as on us MG people. They looked on us with some distaste, as thought we were trying to protect the Germans from the American predations. And I suppose we were. But we were just trying to keep daily life functioning smoothly, even with hoards of several thousands of troops making new demands on them. And these temporarily resident troops couldn't have cared less.

One thing we did do was to conduct "shake-down" inspections to take away from their troops all the loot they had taken from the Germans as they went through their countrysides. The quantity and variety of things they had taken was indeed formidable. Musical instruments were the most vulnerable, but they took everything—typewriters, professional tools, surveying instruments and so much more.

Anything the troops could manage to hide in their duffle bags they kept. But the things that were too big to hide were turned over to the MG detachment. So once again the basement of the Rathaus was filled to overflowing with goods reclaimed from the troops of German possessions. We made some feeble attempts to return those things to their rightful owners. But it was impossible; they had been garnered from all over Germany. When I left Weinheim some months later most of it was still in the Rathaus basement.

Meanwhile the Seventh US Army had moved into Heidelberg and set up its headquarters for what was to become the Army of Occupation for that part of Germany. This headquarters had a lot of military know-how and a lot of authority—even over MG operations. It soon began to bring about orderly procedures from what had been happy-go-lucky decisions.

We had heard about the great Officers' Club that 7th Army had established in the big, historic red castle on the hill. One evening the three of us decided to pay a visit to this fabulous new facility. When we got there, unfortunately, we were turned away. We were not members of the headquarters, hence had no club cards, and therefore could not be admitted. But luck was on our side. Those two Russian officers that we had received so often up in Weinheim recognized us at the door and invited us to come in as *their* guests. As visiting diplomats they were attached to the headquarters and therefore eligible to be members. It still seems strange to me that we US Army officers had to be admitted to the US Army club as guests of Russian officers. (The evening turned out to be not a very great one, as the Russians wanted it to be a contest over who could drink the most. And we successfully avoided this, although our hosts were a little offended that we did not participate.)

The MG office in Weinheim was in the Rathaus which was in the middle of the well-kept city park. It housed several pairs of uncaged pea-fowl. When the males would spread their tail feathers and strut, they were an impressive sight. Their loud and raucous call was distracting until we got used to it.

In the midst of the town were the ruins of two medieval towers. Both of them had storks' nests atop them which were very picturesque sights, particularly when we could sometimes see one of them returning at twilight time. There was also an abandoned medieval-looking castle outside of town on a low hill called the Wachenburg. I had locks put on each one and "No Trespassing" signs, and they were never vandalized while I stayed in town. I'm sure the locals took a lot of civic pride in them.

Our Landkreis was bordered on the west by the city of Mannheim and the Rhine River, and on the east by a range of low mountains called the Odenwald, quite close in and looking very wild and primitive, as they were heavily forested.

Landkreis Mannheim was one of eight Kreises in the area which the Germans called a "Landeskommissariatsbezirk." Our army called it North Baden, and placed an MG detachment in each kreis. One of our neighboring detachments was fortunate enough to unearth a large quantity of Martell VSOP cognac—undoubtedly previously confiscated by the Germans from the French economy—hidden in a cave. Our neighboring MG detachment and we spent several days transporting cases of it back to our own locations. This did not mean much to me, as I do not care for cognac, but it became quite a staple and a barter item among some of our members. Before the cognac was all depleted and dispersed the 7th Army got wind of it and confiscated the rest of it.

We purchased a very good Rhine wine which was plentiful in the area. I think we paid about a dollar a bottle for it in German money—printed and issued by our army. We usually drank about one bottle at each of the lunch and dinner meals. So many years after all this I still remember Rhine wine as something super.

We requestioned the additional vehicles we needed from the civilian economy. I think we had four passenger cars and two small trucks. We really needed these to make our numerous visits to the other towns and villages. Mine was a sporty little black-and-yellow BMW one-seater. There was almost no traffic on the roads other than military since there was no gasoline—the Germans called it "benzine"—available to ordinary civilians. Sometimes in the rural areas big old geese would rush out at the passing cars and bite at the tires, like dogs are wont to do in our country.

The administration of the vehicles and the issue of petroleum supplies was in the hands of one of those local bureaucracies so dear to the German hearts. It gives me the opportunity to expound the longest German word that I ever encountered. I'll put it all on this one line—

Landkreisfarbereitshaftamtleiter.

It means—loosely—"Head of the local office for the administration of wheeled vehicles." And that included bicycles too.

Hidden in a shed and covered with leaves and firewood we discovered one of those huge, open-air official cars that the Germans used to greet and transport dignitaries when they arrived in town. This one undoubtedly was part of the Mannheim equipment. It was a black Mercedes in perfect running condition. Naturally we requisitioned it as being vitally necessary to our MG operations.

One of our pleasures was to ride top-down in this great vehicle in the long evenings after dinner. We would meander around the countryside; and when we spotted one of the large jack-rabbits, one of us would stand up and take a pot shot at it with his service 45 pistol. And we didn't always miss. And the Germans were glad to receive them as meat items for their table.

It wasn't long, however, before 7th Army learned about this too and came up and confiscated it for its own vitally necessary operation. Pretty soon we got a new commander in from the Air Force assigned after the war's end, no doubt from an over-supply of aviators. He knew nothing of Military Government. His only claim for us to admire him was that he had once served in the same unit as Clark Gable. It was something of a blessing that he kept out of our way, as he was a drunk and spent most of his time holed up in his room in our quarters. He didn't last long and was soon transferred out and returned to the U.S. But he was the first of a number who were moved in and out during the following months as transients or as project officers for special details.

The buzzword from the beginning, and it never abated, was "fraternization." That is, contact between our military troops and the German people. It had been decided many months advance that since the Germans were our enemies, therefore when we arrived among them there was to be no social contact. EVER. AT ALL. Our troops could deal with them for business purposes but social activity between the two groups was strictly forbidden. Verboten, as the Germans would say. I don't know what ivory-tower thinker ever conceived this wondrous idea, but it was manifestly unenforceable. Our troops had been in Europe for many many months, and though social contacts with the locals—England, France, Belgium, Holland, etc.—was permissible and even desirable; now here in this new inviting land such pleasurable vistas were to be permanently out of bounds. And the male hormones raged incessantly. Political, social and ideological philosophies existed, but existed on a different level from physical desires. And the German womenfolk were amiable and generally welcoming. Many of them were young war widows or whose menfolk were languishing in Prisoner of War camps. There was no way that the two sexes could be kept apart. Fraternization was widespread, and in effect universal. Among themselves the young German women would refer to "Mein Ami" (my American). And the GI's would routinely call their new friends "my Fraulein." All those who fraternized with the German women ignored the rule, and those who were charged with enforcing it winked at it and even participated. (Most of the German people were on very short rations in those early days, and when the soldiers would take their Frauleins to the officers' clubs and service clubs, they would usually order eggnog as their drinks. That way they would get both the egg and whiskey in the same treat.)

Our MG detachment was not immune from the non-fraternization edict. Living as we did in our very nice houses, it was singularly inviting to entertain there some of the attractive women we had met in the course of our official duties. Consequently it was normal to have social events in our quarters nearly every Saturday night. We would share a nice dinner meal in the dining room and follow it later with drinks and dancing in the big parlor. We would engage the services of a local violinist/fiddler and pianist and sometimes a flutist or reed player. The evenings were relaxing and pleasurable and not infrequently led to exchanges of affection. Some of the liaisons turned out to be long-lasting and touching.

I ought to mention that American cigarettes were a highly prized commodity on the German scene. Each soldier would receive an entire carton once a week—free—as a part of his regular disbursement of treats and goodies. The Germans had none. A tip of a couple of cigarettes left at a table or counter or in return for some small service was gradually accepted and appreciated, I think, more than the paper money in the economy. I was in luck, because I didn't smoke. One time I traded a whole carton of Lucky Strikes for a scandalously large wheel of Emmenthal (Swiss) cheese.

As the summer wore on and faded into the cooler months of autumn the duties of MG became more and more routine. We no longer had to work the long hours and feel like we were continually running from crisis to crisis. The German daily life was approaching something like normalcy—albeit suffering from the hardships of having lost the war. I had peered into all the bank vaults and safe deposit boxes. I was making good progress in restoring to their owners goods and properties which the Nazis had confiscated. The schools had reopened—I got to visit a few classes—under the supervision of a man whom I appointed with a name similar to my own—Arthur Kern. Richard Freudenberg had given up his job as Landrat and gone back to running the works. The new Landrat was Dr. Valentine Gaa; the new Weinheim Burgomeister was named Bruch. More and more our jobs were simply nine-to-five affairs: go to the office after breakfast, go home for lunch and be free after work in the evenings. I got an R&R (rest and recuperation) leave to the Riviera, and drove my BMW to the Alps for a couple of weekend trips. Some of our enlisted men were allowed to attend "schools" at plushy resort areas like Biarritz.

Bob Mayer got a 45-day leave to the U. S., where he got married and brought his new bride back with him.

And one by one we were relieved of our responsibilities which were turned over to the larger MG detachment in Mannheim. Toward the end of the year Guy Wharton was transferred to MG in Karlsruhe to the South. I was transferred to MG Bruchsal and later also to Karlsruhe, the principal city of Germany's Baden province. By the end of December the Weinheim (Landkreis Mannheim) detachment had been completely withdrawn, leaving only a couple of caretakers of the property we had not turned back to the Germans.

I was in Weinheim for about eight months. A brand new second lieutenant, I had never before been thrust into a situation of which I knew so little and was so unqualified. I made mistakes and I paid for them. I feel that because of the experience I eventually became a reasonably competent officer. I am grateful for the experience.

ADDENDUM

As noted above, Kern summarized his travels from March 1944 to May 1945 in a long letter to Kaye, given here. The embargo on information concerning troop movements had been lifted after V-E Day on May 8.

WEDNESDAY NIGHT

MAY 16TH, 1945

My darling wife,

Now I'm getting upset. It's been a whole week since I've heard from you, and I hate so much when I miss out on those few words. It isn't your fault, of course, and it will all catch up soon, I know. But what a nasty mess it is while it lasts. Maybe when all the soldiers get out of Europe and go home—now that they've won the war—our mail situation will be better. I doubt it though.

I see by the *Stars and Stripes* that we are now allowed to tell about our travels up until the time we entered Germany. I don't know whether it will be any of any interest to you, but I'd like to give you a brief sketch of them to fill in the details later.

I left Camp Reynolds [Pennsylvania] on 18 March 1944 and went by train to Camp Miles Standish which is about halfway between Boston and Providence. I thought that we were going to Kilmer right up until the very time I woke up and the train was in Newark. What a disappointment that was. I left Standish and got on the boat in Boston on 23 March 194[4].

Our boat had formerly been one of the less well-known luxury liners, and outside of the fact and we slept in the typically overcrowded conditions and my compartment was directly over the rudder, the trip over wasn't too bad. We arrived at Liverpool on 4 April and lay in the strait for two days waiting for the tide. Got off the boat in the middle of the night and were taken to a little town called Oldham. We were processed there for about two more days and then split up into our various organizations and taken to our destinations. My "billet" was in Didsbury, a little town which is a suburb of Manchester—about 20 minutes on the streetcar. Stayed there for about six weeks and then was pulled out to go work in London where the H-5 section of ETOUSA [Headquarters European Theater of Operations, United States Army] was activated. We started that organization and nursed it like a baby. It was really fun.

In London we lived right smack in the middle of Mayfair. A whole street of houses was occupied by headquarters troops and we were one of them. We lived just two blocks from Hyde Park, and about 10 minutes from Piccadilly Circus. Our office was on Grosvenor Square just one block away from the American Embassy. One night on the German radio, Lord Haw-Haw (gloating about the doodle-bombs) called a shot for the night to land right in the middle of Grosvenor. And he said "and you Yanks over on Green Street, don't think we're forgetting you." Both his predictions failed to materialize, but it was quite a topic of conversation for a while.

I was the junior sergeant of the office and was given the detail of riding with our files of secret papers which we moved to the continent. Consequently I didn't come over with my organization, but only with the truck convoy. We left through Southampton, waited eight days, and landed at Omaha Beach. Lay around in the country for several days there, and finally moved into Paris about a week and a half after its liberation.[9]

---

9. August 25, 1944.

If I had been with the organization, I had orders to go in right behind the combat troops, but I was lost with my convoy and didn't make it.

You know most of the Paris adventure, and what you don't know will take more than one letter to tell. After getting commissioned—thanks to Colonel Hayes, Major Headen, Sergeant Parent, and a half a dozen others—I spent two weeks at the ECAD [European Civil Affairs Division] military government school. It was in a little town called Romilly-sur-Seine about a hundred miles southeast of Paris. Leaving there I was assigned as administrative officer of this detachment and came into Germany on a 2½-ton truck through Chalons, Verdun, and Metz.

You don't know what a relieved feeling it is actually to be able to give specific names and dates for a change. It's like breathing fresh air. I love you very dearly my own Kaye. I hope so much to be with you soon, so we may be together always.

Your devoted,
Kern

My father returned to Germany after a post-War leave in North Carolina in the spring of 1946. During this period, from June 15 to December 29, 1946, he kept a daily journal, transcribed in Kaye and Kern Holoman: Travels *(2023), as "Stuttgart Journal (1946)," pp. 43–77.*

Katherine Highsmith
To Kern with love, Kaye
March 28, 1941

12

KAYE

I

October 1940 – March 1941

I met Katherine Highsmith in the fall of 1940. From that time until her death 57 years later she was the defining entity in my life.

Here's how it all got started:

I was riding with Dub Martin in his (borrowed) family car as he ran an errand on Durham's West Duke campus. "Look, there's Kay Highsmith," he said, pointing out a pretty girl waiting for the bus to take her to East Duke. "Let's see if we can give her a ride." She joined us on the front seat, and we exchanged pleasantries until we dropped her near Washington Duke's statue not far from her dorm. We had never met; she had attended Hugh Morson High, while Dub and I went to Broughton. But the two of them had known each other during high school days at meetings, socials and things.

It was several days later that I received a letter postmarked "Duke Station." It was from a girl whom I had known casually at Broughton. Her name was Ruth Kolb. She had moved away before graduation as her father, a college professor, took a job at another university. To my surprise Ruth's letter invited me to be her escort at Duke's Black and White Ball, a fancy dress-up prom held at or near Thanksgiving time.

I could figure out exactly what happened. The girls in Brown House Dorm had gotten to talking, and Ruth said that she had no date for the event—perhaps not asked or perhaps not interested in anyone who had asked. But, having met me a few days earlier, Kay must have said, "Why don't you ask Kern Holoman? You know him, and he might be glad to come with you to such a fancy party." So Ruth took a chance and wrote the inviting (chancy) letter.

I had been dating sporadically since arriving at Chapel Hill, but had found no one I was interested in—or was interested in me. I was a junior by that time. So I readily accepted Ruth's invitation and asked her for a date at Duke for the following Saturday night.

I found Ruth a moderately attractive girl, intelligent and amiable. And I guess she liked me. We got along well together. Even kissed on the first date—under the gazebo in Sarah P. Duke Gardens.

We successfully attended the Black and White Ball. (It was quite formal; the men all wore dress clothes, and the girls wore gowns that were either black or white.) I sent a floral corsage. Shortly after we arrived Kay and her date came up to greet us, and we socialized during the intermissions. Dances in those days were "boy-break," and I had the opportunity to dance with Kay as well as, of course, with Ruth.

In the days between then and Christmas holidays, Ruth and I dated several times, usually in double-date style with Kay and one of her several escorts. Ruth and I meshed all right, but I couldn't help noticing, even on those dates, what a pretty girl was with that other fella.

When the Christmas holidays came, Ruth joined her parents back home in, I think, Pennsylvania. In Raleigh I resolved that I would seek some new friendships among other girls also home for the holidays. I dated four girls during that two-week period and one of them was Kay Highsmith. Nothing ever came of the other three—I can barely remember their names. But that date with Kay was a red-letter day from the beginning.

We were in my father's car (which was normal in those days). We went to a Bob Hope movie and then had hot dogs and Cokes—curb-service—at the Manhattan Lunch on Hillsboro Street. She wouldn't even let me hold her hand on that first date. But I was fortunate enough to catch a glimpse of a pretty stockinged leg as she got in and out of the car. We parted at her front door with mutual promises of more dates back on the Duke campus.

I didn't believe in love at first sight. I still don't. But I think both of us realized from the first that this was something special. Something that would not go away.

Kay was tall-ish (about 5 ft., 7 inches). She had chestnut brown hair which she wore shoulder length. Her eyes were brown and her lips were full. She had nice, square shoulders (good posture), an ample bosom, slender waist and hips and long, chorus girl-type legs. In short, when she was a college student and a young wife she was one of the prettiest girls I ever saw. From some unknown whim of mine I asked her if I could call her Kaye (with an "e" on the end) instead of just "Kay." She liked that and consented. And so she became "Kaye" until the end of the chapter.

Katherine Herring Highsmith was born June 14 (Flag Day), 1922. She lived with her parents at 832 Wake Forest Road. Her father was Dr. John Henry Highsmith; her mother was Kate Maude Herring. Both of them had their roots in Sampson

County. Her father was an Assistant Secretary of Education for North Carolina. Her mother was an extremely active, capable and influential leader. Both were graduates of Trinity College (later Duke University). Dr. Highsmith had been married before; his wife, Lula, died in the flu epidemic of 1919. He had two children from that union, a son, John Henry, Jr., and a daughter, Lula Belle. Both of them were grown, and had employment sometimes in, sometimes out of Raleigh.

Kaye's younger sister (by two years) was Louise. They were typically affectionate sisters. Louise was from an early age musically talented, and all of her family nurtured her in this channel of interest.

Kaye graduated from high school when she was only fifteen years old. Her parents thought that age was a bit young to go away to college, so they enrolled her for a year in local Peace College. She entered Duke as a freshman, so she was a year behind me, although we both graduated from high school at the same time. She was a self-help student, both waiting on tables at the dining hall and working at her dormitory reception desk. She joined Delta Gamma Sorority early, and was an active and enthusiastic member for her entire time at Duke.

The middle quarter at Chapel Hill was a very bad one for me—one of the worst I can remember. I was terribly anxious to make Phi Beta Kappa on the first selection; and, as it happened, I got trapped in some extremely difficult courses for that term. Also I contracted flu while at home for a weekend; and though I missed less than a week of classes, I found it hard to shake off. I felt miserable and was fighting a fit of depression. The only bright spots were my Saturday night dates with Kaye on the Duke campus. I literally lived for those evenings, would telephone her each night (25¢ on the dormitory phone), and we exchanged two letters a week. I know that already by that time she was a great, important factor in my existence.

Early on Saturday evenings I would stand out on Franklin Street in front of Graham Memorial and try to hitchhike a ride to Duke. It was mid-winter then, and cold on the street. If I hadn't caught a ride by the time the bus came, I coughed up the necessary 25¢ for bus fare. I can still recall the magic thrill of anticipation as I would make my way up East Duke campus to Brown House, where I knew Kaye would be waiting for me. I was in love.

I never dated Ruth after the Christmas holidays. In fact, I don't remember thinking about her very much. She wrote me a bitter, tear-stained letter in which she berated me for throwing her over for someone more attractive. And she was absolutely right. I had. But I couldn't help it if I had found another one to be the object of my affections. I was in love.

The big social event of Carolina for that time of year was the set of dances called "The Mid-Winters." This consisted of a two-day event in which a big-name band would be brought in to play a four-function series: a Friday afternoon concert, a formal evening dance on Friday, a Saturday afternoon "Tea Dance," and then another formal on Saturday evening. The dances were held in the "Tin Can," a monstrous, hopelessly outdated (metallic) structure. It had been built to be temporary in World War I, but had survived (Depression, etc.) as the only place for dances, indoor gymnastics, and other events requiring a big expanse of space. It wasn't much, but it was the best we had. And the committees did a pretty good job of decorating it with miles of crepe paper to make it look festive.

The big band for the Mid-Winters that year was Charlie Barnett and his orchestra. Not as big, perhaps, as Dorsey or

Kyser or Miller, whom we had had on other occasions, but still a "name" to be reckoned with.

The co-eds on campus were routinely available to get to the various events. But the girls who came in from other schools and cities presented a problem, because their escorts would have to find lodging for them on Friday and Saturday nights. In the vernacular of the day they were called "imports."

I asked Kaye to go with me to the dances and she readily agreed. Being dated for these (expensive) dances was a big deal, was something of a "feather," and there were few who refused.

Kaye's parents were quite straight-laced and strict. They insisted that she stay at the Carolina Inn, which imposed the same regulations and curfew hours that the on-campus co-eds had to follow. (Check-in, check-out and be in one hour after the dance was over.) So I made the arrangements, borrowed my Dad's car for the weekend, picked up Kaye at Duke, and ensconced her at the Inn by mid-afternoon of Friday. After the concert (red party dress for her), we strolled around the campus and ended up for dinner at the Carolina Inn, by far the most expensive dining spot in Chapel Hill. We had a lovely, quiet table for two. She was at her prettiest, and endeared herself to me by ordering fried oysters, the cheapest entree on the menu. It wasn't until some time later that I discovered that she didn't particularly care for oysters.

For the dance that night it was a "triple date," with my two roommates and their dates all sharing my borrowed car. Six people in one sedan seems like a lot today, but I think cars must have been bigger in those days. Or else we didn't mind the proximities.

Charlie Barnett's music was just the right blend of swingy pop tunes and romantic arms-around numbers. I didn't dance very well—still don't—but Kaye was a good dancer, and the evening passed with charm and pleasure. At boy-break dances it is the responsibility of the escort to assure that his date has a good time by dancing with a number of young men there, so she would feel welcomed and appreciated—and admired. The way to do this was to approach your friends among the stags (those who had come date-less to the affair) and say, "I want you to meet my date who is with me tonight." Then you would "break" with her current companion, make the introduction, and then leave to find her another dance partner, always assuring that he or she did not get "stuck" with a partner for an overly long time. The good-looking girls would have an abundance of partners during the evening; the "dogs" were something of a problem and perhaps an embarrassment. Kaye was among the good-looking group, though I don't think it would have mattered to her if no one wanted to dance with her. Except me.

After the dance we went to Danziger's, a European style cafe on Franklin Street, where they served Viennese coffee and an assortment of exotic pastries and other sweets. The out-of-town girls always loved to go to Danziger's as an especially glamorous late-evening treat.

We lingered a good while over coffee and goodies and discovered that the Carolina Inn was not at all vigorous about enforcing the curfew rules. All in all a great start to a dear and forever remembered weekend.

The early part of the day on Saturday was consumed in a variety of strolls around Chapel Hill and informal drives through the nearby countryside. Just the two of us.

After the tea dance in the afternoon we repaired for supper to the Carolina Coffee Shop on Franklin Street, which was one of my favorite places for the entire time I was at Carolina.

On the way back from supper I stopped at a secluded spot just off campus. There in a parked automobile I declared to her—for the first time—that I loved her. Kaye's response was, in words that I had never had spoken to me before: "If I ever loved anyone, Kern, I love you."

We drove back to the Carolina Inn for her to change into her ball gown for the final dance that night.

I went bounding up the steps at Steele Dormitory, shouting at the top of my voice to my roommates and to anyone else within earshot, "She loves me! She loves me!"

The rest of the weekend was in a rosy mist of new-found love. We danced the evening away to Charlie Barnett's music as if we didn't know there was another soul in the world.

After the dance we went to a party at the Sigma Nu frat house where we sat in a circle on the floor for refreshments, but still had eyes only for each other. We must have been a completely boring pair. It was the same on the following morning when I checked her out of the Inn and Chapel Hill and returned her to Duke Campus in time for the church service in the chapel.

And that's how it all got started.

II

March–December 1941

The long, dismal winter of 1940–41 finally wound to an end, brightened only by my new-found love of Kaye. And hers for me.

I did realize my ambition to make Phi Beta Kappa on the first pick. In fact, I was rated in the top ten of my class. Pretty soon I received the requisite key—jumbo size—and surprised Kaye by showing up with it hanging on my key chain. In those days it was the fashion to display your honorary society keys on your chain. You hung one end of the chain on your belt loop or in your watch pocket if you had one. You drooped the other end into your side pocket, anchored by an ornamental knife. Then your keys hung freely on the bottom of the chain somewhere near your pocket. If you were a BMOC and had accumulated a number of keys—Golden Fleece, Holy Grail, Gimghoul, etc., they hung in an impressive cluster. Or, you might choose to play it modest and just wear the one key that you valued the most. Which is what I chose to do. Although the Phi Bete key was the only one I had won. Anyway Kaye was suitably impressed. I bought her a showy UNC pin for her to wear on her sweater because I didn't have a sweetheart fraternity pin to give her.

For the spring quarter and for all the rest of my college studies I took only courses in my major and minor—English Literature and Comparative Literature. These were easy for me and presented no trouble in keeping my grades up. In fact, I think I made "A's" on all my courses from then on. It also enabled me to spend a good deal more time visiting with Kaye at Duke. The once-a-week dates on Saturday nights soon developed into twice or even three times a week.

I don't remember that we did very much on those dates, campus movies and plays, campus bowling, etc. But mostly just enjoyed being together. When I would go over in the afternoons we would sometimes take long walks, including the grounds of the Sarah Duke Gardens on West Campus. On those days we would always eat dinner off campus. Our favorite place was the Toddle House a couple of blocks down the street. Hamburgers were fifteen cents in those days, but the pièce de résistance was the dessert there: chocolate meringue ice-box pie. Across the street was a popular hangout, The Ivy Room, which served magnificent ice cream sundaes and sodas.[1]

---

1. The Ivy Room was still doing business in the mid 1960s. Betty and I frequently enjoyed dates there.

Catty-corner across from East Duke Campus was Renaldi's, the only genuine Italian Restaurant south of the Mason-Dixon line that I knew of. There you could get a very acceptable spaghetti plate with meat sauce. It was always busy, always frequented by the students. One time when I was near broke, Kaye introduced me to French fried potatoes with ketchup, the first time I had ever experienced them. Now, of course, it's a routine "go-with" at all the fast-food chains.

For an occasional "big-deal" we would go downtown for dinner at the Tavern of the Washington Duke Hotel. It was oak-paneled and picturesque and featured good steak and potato-type fare. It would sometimes get rowdy later in the evenings; but neither Kaye nor I drank beer, and we usually left before the noisiness started.

The Duke co-eds were a pretty refined lot. Even around campus they generally wore sweater-skirt combinations, saddle shoes, pretty blouses and shirts. Blue jeans and denims were un-heard of. Never even knew they existed. No slacks and certainly no shorts.

For the young women and young men too at Duke—and at Chapel Hill and the other campuses—fashions in wearing apparel were light years away from what they are today.

Dress codes were even stricter when the girls signed out to go into town for a meal, a party or a movie. They were required to wear high heels, hose, gloves and hats. Hats? Gloves? Even in those far-away days that seemed like cruel and unusual punishment.

After dinner our dates usually ended up in pretty much the same way. We would find a not-quite-so-well-lighted bench on East Duke campus and engage in the favorite pastime of young lovers: Petting. Ardently and sometimes fiercely. That was and is an important part of courtship. Isn't it?

Kaye came to visit me several times at Chapel Hill. We liked to take long walks in Battle Park and especially to rent bicycles for a couple of hours around the town. Then, either before or after dinner I would accompany her on the bus back to Durham and Duke.

Kaye's parents no longer insisted that she stay at the Carolina Inn when she came over for the various spring time dances. Some informal at Graham Memorial and some big-deal, big-band affairs. I think it was at about that time that we began to have dances in Woolen Gym. Not air-conditioned, and in the springtime it got hot; but still it was a big step up from the Tin Can. I found a very nice house out in town for Kaye to stay at, run by a lovely, refined lady who didn't care how late she stayed out. And we took full advantage of those relaxed rules. Sometimes I could borrow my father's car for the weekend. In retrospect, I can't believe that he was so lenient and generous with me.

The last set of dances for the school year was called "The Finals," and once again Kaye came over for the Friday and Saturday social events. The big-name band this time really was Tommy Dorsey and his Orchestra. Everybody was agog with the fact that Frank Sinatra was in his entourage, and was rapidly becoming a name as big or bigger than Dorsey's, even though he was still under contract. (Read *The Godfather* to see how this affair came to an end.) Sinatra's vocal group was called "The Sentimentalists," and was making a big hit with "I'll Never Smile Again," on the top ten lists.

After the Friday night dance a group of six of us couples went on a hayride. Our transportation was a wooden wagon pulled by two farm nags and driven by a Chatham County dirt farmer named "Neighbor Creek." We rode along on a dark country road illuminated by a kerosene lantern hanging from the wain. Sometime after midnight we arrived at a lake shore where we unloaded our baskets, spread blankets on the ground and had a glorious evening picnic. We stayed there until the morning birds began to twitter and the grey light began to be born in the East. It was the first time that Kaye and I ever stayed out all night together.

With school out the two of us repaired to our respective homes in Raleigh. We both took summer jobs to earn a little pocket money. Our courtship continued in pretty much the same way except that we transferred our affectionate petting from the bench on East Duke Campus to the swing on the side porch of Kaye's house. Kaye's younger sister, Louise, was wide-eyed that her big sister had a genuine boyfriend. Her older (half) sister, Lula Belle, took an interest in us and encouraged and abetted us. As young lovers will, we had our share of spats, misunderstandings and quarrels. We would break up, swear off, and date other people. But within a few days—or a week or so—we would realize how much we were missing, and would come back together with even more warmth and affection. I don't remember if Kaye vacationed with her family that summer. I remember, though, that a friend of mine motored with me in his T-Model Ford up to a little town near Virginia Beach to visit for a few days a mutual friend. It was a girl. But not a romantic attachment.

I had good evidence that I was "in" with her family in that I frequently was invited to have Sunday dinner at their dining-room table. Big deal for me to feel thus welcomed. For my 21st birthday there was a big celebration at the table with balloons, cake and ice cream and a mock "certificate" prepared by sister Lula Belle, declaring that I was "of age," whatever that means.

I don't remember that we ever had a formal engagement. After so many months we just sort of took it for granted that we would be married some day after we had both finished college, found employment and the prospect of a home. I recall telling her father that we expected to marry, but that was some time later. (I was scared to death of Dr. Highsmith, but he was a fine gentleman of the old school. "Foursquare to the earth," I used to say of him. I am sorry that I never got to let him know how much I thought of him.)

The war was raging in Europe. England continued to undergo air-raid bombings, and the Germans had invaded Russia. Our sympathies were vastly with the British, but I think in the fall of 1941 our over-riding hope was that the United States would stay out of the conflict. We knew that we college students, teen agers and young men would be the ones to do the fighting.

School at Chapel Hill and Duke opened up again in the fall with more of the same routine as in the spring. Kaye moved into Alspaugh Dorm with roommate Eleanor McCray, daughter of a Methodist minister, on a full scholarship. Kaye gave up her job of waiting on tables, but spent increased time working as a receptionist on the desk. Her room was at the back of the dorm, and sometimes I would whistle outside her window. Whereupon she would signal to me and then meet me at the dorm entrance.

One of the things that we would particularly like to do was for me to meet her at East Duke early on Sunday mornings. Then we would ride the bus to the Student Union Building on West Campus, read the morning paper—particularly the funnies—over a nice breakfast in the big Gothic dining hall, then go to the religious service in Duke Chapel. We did this several times.

One day—it was December 7—I had just parted with Kaye and taken the bus back to Chapel Hill. Immediately upon my arrival the word was buzzing around town and campus that the Japanese were bombing Pearl Harbor. This occupied everybody's thoughts and attention, with its implications of what was going to happen to our country, and what was going to happen to us personally. By the next day we were at war.

That fall Duke's football team had had an unbeaten championship season and had been invited to play in the Rose Bowl at Pasadena, California, on New Year's Day, by far the biggest and most important of the bowl games. Since the Japanese had, with ease and undiscovered, bombed Hawaii, the people on the West Coast were terrified that they, too, might be the objects of air raids. Consequently the Rose Bowl Game was cancelled.

But this was too big an opportunity for Duke's magnificent team to let slip away. After some days of meetings and negotiations it was decided to play the "Rose Bowl" game in Duke Stadium on New Year's Day. The West Coast team, Oregon State, accepted the invitation, and the arrangements were made.

As a student Kaye got tickets to the game, and the two of us went over amid all the hullabaloo of watching a national championship game being played right in Durham, North Carolina. It was really a great and festive day, even in the early days of the war. It was the only time in history that the Rose Bowl New Year's Day football game was ever played anywhere but in the Rose Bowl.

Duke lost.

III

CHRISTMAS LEAVE
DECEMBER 1942

In late December of 1942[2] I was just about as elated as anyone in the army could be. I had actually managed to achieve a ten-day leave—they were called "furloughs" in those days—which overlapped Christmas and New Years. Imagine that! A genuine Christmas holiday at home with Kaye and family away from the rigors of army life. I had seen the leave paper on the captain's desk, just waiting for me. I put all my service paper work in "apple pie" order and was just waiting for the document to be handed to me and then to be on my way home.

Then came the catastrophic bombshell. At the last minute all leaves and passes—all of them—were cancelled. It was because of a sudden, impending move of the Fourth Division out of Fort Gordon and to North Africa. All required training exercises had to be accomplished in preparation for overseas movement (POM), and no one could depart until this was done. I still had to fulfill one requirement of marksmanship in firing on the rifle range. And so the leave paper remained in the "Hold" basket on the captain's desk.

My misery knew no bounds. I can't remember any time in my army life that I was so shaken with this news. I paced the field, close to tears, and of course telephoned Kaye that our anticipated Christmas together was off. And she was just as miserable as I.

---

2. See also "A Visit from Kaye" in chapter 3. This was probably in September 1942, before he was transferred in October from Camp Wheeler to Fort Gordon.

But Kaye was determined that we were going to spend Christmas Day together. Wherever. Once again she wheedled permission from her reluctant parents to come down to Augusta and join me, even if only for a day. Perhaps it wasn't quite so difficult this time, because she now had an engagement ring. And these really were war times.

Kaye was to arrive at the bus station in Augusta at about nine o'clock on Christmas Eve. I went into town to meet her and arrange for her stay. Despite the impending move, Christmas Day was a holiday, and everybody had that day off. But the following day I was still required to go back to the post for range firing.

I didn't rent a car this time, but used the local bus transportation. I booked rooms for us at the Bon-Air Hotel, a big resort-type facility on a hill in the suburbs overlooking the city. The architecture was Spanish style, and it exuded a pleasant old-world atmosphere. We had separate rooms with a connecting bath, still observing the proprieties.

In the early evening I went to the largest department store in Augusta—I don't remember the name—and bought Christmas gifts for Kaye. They included—perhaps with other things—white bunny fur slippers and gloves and a necklace of orange, costume jewelry beads. I also bought a potted poinsettia plant. So when Kaye arrived and got off the bus at the station, there I was holding a bag full of gifts and a red potted flower. Both our faces were wreathed in smiles at our good fortune. We were thankful that we were able to salvage this much from our shattered plans.

We took the city bus, the Walton Way route, out to the Bon-Air, where we registered and ensconced ourselves in our new quarters.

Neither Kaye nor I had had any supper, and so, late as it was, we took the bus back into town and ate at a late-night cafe there. I don't remember what we ate; we were so entranced with each other. Probably ham and eggs. Bing Crosby was singing "White Christmas" on the juke box.

Next morning—Christmas Day—after breakfast at the hotel we struck up a conversation and a friendship with a hotel employee who took an interest in us. He was kind enough to take us for a ride in his car to look at the places of interest in Augusta. There weren't very many, in fact, but they did include a drive by the country club and golf course where the Masters' is held.

Christmas dinner at the hotel was a really lavish buffet. We were so euphoric that anything would have seemed good, but this one was entirely festive.

In the afternoon we petted and smooched and enjoyed the hotel's recreational facilities. Late in the day we went to a movie in a downtown theater.

I had to leave early and go back to the post to participate in the range firing that began at daybreak. I told Kaye I would telephone to let her know when and if I could get back in to see her, or if she would have to get back to Raleigh with her own arrangements.

The range firing consisted of qualifying on the new Garand or M-1 rifle. This one was a semi-automatic which fired each time you pulled the trigger, rather than the old Springfield 0-3 which I had trained on at Camp Wheeler. It was a good weapon, but heavy. I shot well that day and finished up by the end of the afternoon.

My requirement completed and my regimental clerking up-to-date, I made bold to ask Captain Spangler if I could now have the rest of my cancelled furlough. Much to my surprise he consented and handed me my signed leave order.

I phoned Kaye from the hotel lobby that I was downstairs and that the rest of my leave time now belonged to us. When

I got off the elevator she was racing down the hall to meet me, wearing a turquoise skirt and a white blouse plus the bunny slippers and the orange necklace I had given her. Once again I thought, "This is the prettiest, most desirable girl I ever saw."

We left by bus first thing next morning. That was December 28. Augusta, like Macon, was not on the main Seaboard line. So the bus ride to Columbia was a "must." Unfortunately the train to Raleigh didn't leave until the end of the afternoon, so we had about six hours to kill. We went to a movie; it was Claudette Colbert and Joel McCrea in "The Palm Beach Story," which I have seen several times since then, and always with the fondest memories.

When we got back to the Seaboard depot I never saw such a crowd. There must have been a thousand people waiting to catch that Northbound train. We had our tickets and did get on, but there was no such thing as finding a seat on this all coach-class train.

Then it was that I had one of the genius ideas of my life. We went to the dining car. There, for the next two and a half or more hours we sat in transportation luxury, enjoying a wonderful dinner with white table linens and dining car silverware. It was another of the highlights of a highlight holiday.

By the time we had unhurriedly finished the train had almost reached Raleigh. Friends and family were there to greet us, and we spent the rest of my furlough in the warmth and happiness of one of our love's most memorable times.

When my leave was over I returned to Fort Gordon to find that the move to North Africa had been canceled. And once again it was "business as usual."

IV

LIVING WITH KAYE IN NEW BRUNSWICK

1943–44

Kaye and Kern were married at Edenton Street Methodist Church in Raleigh on June 22, 1943–a story told at the end of chapter 5, "Camp Gordon and Fort Dix." They lived in New Brunswick from July 1943 until March 1944, at which point Kern was deployed from Boston to England by ship, March 23, 1944; and Kaye returned to live with her parents, the Highsmiths, in Raleigh.[3]

New Brunswick was a grimy little manufacturing town. Its population was mostly Slavic. The largest church in town was St Ladislaus Roman Catholic Church. Other than the university its principal claim for recognition was that it is the headquarters and flagship of the pharmaceuticals giant Johnson and Johnson. There were a number of smaller manufacturers scattered around the outskirts of the town.

Kaye was homesick. Of course, she was happy to be married and happy to be with me. But she missed her loving family and the comforts of home in Raleigh. I'm sure she cried sometimes when by herself, but she tried not to let me know.

The little second floor room with shared bath was pretty grim to say the best. She took her breakfasts with the landlady's family, a Mr. and Mrs. Backus. Mr. Backus ate with his head close over his plate and shoveled his food into his mouth. In the

---

3. The *News and Observer* of March 5, 1944, reported that "Mr. Holoman has recently finished training at Rutgers University, New Brunswick, N. J. Mrs. Holoman will make her home with her parents for a short while." Kern's cohort debarked in Liverpool on April 6, and his military records show him assigned to ETOUSA [European Theater of Operations] from May 23, 1944.

many after years when we would correct our children's table manners, we would say to them, "All right. You're eating like Mr. Backus." They never met the gentleman (nor did I), but we all recognized him as the epitome of the slob.

When the ASTP student body held its end-of-the-day retreat formation Kaye and the numerous other army wives would attend the ceremony. Then after we were dismissed we would have dinner together, either at the Rutgers Dining Hall or more often we would stroll down town and eat at one of the several agreeable restaurants on the main street. We would have, I think, two and a half hours together before I would have to report back for evening study at the dorm.

In war time there were plenty of job opportunities. Kaye took a job with "Tex-el-Tape," a short bus ride out of town, engaged in the production of items like Scotch Tape.[4] Her salary was $100 a month. With that plus her military allotment check and my paltry corporal's salary, we got along very comfortably, although, of course, we had to watch the pennies.

Things began to brighten up when we learned about a vacancy just a block up the street. It was in the Chi Phi fraternity house at 17 Union Street. The brothers had vacated the premises some time earlier. It was a big, colonial style house with numerous individual rooms on the second and third floors and a spacious community room downstairs along with a dining room and kitchen. The arrangement was that the ASTP wives would each have a room (shared with their husbands on the weekends) and together enjoy the rather luxurious facilities downstairs.

The room that was available to us sounded pretty unprepossessing. It was in the basement, but we grabbed at it anyway. When we took occupancy there, we were delighted. It was

---

4. Texcel cellophane tape, which was a competitor to the 3M product Scotch transparent tape.

entirely above ground, and the house mother and building manager, Mrs. Kent, lived in an apartment just across the hall. It is true we had to squeeze by the furnace to get to our place. But once inside, it was as cozy as anybody could wish. There was a short hall, a private bathroom, a kitchenette and a breakfast/bedroom area. We settled into it as a genuine honeymoon nest, and never made a move to try to get upstairs with the others (although, of course, we mingled with them during the various social times). After the noon formations on Saturdays everybody was given a pass, and we had the weekend until Sunday night to be together. You can imagine that on Saturday nights the Chi Phi house rocked with frivolity, merry-making and love-making.

On week nights between the end of study period and bed check I would slip out of the dorm, evade the guards and monitors, and after a five-minute back-alley trip arrive at our little nest for a short visit. Kaye would have either a bowl of Campbell's soup or a dessert and coffee waiting for me. We ate on that brightly colored Fiesta dinnerware, which I still remember with pleasure. These late-night trysts were among the many good things about our life at Rutgers.

After the weekend dismissals at noon on Saturdays there would be a mass exodus of the students, mostly by rail, to New York City less than an hour away. Our budget would allow Kaye and me to visit the Big Apple once every four weeks, and these were always red-letter events with us. New York was friendly to soldiers during these war days, and especially accommodating, we thought, to a young couple like us. We always stayed at the Hotel Governor Clinton. Our favorite places to dine were Caruso's (Italian), Champlain (French), Campus (seafood), and Riggs', a throwback from the Gay Nineties, where the waiters wore tuxedos and waist-length aprons. Then there was the Gripsholm Swedish restaurant with its huge scintillating smorgasbord. But it was expensive ($3.50), and we couldn't go there often. But for another dollar you could get a whole boiled Maine lobster. One time we saw Sonja Henie there, looking like a fairy princess from one of her ice shows. Breakfasts on Sunday mornings were always at the Automat.

We saw the original "Arsenic and Old Lace." We saw Todd Duncan and Anne Brown in "Porgy and Bess" with Cab Calloway as Sportin' Life. We attended concerts at Carnegie Hall and the City Center and Lewisohn (Columbia's) Stadium and were privileged to see and hear a number of the outstanding stars of the day. We rode the open-air red double-decker up Fifth Avenue and Riverside Drive. We had drinks on the lower plaza at Rockefeller Center and in the winter watched the ice skating there. And, of course, there was Radio City Music Hall across the way. Still just a dollar; I think.

One time my brother Chreston and his wife Luna were in New York and we had a grand evening with them. After dinner we went to a racy Broadway musical called "Early to Bed." After the show we had champagne and snacks at Longchamps in the Empire State Building. Then, at Chreston's suggestion and urging, we took the Staten Island Ferry and arrived back at the hotel at three or four o'clock in the morning.

Another time my Dad was in town with his new wife, Virginia. (He had re-married just a month after our own wedding). With us and several of his buyers we went out for dinner and a night-club show. I have forgotten which one.

Those New York City weekends were filled with adventurous pleasure and open-eyed appreciation of the wonders of it all.

The other three weekends in and around New Brunswick also had their pleasures and their charm. Saturday afternoons were leisurely, but they were always followed by a nice dinner downtown. The local chapter of the "Loyal Order of Moose" had a very good white-cloth dining room, as did the Roger Smith Hotel. (Neither of us was drinking anything stronger than wine at that time, but still Kaye had to show her driver's license to prove she was of legal age.) An Italian-type drug store on the main street had a special tutti-frutti ice cream, which was always a festive place for an evening treat. We would frequently go to a local movie or would socialize with the other residents at Chi Phi House for the always-held Saturday night party. We would have breakfast, cooked in the upstairs kitchen. Kaye's butter ration would go only so far on our six pancakes, and we used to look forward to the post-war day when we could douse them with butter. Sunday afternoons [we would often have] a walk in the park or around the old campus or take a bus ride around the pretty, historic countryside.

Kaye's mother paid us a visit, and I am sure that she raised her eyebrow at our basement apartment, but she kept her peace. Kaye's sister, Louise visited us one time, too; but she was just goggle-eyed at our example of wedded bliss.

It was from our house mother, Mrs. Kent, that we first heard the phrase "trick or treat." At about Halloween time she told us, "I'll have to get some trick or treat goodies for the children when they come by." We had never heard of the custom or the practice before, and I guess it came to North Carolina some years later.

We spent a lot of time listening to classical music on the record player that my father had given us. These were the old 78 RPM records where it would take four or five discs to play one symphony. But they were cased in handsome albums. I'm sure we spent too much of our money on records (we gave each other records as Christmas presents), but they were another of our great early-marriage pleasures. We retained these albums until long after they had gone out of fashion and use. I didn't get rid of the last of them until I moved to Whitaker Glen in 2003.

In early December [1943] Kaye got sick. It was a classic case of the flu with congestion, coughs and high fever. Without family or close friends and with my military obligations I was terrified. I was literally benumbed with fear that she might die. That I had brought her away from home to this kind of life then been unable to prevent her perishing in an un-caring town without her loved ones nearby. But Mrs. Kent was caring and concerned and ministered to Kaye during those many times when I was unable to be with her. She also found a doctor who would make house calls. Probably he had called at worse places than ours, but he did come faithfully; and of course the disease ran its course and Kaye recovered in a matter of two or three weeks. In my memory I can still see her lying on her sick bed while I trimmed our first Christmas tree, a tiny one that stood on the little dresser top near our bed.

The holidays over, we returned to our routine existence for what turned out to be the final trimester. The other thing that I principally remember is how cold it was. Just taking a short walk, from block to block or to down town, the cold and the wind would seem to rip into the depths of our bodies. When we would arrive back at our apartment, we were glad that it was so close to the furnace.

When I wound up things at Rutgers and our departure from New Brunswick was imminent, we decided to splurge in New York those last days. We had two or three trips into the city that included a visit to the Palm Court of the Hotel Plaza and dinner at the Grand Ballroom of the Waldorf Astoria. Our plays included the definitive production of "Othello," with Paul Robeson, Uta Hagen and Jose Ferrer; and the next night with Jan Kiepura and Marta Eggerth in "The Merry Widow." Going home from the station, those winds on Easton Avenue had never felt so cold.

After that, it was just a matter of gathering our possessions, heading back to Raleigh and home, and preparing me for departure to Europe.

V

Beautiful Day

1957

Our third son, Christopher Louis, was born at Rex Hospital (the one on St. Mary's Street) on October 14, 1957.

In those days it was routine for the new mother to stay in the hospital for an additional week after the baby was born. New fathers had the privilege of viewing their child—along with the other newborns, through a glass window and trying to identify "which one is mine?" Younger brothers and sisters were not allowed to visit.

So after the requisite number of days had passed Kaye came home to us on a Saturday afternoon. Unfortunately our pediatrician had decided that the baby had not developed sufficiently to come home and must remain behind. Our pediatrician was Dr. Jane Wooten, a distant relative and close friend who attended all of our children from birth to adolescence. And never charged us a penny for all the thousands of services she rendered, including some late-night sessions.

It seemed that the baby had a "bilirubin" count that was either too high or too low, I can't remember which. It has something to do with the liver. And anyway young Chris was jaundiced. Jane thought a couple more days in the hospital with treatment and medications would clear up the problem and he could join his new family at home.

You can imagine how glad Kern and Dick and I were to have our mother back home after a week of "batching" on meals out and miserably cooked meals at home. And just not having "Mamma" at home. That Saturday was a day of great celebration and satisfaction for us.

But not for Kaye. Amid all our rejoicing and attentiveness she was strangely quiet and subdued. We did our best to make her cheerful, but she was not one of the rejoicers.

Then Saturday night, after the boys had gone to bed, Kaye and I were sitting quietly in the living room, and I looked across to her chair and saw the tears just rolling down her cheeks. "What is it, Honey?" I asked.

And she burst forth in sobs, "I want my baby!"

Saturday night and Sunday came and went. And then, first thing Monday Jane called to say that Chris had improved enough to come home, and she had made the arrangements. If we could come over right away she would have him brought out to us. The boys had gone on to school.

So in nightgown and housecoat Kaye was loaded into the front seat of our car. (She was not yet up to wearing dresses.) I pulled up to the side exit of Rex and a nurse brought Chris out and laid him in my arms.

The music on the car radio was playing "O, What a Beautiful Morning" as I carried our newest son down the walkway. I opened the car door and handed him into the loving arms and lap of his mother. As the radio music continued to play.

Beautiful Morning indeed.

The author with his four sons:
David, Chris, Dick, D. Kern, Kern
Luke's Hideaway, Caswell Beach
July, 2002

❦ 13 ❧

LONG BEACH

I
1948

We first went to Long Beach, N. C. (seven miles west of Southport) in the summer of 1948. We went in company with my brother Boyce and his family, with whom we had a very close and friendly relationship at that time. Boyce was five years older than I. We both worked at Boylan-Pearce then, and felt privileged that we could take our two-week vacations at the same time. Boyce's wife was named Lillian (Linnie or Lyn). Their oldest child was Stuart, about five years old, and their daughter was Dorothy, about three.

Our oldest and at that time only child was Dallas Kern, a little less than a year old and usually called "Mike." During the year our families would play bridge almost weekly with the children asleep in the beds of whichever parents were the hosts that night. We picnicked together, shared tickets and passes, swapped tools and all the other things that good neighbors do. Later on, when we had a television set and they did not yet have one, they would come to our house every Saturday night. We would watch "Beat the Clock," "The Jackie

Gleason Show of Shows," "Sid Caesar and Imogene Coca," "The Lucky Strike Hit Parade" and the sign-off playing of "The Star-Spangled Banner." The only station we could get was Greensboro—with our rooftop antenna—and it would usually snow over when an airplane flew overhead. We were close families, and vacationing together was among the many things we liked to do.

We chose Long Beach that year because it was cheap. The real estate lots along the Brunswick County coast were very much undeveloped and prices were much less than those at other vacation beaches like Wrightsville, Carolina and Nag's Head.

Our cottage did not have a name. I'm not sure that the Long Beach cottages *were* named. But we had three bedrooms; the largest was occupied Boyce and his family of four; the middle by me and my family of three—including the less-than-a-year-old baby. The smallest and least desirable room was the domain of the housekeeper that we had brought along for the chores. Her name was Ruth—black, of course. This arrangement didn't really work out very well, because Ruth felt that Lyn and Kaye were hard task-mistresses. She was probably right, as the wives felt that she should do *all* the housework, while she thought that they should do a considerable amount of the tasks. She was not very happy, and let us know so. We certainly did not expect it to be a vacation for her; but even so, maybe we expected too much. Anyway, this was the only time we ever took a housekeeper to the beach with us.

Our cottage was not air-conditioned. I doubt if anyone in those days even considered that beach cottages should be cooled. What we did was throw all the screened windows and doors wide open and let the ocean breezes blow through. When the wind was blowing from the ocean—which it usually was—the ventilation was delightful. On those few nights when the wind refused to blow, it was stiflingly hot. And when the wind would back around and blow from the land, we were treated to the permeating odor of the two menhaden fish factories across the river.

Our garbage can was raided every night by the beach's wild animals. We tried to keep the top securely fastened, but they always found a way. We never did ascertain whether they were raccoons, possums or little wild foxes in which the island abounded. We just called them "varmints."

Long Beach was—LONG. Twenty-two miles from east to west. At the eastern end, across from the Intra-Coastal Waterway and Southport, was Fort Caswell, one of the nineteenth-century coast artillery forts built along our coastline to guard the river entrances against enemy invasions. World War II had proved them all obsolete, and they had been dismantled and deserted, left with only a couple of caretakers. We spent some time walking around the old battlements, but found the adventure hot and uninteresting.

Across the mouth of the Cape Fear River as it emptied into the sea was Smith Island, better known as Bald Head Island because of the abandoned lighthouse on Bald Head Hill known as Old Baldy. As I remember it from that time it was completely undeveloped and deserted. A friend of mine told me that he once went ashore there and hunted for wild goats.

On the road a couple of hundred yards to the west was the Coast Guard station and the Oak Island lighthouse, very much as they are today, except that the station has been moved across the road to be adjacent to the lighthouse. Oak Island lighthouse is by no means the prettiest or most glamorous looking of the lighthouses, but it is the tallest on the entire Atlantic Coast. And in 1948, even as today, it was pumping out its familiar signal: four flashes on and six seconds off in an endless cycle.[1]

The one access to Oak Island was by a draw bridge, or rather a swing bridge. Whenever a boat of any size at all would come up the waterway it would blow its horn and the highway gates at each end of the bridge would come down and the bridge keeper would obediently swing the bridge around to let the boat pass through. The entire process would last for perhaps ten minutes, which was not onerous, as the road traffic was light. And the children would like to get out of the car and watch all the proceedings with great interest.

At the other end of the island—the West End—was the inlet, which separated us from Holden's Beach, the next one over. It was about a quarter of a mile wide, but too deep to wade and with a channel that the little boats would go through with ease. Over on the ocean side of the island was the gentle surf and the wide-ish sand that made our beach such a friendly place to vacation. The end of the island curved around into a lovely lagoon that we all loved to visit. We usually took sand chairs, soft drinks and snacks. The children would delight to paddle in the wave-less water; Lyn would try a little shallow-water fishing; and Boyce and I would crab along the shoreline for the abundant bluefins that teemed in the area. On a good day we could catch enough for a nice crabmeat cocktail at supper time. And in the intervals we all just sunned ourselves and relaxed the way vacationers are supposed to do.

During the twilight several times a week a big, noisy machine would rumble up the road and by-paths spraying a blue cloud of insecticide. It smelled like the spray cans we use today. I

---

1. The Oak Island Light dates from 1958; before that the steel-tower Cape Fear Light, which had replaced Old Baldy, was positioned on the cape just across the inlet from the modern light.

guess it did a good and effective job, as I cannot ever remember Long Beach as being mosquito-y or buggy.

I don't think that the ocean-going cargo ships came in as frequently then as they do now. When we saw one on the horizon it was an exciting event. Then we would all pile into our two cars and hurry down to Fort Caswell—our cottage was about two-thirds up the island—and stand on the wooden pier to watch the ship round the island's end and head up the Cape Fear River past Southport to Wilmington.

The only commercial business on Long Beach was Stott's Store, which doesn't even deserve the description as a general store. It had one gasoline pump out in front beside a stack of crates full of bottled soft drinks and a wash tub full of ice. The shelves inside were stocked with a sketchy array of canned fruit and vegetables. So when we wanted anything—anything—we would go into Southport. I think we went into Southport every day, sometimes more than once.

Southport was a little town that time had forgotten. It was quiet and docile in its riverside clime. The stately old live oak trees lined the streets and walkways, and the ancient houses lined the river front with a quiet serenity, some stately mansions, some small cottages that had withstood the wear and tear of a hundred years. I remember a Leggett's department store, a drug store, a couple of filling stations, and several little cafes and food shops. There were probably other stores too, but I don't remember them. The theater was the AMUZU—we figured out later that it meant "amuse you"—but it was closed and boarded up when we were there. The newspaper was the Southport *Port Pilot,* operated by Jim Harper and his sons, whom I came to know much later. It was published once a week on Wednesdays. There was a small hospital on the road near the town's limit. It was called Dosher Memorial Hospital.

No doubt it was inadequate, but we went there several times for our cuts, bumps, and bruises.

There were two grocery stores in town. One was called Harrelson's; it was much like an old-timey A&P. The other grocery was the Suburban Superette, more like a Piggly-Wiggly. Prices were high and selections were limited.

Southport had a fire department and fire engine. It was a Model-T Ford, painted red and with a ladder affixed to each side. (Probably I am over-emphasizing the sparseness of Southport's attractions. But it was a *really* sleepy town, very much undeveloped as a tourist spot or a vacation mecca.)

We took our dirty laundry into the Baptist Washerette, a fund-raising project of the local church to build their new sanctuary. The man in charge there was a very friendly and helpful person whom we quickly came to like. Very shortly he announced to us, "On weekdays I'm the laundry man. But on Sundays I'm the preacher."

It is seven miles from Long Beach to Southport. The road goes straight into town and comes to an end at the Cape Fear waterfronts. There sat Mac's Seafood Shack, identically the same place as the present Ship's Chandler Restaurant. We ate many of our evening meals—at least half—in Southport, and Mac's was our favorite, better than "Quack's" up the street. Mac was always either in the kitchen or behind the counter. Everything he served was good, but we especially liked his place because he served a variety of fresh vegetables, whereas all the other places served only French fries and cole slaw. And no place could ever equal his broiled flounder, which he cross-hatched and stuffed with crab meat. Mac's name was McGlamery, and after he sold his business he retired and lived to a ripe old age.

Adjacent to Mac's was a fifth-rate motel where the fishermen used to stay the night before going out on their deep-sea trips and breakfasting at Mac's shack before they left.

Frequently in the evenings after dinner we would take long rides in the dusk and darkness. All of the countryside was much undeveloped and unlighted. I remember one night coming unexpectedly upon a ghostly looking country church framed in Spanish moss. With the moon racing overhead, it would have been a perfect setting for a ghost story. But it never got written.

One day on the unpaved road that led toward Orton Plantation I came upon a large-ish patch of Venus fly traps growing right there on the shoulder. It was, I guess, about fifty inches in diameter. I dug up a specimen and took it back to the cottage to show the others. Boyce and Lyn promptly wanted to be led to the same spot, where they took up more on the return trip. Eventually we ended up digging it all up. I think we must have had the idea of raising them back in our own homes in Raleigh. But, of course, they all died.

Well, our vacation with all its assets and liabilities came to its two-week end. We did not return to Long Beach for a number of years, really not until after Hurricane Hazel in [October] 1954 leveled the place and destroyed just about everything. But it never ceased being a favorite vacation place in our minds. So that in the long run it was the place where both our families regularly visited for about fifty years. We were frequently at Long Beach at the same time, but this was the only time our two families shared a cottage.

On the way home Boyce and his family drove straight back to Raleigh. (Cottage rentals in those days ran from Sunday to Sunday.) We stopped off in Wilmington and had Sunday brunch at Fergus's Ark, an old boat that had been converted into a restaurant permanently docked at the Cape Fear waterfront. It was a favorite and festive way to end our vacation, and we did it traditionally and regularly as long as Fergus was in business.

II

After Hurricane Hazel

After that first summer in 1948 we did not return to Long Beach for a number of years. We did vacation with brother Boyce and his family for three more years, once at Nag's Head and twice at East Cherry Grove Beach (now a part of Myrtle Beach). Kaye and I had two children by then. We continued to call our oldest "Mike," though one relative grumped, "If you're going to call him Mike, you should have named him Mike." When he grew to the age of decision-making, he chose to use the name, "D. Kern," the "D" being to avoid the title of "Junior," and to distinguish it from my own name. He did, however, choose to name his son Michael, so I guess he did have some affection for the nickname.

Our second son, Dick, was an early riser and a very active one. It fell to my responsibility to be up with him in the dawn-like hours while the rest of the household slept. I can still remember wakefully trying to keep Dick out of trouble while struggling with the overpowering desire to doze off.

After those years our two families no longer vacationed together. We went to different places at different times. My family went twice to Topsail Beach because Boylan-Pearce had a branch store in Jacksonville. We took one travelling trip to the North Carolina mountains, and another one all the way to Quebec, Canada, and Niagara Falls. Twice we stayed home because we had incurred household expenses and didn't feel that we could afford a trip.

One time we went back to Nag's Head, and arrived just a few days before a hurricane was predicted to strike. I thought it would be a fun thing to stay down there and experience a genuine heavy storm. It was not a great idea. The day was spent in observing the ominous grey clouds assemble overhead and seeing the two storm flags flying at the Coast Guard Station at Manteo. The hurricane came ashore at about Hatteras and beat its way up the Outer Banks. At about 9:00 PM, it hit us and everything went: electricity, lights, radio, running water, telephone, cooking. The works. The wind blew ferociously for hours. Windows blew out and water began to creep under the doors. We sat there in the dark while I kept saying to myself, "You fool! You monumental fool! To deliberately subject your family to this kind of hardship and danger just for the sake of a cheap thrill. You'll never pull this kind of stunt again." I never did, though I made my share of other stupid mistakes.

The eye of the hurricane must have passed directly overhead, because in the wee, small hours of the night, it got dead calm. People began to come out on the streets and reassure ourselves and each other that we had survived. Pretty soon it began to blow again. But never as strongly as the first round.

The next morning everybody began to clean up. It seems to me that the utilities were restored in a relatively short time (about two or three days, I think), and we managed to have a fairly nice vacation for the rest of our time there. I believe we even went down to the Forest Theater in Manteo and saw a brave production of *The Lost Colony*.

This was not the same storm as Hurricane Hazel in 1954, I think, which leveled Long Beach and destroyed just about everything on Oak Island. It was several years after that that our families ventured to it again.[2] And we found it completely different from what we had experienced before. The old inlet was gone, and a new one broken through about a quarter mile to the East.

A new line of cottages had sprung up along the shore line and across the Long Beach Road. Everywhere there were bustling signs of optimism and energy and a spirit to make things even better than they had been before. We liked what we saw, and this strand has been our favorite mecca ever since.

Once again Boyce's family and mine vacationed at the same time but took cottages about a mile apart on the beach front. We used to walk down the sand to them and enjoy sporting in the surf and dabbling in the sand. Boyce died in 1972, which put an end to those arrangements. But Chreston's widow, Luna, for a few years rented a cottage for four consecutive weeks and invited her two children to come and spend two weeks each there with her. Those bygone days with departed loved ones remain warm and dear in my memories.

After crossing the bridge onto the island you first came to the town of Yaupon Beach. It was developing into a little commercial community with a fair amount of little shops and fast-food cafes. There were two motels and a tiny amusement park with a merry-go-round, bumper cars, and take-a-chance concession booths. There were Baptist, Presbyterian and Methodist churches at various locations, and some time later the beginnings of a nice library.

The town of Long Beach made its share of progress in a more sedate way. After exiting Yaupon Beach, you took a sharp left turn to get onto the beach road. There were now only three stores plus the Long Beach Pier not far from the

---

2. August 1958. Chris was less than a year old.

end of the island, built several hundred feet out into the ocean, and a drawing card for fishermen. The city government seems to have been in the hands of three men. There was Shannon, the postmaster and also chief of the volunteer fire department. There was Ferrell, the mayor, who was interested in developing real estate tracts. And there was Schuler, the garbage collection man. He had a little Hitler-style mustache and a perpetual sneer as if he were eternally sniffing the products of his trade. Each of them ran a store on the beach. Ferrell, I believe, later got rich selling beachfront property and permanent residential lots back closer to the Intra-Coastal Waterway which ran behind the island. After a number of sales, trades, etc. Ferrell's eventually became Oak Island Accommodations.

Up at the east end of the island the Baptist Conference bought (or were given) the Fort Caswell property. They left the old ramparts and battlements in place, developed the internal buildings into a religious training ground and a Baptist recreational spot mostly for their youth. Unfortunately (for us) they soon put up a gate house at the entrance to keep out undesired visitors. This was a disappointment to us, for going to the wooden pier at the back had been one of our favorite spots to watch the boats go by.

One of the big events was the arrival [autumn 1961] of the battleship North Carolina. "The Immortal Show Boat" of World War II, it had been decommissioned some years earlier and was headed for the scrap yard. But a consortium headed by Wilmington native and well-known entrepreneur Hugh Morton purchased it for a song and made plans to dock it permanently on the Cape Fear River at Wilmington as a tourist attraction. The news stories followed it as it was towed down the coast line, and there was a lot of interest and anticipation of its coming. Governor Terry Sanford was to be on hand for its scheduled arrival on Sunday morning. My family of four drove down to Yaupon Beach on the previous Saturday night and stayed at one of the two motels. Sunday morning was a big thrill as we looked off the porch and saw the battleship's great hull looming on the horizon.

As the announced time approached we drove down to the wooden pier at Fort Caswell to observe the towing in. Unfortunately the weather was stormy with a brisk, rainy gale blowing, and we learned that the North Carolina's arrival had been postponed until the next day. Since we had school and work obligations we had to return to Raleigh on Sunday, and so we spent a rainy day walking around Southport and later on Wrightsville beach.

The ship was actually towed in on the following day amid delayed fanfare and welcome speeches. In maneuvering into its space on the far side of the river opposite the Wilmington docks, it nicked the side of Fergus's Ark. For a number of years thereafter Fergus advertised that he ran the only restaurant in the world that had been hit by a battleship.

Another big event on Long Beach was the opening of the first real grocery store. The Red and White chain established a medium-sized facility at the corner where you turn off to get onto the beach strand. It also had a hardware department. The prices were atrocious, and the selections were skimpy and sketchy, but, by-gum, we had a place we could buy groceries without going into Southport every day, although we still made frequent visits there. The Red and White soon became the center for a number of small shops along the same block, many of which still endure.

Across the street from Red and White came the first real seafood restaurant. It was (and is) Jones' Seafood Restaurant, which is still in business today. It advertised "Calabash-style" cooking, which means that everything is deep-fried in oil. But it remains popular.

Calabash is on the waterway in South Carolina, some fifty miles down the road. The town consists entirely of some two dozen restaurants all cooking Calabash style. We would usually go down there once during our two-week stay, including a stop at the fireworks store, and sometimes a short boat ride up and down the waterway. It was at a Calabash restaurant, Captain Juel's Hurricane,[3] that I first saw a salad bar. Today, of course, salad bars are ubiquitous, but it was an unexpected treat forty or so years ago.

Our favorite crabbing spot on the island was at the then-undeveloped Bluewater Point on the fringe of the waterway. For some reason the crabs seemed to abound there, and we were always lucky. One day we were particularly lucky when a little commercial fishing boat drew up nearby and one of the crew members called out "you want some crabs?" "Sure," was our reply, and he obligingly dumped a load that filled our crab basket to overflowing. Bonanza! For the rest of our stay that year we had all we could handle, and we feasted on crab cocktail, crabcakes, and panned-fried crab meat (Kaye's favorite).

Dumped out with the crabs from the little boat we found an all-metal knife that was and is useful. At the end of our vacation it found its way into my knife drawer. After all these years, it's still there among the others, and I think of the good days at Long Beach every time I see it. They really were (and still are) the good days.

---

3. Calabash is in North Carolina, just before the state line. Juel's Hurricane is a few miles south, in Little River, South Carolina. The salad bar was set out in a rowboat full of ice.

III
Later Visits

We never did seriously consider buying a place of our own at Long Beach. Probably, over the years, we paid a good deal more in rental money than we would have if we had purchased, particularly if we had put it up for rent during the times that we were not occupying it. But we liked the idea of being able to walk away from it at the end of a vacation without worrying about maintenance, storm damage and the mechanics of leasing. Besides, as our family continued to grow, we increasingly had need for larger cottages.

We rented so many different cottages that I can't remember them all. There were the Rhoney Cottage, the Troxler Cottage, the Maner Cottage (for five summers or more) and the "Real McCoy." Then there were the ones that had individual names: "Sea and Sand," "The Sandpiper," "The Tuna Hut," "The Olive Bowl," "Lazy Daze," "The Red Anchor," and others.

Meanwhile the commercial side of the island continued to build up. The Beach Drive paralleling the shore line became almost solid stores, shops, eateries, gas stations, souvenir stands and the like. The town of Yaupon Beach was the most commercialized, but the town of Long Beach was not much behind. The town limits of the two were contiguous. Also the road from the highway turnoff to the island was similarly built up.

We began to look for accommodations at less built-up places on the island. We found them at the Town of Fort Caswell Beach on the east end. When you cross the bridge, instead of turning to the right, you follow the curve of the road around to the left to find a community of cottages and condominiums without commercialization of any kind. There was a country club across the road, and beyond that, past the Coast Guard station and up to the Baptist Assembly Ground at old Fort Caswell, there were only private cottages and condos. In fact, once settled in a cottage, it required a drive of two or three miles just to get to the store and filling station, just to buy a morning paper. And we liked it that way.

I don't remember when we decided to take our vacation cottages at Caswell.[4] But I recall that at one of the early-on locations at an un-named cottage Mark [Holoman, b. June 18, 1975] was with us as a baby only a couple of months old. After that we stayed at several cottages as they seemed appropriate each year. The last one that accommodated the entire family was "Four Square," which we occupied upstairs and down.

By that time it was evident that with sons grown and married, children coming along and an occasional friend invited, it would be very difficult to find a place that would hold us all. That's when we began to rent a second cottage, conveniently located, across the road if possible, but sometimes as much as a mile away.

We finally latched onto "Luke's Hideaway," a beach-front cottage painted gray, trimmed in red. It was not the most prepossessing-looking facility, but it had a couple of features that we really liked. It had a great room in the center with high, sky-lighted ceiling, large enough to hold comfortably all of our gathered family. It had a number of niches and sleep-on sofas

---

4. The first Beach Bulletin that Kaye issued was in 1983, giving directions to the Olive Bowl in Long Beach. In July 1988 the directions are to Four Square in Caswell Beach, as though that were a new destination. The two 1990 bulletins concern Luke's Hideaway "where we have been twice before." Luke's in fact held everyone for some years before a cottage across the street came into the picture. Our first visit to the beach with our daughter Kate was in 1983, when we drove across the country to join the merriment.

that could easily take in an unexpected guest or two. And it had a huge dining table where we could easily seat twelve and more for a meal. We kept coming back to Luke's, year after year. It had some drawbacks, but at least we knew what we were returning to. We continued to use it each summer until 2004, when the owner made it not available.

Kaye—grandmother to everybody else—died in 1997. At that time I sincerely thought that everybody would decide that with her gone, they no longer wanted to continue the annual vacations to the beach. I was wrong. Unanimously they decided that they wished to continue to come back each year. The times were full of sentimental associations and dear remembrances. Besides that, with our families scattered far and wide, they liked the one opportunity each year to re-join cousins and in-laws, catch up on family doings and watch the grandchildren grow up.

It wasn't the same without Kaye—certainly not for me. I particularly missed the annual birthday parties she used to have for the children around the big table. But it was still very good indeed, and a genuine time of happy togetherness. Over all those years and among those twenty or more relatives, I recall that there were very few disagreements or unkind words spoken. The co-operation and kindness among the daughters-in-law was especially notable.

Although there were many memorable meals, one we always looked forward to was when it was Dick and Sandy's turn. They would bring in huge quantities of shrimp which they served cold-boiled in big bowls spread out on newspapers on the table. Just shrimp, with few if any "go-withs." Never any left over. At the end of dinner we would look at those empty bowls and couldn't believe we had eaten so many shrimp.

Grandaddy's big deal—mine, that is—was the "Happy Hour" held almost every evening on the ocean-front pier of Luke's. One by one we would begin to assemble for drinks and snacks, and before long were all packed in for shared conversation and family friendships. The folks across the road would join us at all times, and we would do our socializing, "beaching" and dining at Luke's. Breakfast was served at nine each morning for whoever would show up. Lunch was independent, informal and on-your-own. Each family would take turns in preparing dinner, and—I suspect—would try to outdo one another the specialness of the feast for that evening.

An event that bears recounting was the arrival in the locale of big, genuine, chain grocery stores, one on each side of the road at the turnoff from the highway. There was a Lowes and, I think, a Harris-Teeter. They brought complete selections at competitive, big-city prices. [This was] a great development, and afterward we did the great majority of our shopping there. The center also featured hardware stores, book stores, branch banks and a movie theater. Really, our once-countrified vacation spot now offered all the modern conveniences one could wish for.

Southport, too, had been building up with stores, cafes and tourist attractions, with really a surprising number of art stores and souvenir shops. About the only reason we went into Southport any more was to dine fairly frequently at one of the several restaurants. Mac's Seafood Shack had been converted into a rather upscale facility called the Ship's Chandler, with full glass windows looking out on the Cape Fear River. It remained our favorite, although prices were about triple of what Mac's had been. Popular with all of us was down the street on the waterfront a very informal eatery called the Yacht Basin Provision Company. It was semi-outdoors with a ceiling and overhead fans. It featured crabcakes and shrimp, but offered a variety of other choices. The order-taking seemed a mass of confusion, but somehow they would get our orders to us efficiently and in a minimum of time. On the main street was The Pharmacy, formerly a drugstore, but one that had been re-modeled into a genuinely upscale restaurant featuring gourmet dining. It was Jackie Harper's pleasure to entertain the group there for a lavish luncheon.

The other notable activity in Southport was to drive along the picturesque waterfront. Southport has a lot of self-respect for its historic past, and has been diligent in preserving its beautiful houses, some mansions and some charmingly small ones. A mile beyond the city limits was the ferry across the Cape Fear River to Fort Fisher and the North Carolina Aquarium. It's an interesting twenty-minute ride, and most of us would take the trip over one time, if only to show the young ones and the newcomers.

One activity that has become a tradition is our annual boat cruise. It developed in different ways. Early-on on we would drive to Calabash, S. C.,[5] for a seafood dinner and a cruise on the Inland Waterway. For two or three years we would rent a "party boat" mounted on pontoons for our family members to putt-putt up and down the rivers, creeks and waterways. For my 80th birthday they chartered a boat for a big on-board to-do in my honor. More recently we have been going into Wilmington for a luncheon cruise on the Cape Fear, our vessel looking like an old-timey Mississippi riverboat, called The Henrietta.

We don't seem to go crabbing any more. Connie still likes to surf-fish. We go "ooh and ah" when she hooks a small shark.

We drive down to the end of the island, stopping for a look at the rent-a-boat activities at Bluewater Point. Then on to the inlet, a new one cut by one of the more recent hurricanes.

---

5. Again: Calabash is in North Carolina.

The towns of Yaupon Beach and Long Beach have now merged and entitled themselves Oak Island Community, although they still struggle to maintain their individuality. The town of Fort Caswell Beach has chosen to continue its independence from the others.

The island, which is now called Oak Island, has endured a number of hurricanes and tropical storms since we have been going there. The cottages on the beach have suffered varying amounts of damage, depending upon the severity of the storms. But somehow the owners and maintenance people seem to get them ready for our occupancy by our vacation times. We have never taken trip-cancellation insurance, and have had our trip interrupted only one time. That was when the hurricane came about the middle of our first week there, and we vacated the cottage and went back to Raleigh. But the storm had passed by the weekend, and on Sunday we returned and enjoyed a delightful second week.

As this episode is being written in the fall of 2004, I have gradually relinquished my responsibilities for making the vacation arrangements. Dick is now in charge of that aspect. We have reservations for a week next summer at "Beach Buzz" cottage on the waterfront and at "We Did It!" across the road. They are both two-story cottages which we occupied last summer, found pleasant, and are looking forward to enjoying again. Everybody gets older one year at a time. Families are fragmented and interests become divided. But there still seems a continuing desire to keep the old tradition going. Nobody seems to want to call it to an end. So I guess we will continue to reassemble there for beach vacations as long as a substantial number of our family wants to make it happen.

IV

Crabbing

If you want to go crabbing—amateur style—you will need the following: length of sturdy string or cord—about fifty feet; lead sinker—three or four ounces; medium size cardboard box; and a crab net—string basket on a broomstick: buy one at a fish tackle shop.

Find a wave-less body of water, still, not stagnant, with some access to the ocean and a gentle sandy slope away from you.

Fasten the sinker to the end of the cord. Then attach to the cord at the sinker a piece of bait about the size of your fist or smaller, a chicken neck and head or a dead fish or a hunk of meat. Just wrap the cord around it and pull it tight so it won't fall off. Fasten the other end of the cord to your belt loop so it won't fall off into the water.

Then swing your baited sinker in a vertical circle, and let it fly out into the water as long as its length will allow.

When you feel it touch bottom, begin to pull it toward you slowly and gently. Pretty soon you will feel the weight of the crab as he takes hold of the bait on your line. Continue to pull toward you gently—GENTLY, I SAID—or else the crab will let go and you'll have to start the whole process over again.

When the crab gets about three to five feet from you, you will see it in the water. Then take the crab net and with a quick—QUICK—downward motion scoop up the crab—with sinker and bait. Shake the crab net over the box until the crab lets go and drops in. Then go back to the water to catch another one.

If the crabbing is good, you should catch one every ten minutes or so. The ones in our waters are blue-green in color, and the good ones are about the size of your palm.

After you have caught as many as you want—or have gotten tired or the catch has become meager—you have a decision to make. You can either release your catch back into the water to live out their lives and provide recreation for a future crabber. Or you can (preferred choice) take them back to the cottage and drop them one by one into a big pot of boiling water and crab-boil powder. Like most crustaceans they turn a brilliant red when boiled. Put them in the fridge until you are ready to prepare them to eat.

Picking the white crab-meat is time-consuming and tedious. But it is well worth the effort. The fresh crab-meat cocktails are simply delicious. Or, if you have had a big catch, pan-fried crab-meat or crabcakes make unforgettable delicacies, and an extra bonus reason for a beach vacation.

Sometimes, just for the fun of it, after dark you can take your crab net and box and with a flashlight you can walk along the surf and scoop up any number of the brown speckled crabs. But they are worthless and fit only to be thrown back into the ocean.

Dallas Holoman, Sr.
in his early 20s, c. 1905

14

DALLAS HOLOMAN, SR.

These are some of my recollections of my father, Dallas Holoman, Sr., who died on May 17, 1958, at the age of 73. Like most recollections, they have become blurred by time and probably contain some inaccuracies. I regret very much that while he was living I did not have enough curiosity about my father's life to ask him more about his early days or listen closely to the stories he told of his childhood and youth.

Dallas Holoman was born on a farm in Northampton County, N. C., near Jackson. He was the ninth in a family of ten children, all but one of whom lived to maturity, most to old age. He said his birthday was September 1, 1884, although he once told Dallas, Jr., that he was not sure of the actual day; he just picked a convenient one about that time. Anyway, September 1, 1884, is the date he wrote in his own hand in the family Bible. He was christened Dallas Wingate Holoman, but he disliked the name Wingate and early dropped it. (Many years later he had a woman working for him at Boylan-Pearce named Wingate, whom he detested. I never decided whether he hated the name because of her or thought less of her because of the name. Both are reasonable possibilities.)

His parents were George Dorsey Holoman and Mary Ann Temperance Boyce. His father had been married twice before, and there were children by both of these previous marriages. We never knew them well and have lost track of all of them. George Dorsey, basically a farmer, seems to have been a rather skilled amateur blacksmith; he said he made the hinges and other hardware for the farmhouse in which Dad was born. He had been a captain in the Confederate army and had trained troops at the camp at Garysburg. Some years after the Civil War he was a member of the N. C. General Assembly. *His* father was named Jeston, and the family can be traced back pretty definitely to the 1650s, when a Christopher Holoman [or Hollyman] was on record as living in Isle of Wight County in Virginia. We think he emigrated from the island of St. Kitts in the Caribbean. There is some evidence that Christopher was the son of a John Holoman who lived in Tring, England. (Anyway, if you want to be a member of the D.A.R., there is ample proof that the Holomans were here before the American Revolution.)

Dad said that his mother used to keep moldy bread around to put on cuts and open sores to prevent infection; therefore, she was the real discoverer of penicillin. Another story he liked to tell was that he once pretended to be sick in order to avoid an unpleasant chore. He woke up three days later after having been delirious with fever for all that time.

You can imagine that at least ten children on a dirt farm did not make for a very prosperous existence. Dad left the farm at an early age and never went back there to live. He may have been 14 or 15 years old, perhaps as young as twelve. I have been told that be worked for awhile at a store in Elizabeth City. We know for sure that be lived in Norfolk, Va., for at least a year, probably working in a store, living near City Park. Some time later he was living in New York City, still a teenage boy. Apparently he got some help from home. He told one story about the money that didn't arrive on time, and he went hungry over an entire weekend. He found an unused two-cent stamp on the street and traded it in at a bakery for one piece of pastry.

Dad went to Europe at least once, I think twice, working his way across on a freighter. I remember that he said he had been to England, France and Belgium, and that in Ireland he had kissed the Blarney Stone.

About the time he reached manhood, our father was working at Canane Brothers Department Store in Springfield, Ohio.[1] I think he was something like a stock clerk. During this time he attended night classes in window decoration and sign painting at Wittenberg College in Springfield, the only higher education he ever received. Dad said that on more than one occasion he and some friends would go over to nearby Dayton on Sunday afternoons and watch in the field as the Wright Brothers would try to get their airplane off the ground. (Many years later in the late 1930s, Dad and I re-visited the old store in Springfield, now with a different name, but owned and operated by his old supervisor. Mr. Tiehan said he remembered Dad, but I doubted if he did.)

By 1907 Dad was living and working in Richmond, Va. I don't know if it was his first job there, but he was soon working as a traveling salesman for Richmond Dry Goods. In Richmond that year he met and married Edna Pleasant Lockwood, a native of the city. She was 18 years old. He said he decided to marry her the first time he saw her and followed her until

---

1. Kinnane Bros., later Kinnane & Wren. The visit was to Edward A. Tehan, of Fahien & Tehan Co. In the Springfield city directory of 1906 Dallas Holoman is listed as "window trimmer" at Kinnane Bros. with rooms in the historic Arcade Hotel, proximate.

she spoke to someone he knew, whom he later got to introduce him. It seems a rather unusual way to meet your future bride, but most people have a story about how they met their mate. They were married on July 29, 1907, and their first son, Dallas, Jr., was born the following May.

In those days, traveling salesmen went by train, carrying their trunks with them and "setting up shop" in sample rooms of the local downtown hotels. Dad said he decided to give up that occupation after staying at Hickory, N. C., for three whole days and selling one $15 bolt of Fruit-of-the-Loom muslin. He accepted a job in the piece goods department at Miller and Rhoads, so he could spend more time with his growing family.

Dallas, Jr., had been born on May 11, 1908, George Chreston on October 5, 1909. Stuart Boyce was born on April 20, 1915, and I, William Kern, on August 10, 1920. Some time in that period Dad gave up his job as piece goods buyer for Miller and Rhoads and became a floor manager or a division merchandise manager for Thalhimer's.

When I was born we were living at 1414 Floyd Avenue in Richmond, within walking distance of downtown. The character of the neighborhood has changed steadily since then. When I used to visit it as a teenager, I thought it looked very "slummy." Nowadays it has been renewed and is considered quite a desirable place to live. Were we poor? Well, we didn't have a car until 1924—a Chevrolet sedan; no television, no refrigerator, no central heat. We had electricity, but we also had gas jets in the wall. I can remember Dad with earphones and fiddling with the dials of a box-type radio. He let me listen to what he said was a speech by President Coolidge, but I couldn't hear anything. We had a classic "parlor" that we hardly ever went into. It was so cold in there that (as all of us like to tell) we kept the Christmas tree up one year until past Easter.

In my childhood I don't have any feeling of ever having been "deprived" of anything. But I knew that when Mother had to have surgery in the early 1920s—from which she never completely recovered—Dad had to go heavily into debt to pay the doctors' bills.

My earliest recollections of my father were of his coming home in the evenings as the typical family breadwinner and of taking us to church at Grove Avenue Baptist around the corner on Sundays. He was not a tall man, about 5'7" or 5'8", and he had the blue eyes characteristic of all his brothers and sisters. His hair had been sandy blond, but for as long as I could remember he was both very bald and blind in one eye. He told me he lost his hair about the time of his wife's illness. The eye he lost was as a result of either using the wrong eyewash or from too strong a solution. He was optimistic and never gave up the hope that he might get back both his full eyesight and his hair. I recall many times when he would hold his hand over his good eye and say, "I can see a little cloudy light and even some vague shapes." I would hate to think of how many hours and dollars he invested in patent medicines, salves, nostrums and other hair-restoring devices. I remember seeing him sitting in the dark at the end of a day wearing an electric cap containing an ultra-violet light bulb. Of course, nothing ever worked; his baldness was to me just a part of Dad. And he functioned completely normally with his one eye for forty years. He was of medium build but grew heavier in his later years. He had four rather prominent wrinkles in his forehead. He said there was a wrinkle for each of his four sons.

In 1925 Boylan-Pearce was Raleigh's—and perhaps North Carolina's—outstanding department store. Thirty feet wide, four stories tall, on the second block of Fayetteville Street, people came here from all over the state to praise the quality of its merchandise, the taste of its fashion. It was run as a stock company by a group of prominent Raleigh business and professional men with a hired manager. Upon the death of William Perlstein in that job, the Board of Directors contacted Dad and offered him the position. It did not take much persuasion, for Dad had found William Thalhimer, Sr., a hard taskmaster, for which he never really forgave him. Dad accepted the job of General Manger of Boylan-Pearce in the early summer of 1925 at a salary of $10,500 per year, a princely sum in those days. At that time, Dallas, Jr., was just graduating from high school; Chreston was still in high school; Boyce was in elementary school; and I had not yet begun.

The family stayed in Richmond until school was out and moved to Raleigh in August, living for a month at the old Hillyer mansion (now demolished) on the corner of Hillsboro and St. Mary's Street. Then we moved to the downstairs of a two-family dwelling on Halifax Street, just a block away, I might remark, from the home of Bessie Gray and Hubert Gill.

Without formal schooling and with only on-the-job training, Dad was never a "book" merchant. Mostly he flew the store by the seat of his pants with sound business instincts and with a steady succession of astute purchases. He would send his buyers to the market—always New York in those days—for routine stock purchases, but his own trips were prowls through the entire wholesale market for those "hot" items that would produce the extra prominence and bring the extra profits. So successful was he that in a lifetime of business uncertainty—Depression, war, repeated sale of the business, and the flight to the suburbs—during his association with the business, Boylan-Pearce never failed to make a profit every year.

Dad was prominent in the business life of Raleigh. He joined Rotary shortly after coming here—and ever afterward complained when the luncheon menu was chicken, mashed potatoes and green peas, which it usually was. He was an officer of the Chamber of Commerce and instrumental in having signs erected to identify most of the public buildings in Raleigh. He was afraid his fellow merchants were going to run him out of town when he had the brazen audacity to suggest that it was not necessary for US Highway Number 1 and all the other routes through Raleigh be directed right down the entire length of Fayetteville Street. In 1927 or 1928 he was elected president of the North Carolina Merchants Association; and during his tenure there he visited every local merchants' association in the state, the first time this had ever been done. He fought bitterly against the impending 3% North Carolina sales tax and was such a formidable opponent that Governor Ehringhaus summoned him to his office in the State House and threatened dire consequences if he did not slacken his efforts. But he actively supported Ralph MacDonald, a sales tax opponent, in the gubernatorial primary. The Democratic nomination, though, went to Clyde R. Hoey, then tantamount to election, and the sales tax became a permanent reality in the state.

I think one of my father's outstanding characteristics as a businessman was his ability to establish warm personal relationships and lasting ties with his employees. His close friendships with Office Manager Kim Weathers, with Head Bookkeeper Louise Farmer—who at first wouldn't trust him with the combination to the safe—his bridge evenings with Louis Sitner and Ida Smith, with Anne Moore, with Thelma Alford, with Bill Didenhover, were legendary. He truly regarded the Boylan-Pearce staff as his "family," and many were frequent guests in our home. He was tenderhearted in the extreme, and would never fire anyone except for dishonesty or the grossest malfeasance. This, in turn, promoted fantastic loyalty and support on their part, so that stability and goodwill were the usual atmosphere in the store. Many stayed on who could probably have found more lucrative jobs elsewhere. They just liked the working conditions under Dallas Holoman. The traveling salesmen, too, were his friends, always welcomed in his office, and frequently invited out for a home-cooked meal or a picnic nearby.

In 1927 he bought the house at 2123 Woodland Avenue, where he and his family lived for some 25 years. It was just outside the city limits then, near the end of the street car tracks. The lot was heavily wooded and poorly landscaped, and he and Mother spent a great deal time and money in beautifying it. He had a project of sprigging the entire lawn with centipede grass and put in long hours on his hands and knees putting it in place. (When I drive by my old boyhood home these days and see the excellent stand of grass there, it brings pleasant memories of the one who got it started.)

We had a little fox-terrier dog named Terry. Dad kept a picture of him in his wallet. When we would eat out at a restaurant, he would bring out the picture, show it to the waitress and beg some table scraps to take home to his "poor, hungry little dog"—which were always forthcoming with a smile.

The business went swimmingly well until the Great Depression that began in 1929. After that nobody had any money for years on end. The money simply wasn't available, and the customers didn't come. The stockholders of Boylan-Pearce had lost heavily in their other investments. Pinched for cash, they began to sell off their stocks. Shortly afterward the business was reorganized and came under the control of an out-of-state investor. In the ensuing years ownership of Boylan-Pearce changed hands several times; it was a period of great instability as well as greatly depressed sales. I think my clearest memory of Dad in those days was at home in the evenings when he would pace the floor, his hands behind his back, wondering how he could keep the business going for a few more weeks, wondering if he would still have a job day after tomorrow. It is to his great credit that during the entire Depression he never laid off any of the Boylan-Pearce employees to effect economies. He did impose drastic salary cuts on everybody and took the biggest percentage cuts for himself, reducing his income by more than half.

Although the vast majority of his time was spent on concerns with his business, Dad loved his recreational times. He was an avid fisherman, a good billiards player, enthusiastic in bridge, and enjoyed the occasional penny-poker games around our dining room table, usually with Boylan-Pearce employees and salesmen. He had time for bikes, picnics and weekend travels with his family, and he loved to play caroms and checkers with Boyce and me in the evenings—although he was so kind-hearted that he would rather lose to us than win, and would frequently "throw" a game when he could have easily won. As long as I knew him, he smoked at least two packs of cigarettes a day, and he had a persistent smoker's cough. (If I heard that cough anywhere in heaven or earth today I would recognize it instantly.) He drank socially with his friends, but was not a heavy drinker. He kept one or two bottles in the house, but they would usually stay for months. The tradition and the recipe for eggnog at Christmas, which has spread through the families, began with Dad; and dozens of people would come to the house all day and all evening for greetings and a cup of Christmas cheer.

On his fiftieth birthday my father was seized with an attack of appendicitis, which ruptured on him before surgery could be performed. For several weeks he lay close to death.

Although he did finally recover, left with huge incision scar in his abdomen, he told me later that in the hospital he had had one of those near-to-death experiences in which he felt a great sense of peace and euphoria to be leaving the cares of this world for a better existence. He returned to consciousness to find a concerned nurse bending over him saying, "your heart stopped beating there for a few seconds."

Upon his recovery most of his concern and care were for his ailing wife, our mother, Edna. She had been ill and in pain for many months, growing progressively worse until she finally gave up this life in October 1935, at 46 years of age. After an initial period of grief, he renewed his business and social activities with increased concern—for his employees, his friends and family.

Especially for me. At that time I was the only one of his four sons who was still a child. Perhaps because I was his only real dependent, he lavished on me an affection and generosity of his time and money that was truly touching. I know that he was responsive, appreciative and loving toward his other three sons; but, all during my high school, college and active duty in the Army, his attentions to me were abundant indeed. I knew I was not deserving of so much, and sometimes reacted poorly, but even then I was fully grateful for it.

By the late 1930s Boylan-Pearce's situation was sad indeed. Its ownership had passed into the hands of a manipulator who systematically milked the business of its assets. The building was sold to produce cash; operating capital was diverted to finance outside projects; and all the cash was drained into huge "loans" which everyone knew had no chance for repayment. Our father felt helpless to stem this tide as he strove desperately to keep the business alive and continue the jobs of 100 employees and himself. Finally, with no assets left at all except its merchandise and with a mountain of unpaid bills, bankruptcy and possible legal action were a looming spectre. Dad re-mortgaged his home, scraped together about $15,000, secured financial backing from a local investment company and bought out the owner, acquiring controlling stock in Boylan-Pearce. It was the first time that he had held any ownership in the business. Everything before had been as a hired manager.

The problems involved in paying off such monstrous debts seemed insurmountable. But shortly afterward World War II began, shortages developed everywhere, and stores could sell about everything they could get their hands on. Our integrity and position in the wholesale market had remained good, so that the store was able to obtain merchandise even in the face of severe shortages. Boylan-Pearce prospered, and in an astonishingly short time the debts were paid off, the ownership became clear and the company was taking in handsome profits. For the first time in his life, Dallas Holoman was really independent and financially secure.

I don't want to give the impression that Dad had been a Gloomy Gus or a worrywart. Other than occasional periods of despondency, my overall recollection of him was with a sunny disposition and a warm, outgoing attitude toward his family and widening circle of friends, always marked by his generosity. I never saw anybody quicker to pick up the dinner check or to fight to pay the costs than he was. Although he had had almost no formal education, Dad was a voracious reader, leaning mostly to biography and classic fiction. He was a great admirer of Charles Dickens and O. Henry and bought the complete works of both. Over the years he acquired a formidable library and also showed some remarkably good taste in obtaining contemporary art reproductions. He cared nothing for classical music but could discuss English and American literature with anybody. In history, I suppose his hero was Robert E. Lee, and one of his cherished possessions was Douglas Southall Freeman's definitive biography of Lee, given him one year by his sons.

With complete responsibility for Boylan-Pearce, Dad now turned his attention to assistance in managing the business. He turned to his sons, in whom he had great confidence. His dream was for all four sons and himself to be active in the store, convinced that there was opportunity for expansion and prosperity for all. "This business is a little gold mine," he used to like to say.

Chreston had come in earlier as a shipping room clerk and had soon shown a flair for merchandising unequalled by any of the rest of us. By 1940 he was general merchandise manager. Boyce came from Pine State Creamery to be office manager, and in 1942 Dallas, Jr. gave up his career with New York Telephone Company to be comptroller. I worked in the shipping room in the summer times.

All the time Dad was consolidating his grasp on Boylan-Pearce I was away at college. I graduated in the summer of 1942 and was immediately drafted into the Army. These were emotional times for all of us; after fifty years it is impossible to describe how nearly everybody lived every day near the edge of his emotions. I was in the Army nearly five years, and I believe that Dad regularly wrote to me twice a week for the entire time and regularly deposited money to a special account for me while I was unable to earn the kind of income the rest were earning. When I would come home on leave, Dad would always—always—celebrate with a lavish steak supper for a combination of his friends and my friends at Proescher's Restaurant, the only steak house in the area at that time.

After a year in the Army, I married Kaye in the summer of 1943. With his last son married and gone from the fold,

Dad remarried, too, less than a month later. His choice was Virginia Barber of Windsor, N. C., who had been a worker at Boylan-Pearce for a number of years and had served during the more recent years as his secretary. Virginia was—and is—a tall, very beautiful brunette with excellent taste and solid good sense. She provided a lovely, comfortable home for him on Woodland Avenue and later on Rothgeb Drive, lived with him in affection and concern, and took good care of him as a caring companion in his declining years. All of us are grateful to Virginia for her place in the life of our father for his last 15 years.

When I returned from the wars in 1947 to a rousing barbecue he gave in my honor at the Neuseoca Fishing Club which he had joined, I found his age was beginning to tell on him. He was 63. As I, too, began work at Boylan-Pearce, I saw that he had relinquished almost all of the real management of the business to his sons. Gone were the dynamic buying trips to New York; gone were the close, day-by-day inspections and supervisions of every detail. He considered himself a sort of elder statesman with lots of observations and experience, but with little zest for incisive actions. "This is your business now," he used to tell us. "Run it the way you think it ought to be." Nevertheless, he could not help being frequently wistful if we should happen not to run it in the ways that he would have.

Increasingly he found pleasure in his yard, his Boston terrier dog, Butch, and his little wooden bird call with which he would summon the wildlife for their daily feedings. He was devoted to his grandchildren, all of whom lived in Raleigh, and it was his great pleasure to provide each of them with "ice cream money" for the coming week. I think the going price then was $1.00 a week to pay for a cone every day. How times have changed! That wouldn't even buy one decent trip to Baskin-Robbins these days.

Our father had earlier renewed many of his contacts with his own family, mostly still in rural Northampton County. His mother and father were, of course, long since dead, but most of the others were still around, in general a long-lived clan. He loved to visit them on their farms and simple country or small-town homes. He paid for cleaning up the old family burial ground, and I am sure he gave financial support to some of them, including to a family that was then living on the old home place. He was deeply affectionate to his two living sisters, "Aunt Weedie," nearest to him in age, and "Aunt Kate," older, who had helped rear him in his early years at home. With "Uncle Henry," his next older brother, there was a particularly warm friendship; and on several occasions they took vacations together, including one to Florida and Cuba. As time went by, however, most of the visits to Northampton were on the occasion of funerals, as one-by-one his family and their spouses retired to their graves.

In the early 1950s came the first of a long series of heart attacks that felled him, incapacitated him and eventually carried him away. My recollection of Dad in those days was mostly of visits to a hospital room, to oxygen tents and slow recoveries marked by his frustrations over his illness and his awareness that he *was* ill and not really recovering. As long as he could, though, and whenever he could, he came to work every day and took great pleasure in observing the workings of the store from his open office on the balcony of the Fayetteville Street store. In those days the store owned a company sedan, and the five of us used to ride to work together, since we all lived within a mile radius of one another.

Dad's health was too poor for him to participate very much in the plans to transfer our operations from Fayetteville Street to Cameron Village, but he supported the project whole-heartedly and gave us all continued support and encouragement when we might have faltered at the enormous risk of being the first major store anywhere (so far as I know) to move its entire operation from Main Street to the suburbs.

As we all know, the move was a glowing success from the first day, and the Boylan-Pearce in Cameron Village had—and still retains—a beauty and distinctiveness that we continue to take pleasure in. Dad was truly enchanted with it. He said, "This is as close to going to heaven as I can possibly imagine."

We established him in the large front room of our executive offices on the main floor. "D. Holoman, President," said the sign on the door, I think the only time he ever had his name on a door. He continued to come to work every day when his health permitted. There was a television set in his office which occupied some of his attention. But what he liked best was for his sons and his old-time employees and co-workers to drop in on him to reminisce, to share experiences and to ask his advice. By that time I was a buyer and merchandise manager, and I used to try to do the same things on the New York market that he had done. Buying trips were always grueling occasions to me, and I would usually come home exhausted and full of doubts over the decisions I had made. My most comforting times were to spend most of mornings after my returns in his office telling about what I had done and why and always being given understanding and encouragement. I am sure those are my dearest memories of my father's last days.

The last heart attack that killed him occurred on Saturday afternoon in late May. He was stricken while at home with Virginia and died before the ambulance arrived. I made the announcement on the store's P. A. system, and we closed immediately, not reopening until the day after the funeral the following Monday. The store employees insisted on giving the huge blanket of roses for the casket. His funeral was held at First Baptist Church, and he was laid to rest beside our mother in Montlawn Cemetery. I think his obituary included the well-known litany for men of his time and area: "He was a Baptist, a Mason, and a life-long Democrat."[2]

For me, his memory is of the kindest and most generous man I have ever known. I still miss him.

MAY 1986[3]

---

2. This was actually said in the obituary of my other grandfather, J. Henry Highsmith: "He was a Phi Beta Kappa, a Mason, a Rotarian, and a life-long Democrat" (*News and Observer,* May 9, 1953).

3. Written for a reunion of descendants of Dallas Holoman, Sr. on the occasion of the 100th anniversary of his birth. The event was held at the Sampson County farm of Laura Holoman Murphy, his granddaughter.

OTHER WRITINGS

My Father and My God

My father was not an unusually gifted man. In most respects he was not really extraordinary at all. His successes—and he had some successes—were owing to his industry, his perseverance and to a certain rock-ribbed integrity. He is extraordinary to me, though, in a very special way.

My father was born on a poor-to-middling farm in Northampton County. He was the ninth in a family of ten children. He had no education beyond the most elementary of elementary schools. I think he must have decided at an early age that there was no way for such a poor farm to support so large a family. So while he was still quite young (perhaps 12 or 14?) he took a job in a store in a nearby town. He was associated with retail sales for the rest of his life.

I was a sixteen-year-old boy when my mother died. By that time my three older brothers had grown up and left home. From that time until my emergence into manhood my father lavished on me a bounty of love and care of which I was unworthy and totally undeserving. I was, of course, gratified for all these goodnesses, but even then I was aware that they were far beyond anything that I had any right to expect.

I am sorry to say that most of my recollections of my father are so painful to me that I cannot recall them without sense of regret over my failures in our relationships. On countless occasions, in so many ways, I disappointed and hurt him by my callousness and lack of consideration for his feelings.

I cannot escape from the memories of my falsehoods, my deceptions, my broken promises, my disobediences, my failures to do what he asked and expected of me. In my mind they make a patchwork that forever sullies the fabric of our lives together.

No doubt there were many things that he never knew about. Perhaps there were others that he knew, but chose not to confront me about. For those he did discover he rebuked me. But he never punished me, even for the more serious ones, when doubtless he should have.

And through it all he was kind, understanding and forgiving of my shortcomings. Even though they must have been painful to him then. As they are to me now.

And generous to the point of excess. I never lifted a finger to pay for my college education. I had no allowance, but drew without restriction on the special bank account that he set up for me. His only automobile was available for me whenever I asked for it. He made weekly deposits for me in a savings account all the time I was in the army. I am not sure I ever reimbursed him for the money he advanced to pay for the engagement ring for my wife-to-be. In everything I was so much less than I should have been; he was so much more than he had to be. All this remains painful to me. Time has not healed the ache.

Toward the end of his life, as his health was declining I became very close to my father. In long sessions we would sit together and exchange "war stories" about life in the department store business. We never discussed the tribulations of the past;

and I take much comfort from the feeling that there at the end was reconciliation and loving warmth between father and son.

How could anyone have been so good to me who was so undeserving? And that makes me think about God. Although I am an active and supportive member of my church, my personal faith is not very structured or formalized. I regard myself as a child of God—one of His myriad human creations—and I believe that I will be in a loving relationship with Him forever. I know that I had a loving father. And I know, too, that I have another Father who is even more loving, even more understanding, and even more generous than my earthly father. For, as a child of God, I know that He lavishes on me a love and care far greater than human minds can ever conceive. In my prayers I daily thank God for the lavish gifts He showers upon me. My faith says to me each day that surely God's goodness and mercy shall follow me all the days of my life. I only know I cannot drift beyond his love and care.

I am reminded of the parable of the Prodigal Son, which I call the parable of the Forgiving Father. But more than this, I am reminded of these words of Jesus (Matthew 7:8–11): "What man is there of you who when his son asks for bread will give him a stone? Or if he asks for a fish will give him a snake? If you, then, who are evil, know how to give good things to your children, how much more will your Father who is in heaven know how to give good things to those who ask?"

And these words are a cornerstone of my faith.

I have personally experienced my own father's goodness and forgiveness here in my own life. And I take total comfort in my faith that even more goodness, understanding and forgiveness is offered to me by my Father who is in heaven. And in this faith I shall abide in the house of the Lord forever.

Halloween Story

It isn't very remote. Only about ten miles from Siler City, near the center of the state. And it isn't very large either. Only a circle about fifty feet across. And yet the rural farmers of Harper's Creek Road avert their eyes and hurry past it on their way to tend their fields. The hunters will detour a half-mile to avoid crossing this barren, forsaken spot surrounded by pine, scrub oaks and underbrush. For nothing will grow there. No weeds or wildflowers spring up from its soil. Deliberate attempts to plant or cultivate it are dead by the next morning. Sticks or other small objects placed within its orbit have disappeared by daybreak.

And why? The natives say that the Devil has a favorite haunt on earth, and it is here. They say he pays nocturnal visits to this lonely spot. It is his nightly presence that prevents the growth or living of anything fresh or green. Or good. Round and round each night he paces his well-worn path and tramples the good things that would challenge his domain as he concocts his evil snares for mankind.

Perhaps, then, it is no coincidence that the last evidence of the disappearance of Edgar Torrence was found here. His Volkswagen sedan had pulled to the shoulder of the dirt road about a hundred yards down from this Devil's Tramping Ground, but no trace of Edgar was ever seen or heard from again. To the dismay of his avid and admiring readers.

Edgar Torrence was a wildly best-selling author and purveyor of horror stories. With each new novel or essay he would present a panoply of spine-tingling chills that would assuredly produce nightmares among his readers for night after night to come. Those devotees would eagerly await each new tale of terror, and would again ask from whence came his inexhaustible knowledge of the grotesque and the horridly bizarre. His fan mail was enormous, and nearly every one posed the question, "How can you know so much of the evil that lurks within, beneath our surfaces?" To which he always responded that he plumbed a well of occult lore not available to the rest of humankind.

It was on an interview with North Carolina television personality Bob Warner that he confessed that all of his images of terror were stirred up from his own fertile imagination. He said "I scour the depths of my personal psyche, and from them conjure up vistas that wrack the readers' souls with horror." "No gazing upon the face of evil to obtain your sources?" asked Bob. "No, was the reply. "I sometimes wish that I *could* gaze upon the face of evil itself, rather than dredge up everything from within."

"Have you never gone on a safari to seek out that face of evil which you say you long to see?" "No," replied Edgar, "Wherever would I go to look for the face of evil for myself?"

It was near the end of the interview that Bob asked, almost jokingly, "Why don't you look for him at the Devil's Tramping Ground in my own home state of North Carolina? They say he goes there every night to build more schemes and beset mankind." "Maybe I'll seek him there," promised Edgar in a somber tone that was only half in jest.

And so it was that not too much later, on an autumn night—it was All Hallow's Evening of all nights—that Edgar with the aid of flashlight and road map pulled his Volkswagen to the road shoulder of that dark, drear spot.

It was an apt stage for an evil, macabre encounter. A wisp of cloud floated down through the pines, while overhead the full moon was a ghostly galleon sailing the seas of the sky. The bob-whites called softly in the undergrowth, while from the nearby hills the nighthawks and whip-poor-wills shrilled their persistent cries, as if to announce the presence of a newcomer in their midst.

Edgar felt his way through the low pines, searching for the evil Promised Land. There! He arrived at the forbidden circle. The dark figure treading the pathway saw him first and began to advance sedately toward him.

He was a towering personage—much taller than Edgar—and dressed all in black. His immaculate visage bore a small T-shaped beard. On his head was a Robin Hood-style cap with a long, black feather. He seemed an ordinary, if overly tall, man. Except. Could those possibly have been little horns peeking out from his cap? Was that just a hint of a long, forked tail only half-concealed under his cape? Then, too, there was the faint odor of a he-goat, mingled with the unmistakable aroma on his breath of burning brimstone. From the beginning Edgar had no doubt of the identity of this forest apparition who approached. He whom Edgar had come to seek had arrived promptly for an unappointed tryst.

When the figure spoke, it was with the compelling authority of a proprietor. "What seek you here in this circle that is distinctively mine in all the universe?" An imperative demand that boded no refusal. "You are then, the master of this place? You are that Prince of Darkness who has confronted human-kind through the ages?" Edgar asked. "I am he," was the reply.

"I am called by many names. Your Bible calls me Satan—the adversary. Milton said I was Lucifer, the fiery fallen angel. Beelzebub, Belial, Mephisto—they are all one to me. I come in many guises, but I am ever the same—unchanging."

"What shall I call you then?" asked Edgar.

"You shall not call me anything. You shall answer to me why you thus invade my domain."

Edgar felt the merciless chill of this demand. The whip-poor-wills shrilled in the distance. He felt his own impotence beneath the imperious voice of this powerful host. He hung his head.

"I thought that this night in this place—with you—I might gaze upon the true face of evil."

"What reason made you think thus? What compulsion made you desire thus?" Harshly demanding. Penetrating.

Edgar said "All my literary life I have scoured the depths of my own evil soul. I have dredged up every horror, every terror that my own mind could conceive. I have presented them—for profit—to an appreciative public. I come here hoping to look upon an evil outside myself. An evil that exists beyond the wanton grotesqueries of my own conscience."

"And do you think you have found that which you seek? Here? Tonight? With me?"

"Thus far I have seen only your appearance. Heard only your voice. Have you nothing more to show me?" Edgar confronted the reality of this presence before him.

The Devil emitted a snort and scowled. His face glowed darkly in the full moon's light. "Look you. You wish to gaze upon *my* evil? I can show you more evil than your feeble mind can ever hold. I can summon forth all spirits from the vasty deep. *All* evil dwells with me in my palace at Pan-Demonium."

Edgar persisted. "I want to gaze upon a face of evil not my own. I want to *see*."

"Then behold!" With his arm he flared his black cape. And immediately the moonlight overhead dissolved into a silvery pathway before the feet of the two of them. And before them began to pass, as if in review, such a parade of phantasmagoria as Edgar's mind had never conceived. Each fixated his eye with a glowering stare as he passed. And Satan announced the name of each, though many were already known to him as objects of his own terror-filled, horror-filled past.

"Look upon this monster that Dr. Frankenstein builds in his laboratory from human parts purloined from the grave. And then released to prey upon the peasantry. Behold ashen-faced Voivode Dracula, who sucks out the life blood of beautiful women with his kisses. This blazing-eyed serpent is the same who proffered the apple of perdition to Eve. Look upon this hag from Endor in Galilee who summoned forth the saintly Samuel from his tomb."

The passing parade continued with leaders of their own people. "Here is Atilla, who slew his thousands. Genghis Kahn, who slew his ten thousands. Adolph Hitler, who slew his millions. This hunch-backed villain who smothered his princely nephews in London's Tower as he clawed his way to England's crown."

There seemed no end to the drear procession. Satan's feather waved in the moon light as he nodded approvingly on his creations as they passed.

"Look at these goblins who raced Tam O' Shanter for his soul to the kirk at Brig o' Doon. See this headless horseman who terrorized the hapless school master of Sleepy Hollow. And pirate Teach who lighted his Black Beard to appall the citizens of Bath."

Then followed countless un-named lesser spirits who all engendered fear, loathing and despair in the human-kind which they beset: Furies, harpies, poltergeists and every kind of demon to wrack the mind with dread. As far along the moonlit path as Edgar's eye could see.

Slithering along beside their feet came hoards of serpents, snakes, adders and vipers of every description. And they were followed by packs of slavering wolves, by teeming herds of attic rats and flights of vampire bats.

"Enough! Enough." This was more evil than Edgar had

ever encountered in the sum of all his demented dreams. His fevered mind could no more hold all that Satan had shown him. He turned away from the stark visions on the path before them. He addressed his host with revulsion of what he had been shown, and remorse that his own writings had encompassed these same forbidden evils.

"From this moment, henceforth," vowed Edgar, "I renounce all that you have shown me tonight. I renounce every jot and tittle of all that I have ever written that has to do with evil and its spirits. Never again will I turn with pen or mind to that dark domain which is eternally your realm. I leave you now to depart to my own home which will henceforth be a brighter place."

"Nay. Not so," the Devil countered. And he seized Edgar's wrist in a deadly grip so powerful that no human could repel it.

"At this place you are closer to *my* home than to your own. Tonight you will go home with me. And abide with me and my dark spirits for all the nights to come. Forever."

WHITAKER GLEN
OCTOBER 2004[1]

---

1. For the popular "Scary Stories Night" at Whitaker Glen retirement community. Dad would often tell other people's stories, but this one was original work based on the old North Carolina legend of the Devil's Tramping Ground. We made family trips there on several occasions.

Joyeux Noël In Paris

It was Christmas Eve, 1944. World War II was still going on. I was stationed in Paris as a part of the American Army fighting in Europe. We were comfortably quartered, cozy and warm in an abandoned school building. Then suddenly we weren't comfortable any more. The word came down that we were to evacuate **IMMEDIATELY** to make space for an emergency hospital to receive our casualties from the front. It was what became known as "The Battle of the Bulge."

So we packed everything we owned into our one duffel bag, and in the middle of the night we were trucked downtown and dumped off at the Petit Palais, an empty museum just off the Champs-Elysées, which had been denuded of its art works for storage during the war. Inside it were field conditions all over again—no running water, no toilet facilities, no electricity, just drafty old rooms and corridors. Of course it was a lot better than our troops' condition on the battle field, and even in the midst of our own little miseries, we were thankful that we could have this much of a Merry Christmas Eve.

Things began to look a little better for me the next day when I had the opportunity to attend the Christmas Mass at the Cathedral of Notre Dame. It was a sunny day, and light came streaming through the glorious stained glass windows.

There was still sunshine and beauty in the world.

Whitaker Glen
December 2003[2]

---

2. For the Christmas newsletter at Whitaker Glen.

The author with four great-grandchildren and their parents:
Ayla, Mark, Reese, Kern, Charlie, Jeff, Kate, Jackson
Seaford, Caswell Beach
July 2009

APPENDIX

Correspondence with Jeff Holoman

As noted in the introduction, my father's interest in his memoirs and in the publication of his letters from Europe was particularly fostered by his grandson, Jeff, beginning so far as I know at Caswell Beach, N. C., in the summer of 2003. (Dad would turn 83 that August.) Jeff would prompt his grandfather to tell his stories, then send him away at the end of each vacation with an admonition to keep typing–which he did.

30 September 2003

Dear Jeff—

This is the only significant thing I have written since we came back from the beach ["My Father and My God"]. Please include it with the other "Memoirs" of me that you have.

    I was particularly anxious for you to see this one, as it says something about my beliefs and my personal philosophies. I hope it will be meaningful to you. How are you coming with making copies of those "Memoirs" that you already have? I'll be glad to see them.

Love
Grand Father

28 October 2003

Jeff—

Thanks for returning my stuff to me. Some of them were the only copy I had, and I needed them. The first enclosure is the first of a three-part series on how the army sent me back to college. The second is one I wrote 60 years ago about one of the army's mandatory sex education classes. I thought it was funny at the time I wrote it. Now, I'm not so sure.

I will be going to visit your dad in Plano next week.

Love
Grand Father

29 December 2003

Dear Jeff—

Here is a brief biography that I wrote on my father, your great-grandfather, that you said you were interested in. I wrote it on the occasion of a Holoman family reunion on what would have been his 100th birthday.

I also enclose a photo of my dad when was about 70 years old.

Please be sure to return these to me when you have seen them. They are valuable and dear to me. Warmest regards and best wishes for the new year.

Grand Daddy

19 January 2004

Jeff

Here is the second (of three) accounts of my life when the army sent me to study French at Rutgers. Here is also one of the WW II letters written in Paris in Oct. 1944. The typing and the copying are bad, but you can puzzle it out if you think it worthwhile to spend the time.

Hope you will have a great Thanksgiving time with Mark, Jenner[1] and your Dad. I will be in California with D. Kern.

I am proud of Auburn's football team.

Love
Grandfather

20 July 2004

Here is a little item ["Joyeux Noël in Paris"] that I wrote for our Whitaker Glen publication last Christmas. Thought you might like to see it.

Grand Father

Enjoyed seeing you and Katie at the beach last week.

---

1. Jena, he means: Mark's wife.

16 August 2004

Dear Jeff

I am sending you, enclosed, another one of my "memoirs." I am writing on them, now, with some regularity and expect to be sending them to you with a fair amount of frequency.

I would appreciate knowing what you think of them. Write me.

When you have read and finished with them, please send them on to your Dad, who has also expressed some interest. Tell him to return them to me when he is through with them.

I am sorry there are so many errors and typos in these pages, but I am a poor typist, and this is the best I can do.

With love and best wishes.
Grand Father

1 September 2004

Dear Jeff—

Thanks for your letter / note. I was glad to get it. Everybody likes to be appreciated for one's efforts.

These writings are a labor of love, but they do take time and effort. After the first batch, you do not need to send them back to me. I am keeping copies for myself now.

But do send them on to your Dad—and Mark too if he is interested.

Lots of love,
Grandfather

I expect to send you a new letter each week or so. W.K.H.

9 September 2004

Jeff—

This paper [Richmond] includes my earliest recollections.

Grand Father

29 September 2004

Jeff—

The attached was written the day after the Armistice Day parade in Paris nearly 60 years ago.

The copy was on onionskin paper which has not withstood the sands of time.

After you have made a copy (and if you want one) please return this to me.

Love
Grandfather

6 October 2004

Jeff—

This is one of my very early letters from Paris. It was written in September, 1944, over sixty years ago. Don't forget to send me these writings after you have finished with them. I haven't received any yet.

Love
Grandfather

28 December 2004

Dear Jeff—

Thank you for sending me back the copies of the "Memoirs" that I have previously sent to you. And for the appreciative and touching note that you sent in accompaniment. It really was not necessary for you to have spent that kind of money to get it to me quickly. There was no hurry; I just like to have them back sometime. I am glad that you find them interesting and enjoyable. I am having fun writing them, and take pleasure in the thought that others find them worth reading.

I am sending you in this envelope two more for your perusal. One is the third and last installment of my time at Rutgers. This one has to do mostly with the "honeymoon nest" that Kaye—your grandmother—shared while we were there. The other letter is another from the series that I wrote in Paris in 1944–45. This one is about the "mess hall" where we dined in Paris.

I am also sending you a list of all the writings that I have done so far. I intend for there to be more to follow. I thought I could remember which ones I had sent and to whom. Alas, my memory is far too leaky for that. Please look this sheet over carefully and let me know which of them you have already received. Just put a check mark to the left of the line/title if you have already received it. If you have not yet received it, put an "x" to the left. And, of course, if you would like to have it, draw a circle around the X. The return it to me, and I'll try to keep up with it better in the future.

Anyway, I hope you are having a happy holiday season, even though you are not in Plano with your father and Mark and Jenner.[2]

---

2. See n. 1.

It will be a pleasure when I hear from you again. And better, yet, when I see you.

With love,
Grand Father

8 December 2004

Jeff—

Here is the third—and last—installment of the Long Beach Memoir.
    Here also are some of my writings from Paris in 1944.
    Have a good Christmas.

Grand Father

11 January [2005]

Jeff

I am sending you a copy of a Halloween ghost story that I wrote for Whitaker Glen this year. I hope you enjoy it.

Grand Father

24 January 2005

Jeff—

I have not sent you any of my writings recently, but I have been working on transcribing some old ones. More will be forthcoming if you continue to be interested. Here is one that I just finished last week, so I know you haven't seen this. It is long, telling about my voyage to England on a troop ship, etc.

Please do return to me that sheet I sent you and tell me which of these "memoirs" you have received, not received and would like to have. I have completely lost track of which ones I have sent and to whom. So I need this information so as not to burden you with duplications.

Sorry I didn't get to see you during the holiday times. Will hope to be with you during 2005. Meanwhile I hope that all is going well to you and that the world is treating you O. K.

Warm regards to Miss Kathy—or is it Cathy?[3] Anyway, lots of love to you both.

Grand Father

---

3. Katie, he means, who was to marry Jeff in 2007.

AU VIEUX LOGIS

Kate M. Herring
Mrs. J. Henry Highsmith
Collected Writings
2020

Kaye and Kern Holoman
*Travels
and Other Journals in Their Archive*
2023

Kern Holoman
*Memoirs
and Other Writings*
second edition
2023

D. Kern Holoman
Philharmonia: A Memoir
forthcoming

www.ingramcontent.com/pod-product-compliance
Lightning Source LLC
Chambersburg PA
CBHW031059080526
44587CB00011B/750